Studies in Jewish and Christian Literature

Messiah and the Throne, Timo Eskola
Defilement and Purgation in the Book of Hebrews, William G. Johnsson
Father, Son, and Spirit in Romans 8, Ron C. Fay
Within the Veil, Félix H. Cortez
Jude's Apocalyptic Eschatology as Theological Exclusivism, William Wilson
Intertextuality and Prophetic Exegesis in the War Scroll of Qumran, César Melgar
The Past Is Yet to Come: Exodus Typology in Revelation, Barbara Isbell

AT THE END OF ALL THINGS:
IDENTIFYING THE IDEAL READER OF REVELATION

At the End of All Things: Identifying the Ideal Reader of Revelation

Jason P. Kees

Fontes

At the End of All Things:
Identifying the Ideal Reader of Revelation

Copyright © 2023 by Jason P. Kees

ISBN-13: 978-1-948048-76-7 (paperback)
ISBN-13: 978-1-948048-77-4 (hardback)

All rights reserved. No part of this publication may be reproduced, stored in a retrieval system, or transmitted in any form or by any means—electronic, mechanical, photocopy, recording, or any other—except for brief quotations in printed reviews, without the prior permission of the publisher.

Typeset by Monolateral.

FONTES PRESS
DALLAS, TX
www.fontespress.com

Contents

Abbreviations ix

1. The Canonical Approach in Retrospect 1
   Introduction 1
   What is the Canonical Approach? 4
   Intertextuality within the Canonical Approach 6
   Shape and Its Influence Upon Interpretation 8
      Brevard S. Childs 11
      John Sailhamer 15
   Canonical Approaches to the New Testament 19
   Critiques of the Canonical Approach 24
   A Need for the Canonical Approach to Revelation 29

2. The Problem of Interpreting Revelation 33
   Introduction 33
   Conceptual Background for Interpreting Revelation 36
   The Role of Historical Background Information 39
   Case-Study in Colossians 41
   Conclusion 44

3. Revelation in the Context of the New Testament Canon 47
   Introduction 47
   The Concept of Canon 48
   The Development of a Canonical List 51
   The Canonical Order of the New Testament 53
   Revelation in the Context of the Canon 59
      Approaching Revelation Canonically 61
      The Structure of Revelation 61
      The Content of Revelation 64
         The Prologue (1:1–8) 65
         The Vision of Christ (1:9–3:22) 65
         The Vision of Heaven (4:1–16:21) 66
         The Vision of the Wilderness (17:1–21:8) 71
         The Vision of the Mountain (21:9–22:5) 72
         Epilogue (22:6–22:21) 73
   Conclusion 73

4. Revelation's Usage of the Synoptic Gospels and Acts 75
   Introduction 75
   The Gospels and Acts 76
      Revelation 1:1; Matthew 24:6; Luke 21:9 77
      Revelation 1:3; Luke 11:28 78
      Revelation 1:3; Matthew 26:18 80
      Revelation 1:7; Matthew 24:30; 2 Corinthians 1:20 80
      Revelation 1:16; Matthew 17:2 83

        Revelation 2:7; Matthew 11:15; Luke 8:8; 14:35; Mark 4:9 84
        Revelation 2:20, 24–25; Acts 15:28–29 85
        Revelation 3:3; 16:15; Matthew 24:42–43; 1 Thessalonians 5:2 87
        Revelation 3:5, 8; Matthew 10:32; Luke 12:8; 1 Corinthians 16:9 89
        Revelation 5:5; Luke 7:13; 8:52 91
        Revelation 6:4; Matthew 10:34 92
        Revelation 6:10; Luke 18:7–8 94
        Revelation 6:12–13; Matthew 24:29; Mark 13:24–25; Luke 21:25 95
        Revelation 6:15–16; Luke 23:30 97
        Revelation 6:17; Luke 21:36 98
        Revelation 9:20; Luke 18:11 99
        Revelation 11:3, 6; Luke 4:25; James 5:17 100
        Revelation 11:15; Matthew 4:8 102
        Revelation 12:9; Luke 10:18 103
        Revelation 13:11; Matthew 7:15 105
        Revelation 14:4; Luke 9:57 106
        Revelation 14:7; Acts 4:24; 14:15 107
        Revelation 17:14; Matthew 22:14 108
        Revelation 18:24; Luke 11:50 110
        Revelation 19:7; Matthew 5:12 111
        Revelation 19:9; Luke 14:16–17 112
        Revelation 21:10; Matthew 4:8 112
    Concluding Observations 113
5. Revelation's Usage of the Pauline and Catholic Epistles 115
    Introduction 115
    The Pauline Epistles 115
        Revelation 1:4; Colossians 1:2 116
        Revelation 1:5; Colossians 1:18 117
        Revelation 1:5; Galatians 2:20 118
        Revelation 1:18; 2 Corinthians 6:9 119
        Revelation 2:9; 2 Corinthians 6:10; James 2:5 121
        Revelation 2:24; 1 Corinthians 2:10 122
        Revelation 3:14; Colossians 1:18, 15 123
        Revelation 3:17; Colossians 1:27 124
        Revelation 3:21; Colossians 3:1; Ephesians 2:6 125
        Revelation 7:3; Ephesians 4:30 126
        Revelation 14:13; 1 Thessalonians 4:16 128
        Revelation 17:14; 1 Timothy 6:15 129
        Revelation 18:4; 2 Corinthians 6:17; Ephesians 5:11 130
        Revelation 21:4d–5b; 2 Corinthians 5:17 131
        Revelation 22:21; Ephesians 6:24; Colossians 4:18 132
    The Catholic Epistles 133
        Revelation 1:6; 1 Peter 2:9 133
        Revelation 2:10; James 1:12 135

	Revelation 7:17; 1 Peter 2:25	136
	Revelation 13:8; 1 Peter 1:19–20	137
	Revelation 16:19; 1 Peter 5:13	138
	Concluding Observations	138

6. AT THE END OF ALL THINGS: THE IDEAL-READER OF REVELATION 141
    Introduction 141
    Summary of the Study 142
    The Ideal-Reader of Revelation 144
    Contribution to the Field of Study 145
    Suggestions for Further Research 145
    Conclusion 146

BIBLIOGRAPHY 149

INDEX 161

Abbreviations

AJBT	*American Journal of Biblical Theology*
BECNT	Baker Exegetical Commentary on the New Testament
BBR	*Bulletin for Biblical Research*
Bib	*Biblica*
BR	*Biblical Research*
BSac	*Bibliotheca Sacra*
BTF	*Bangalore Theological Forum*
CBQ	*Catholic Biblical Quarterly*
CBR	*Currents in Biblical Research*
DaLog	*Davar Logos*
EGGNT	*Exegetical Guide to the Greek New Testament*
HTR	*Harvard Theological Review*
ICC	International Critical Commentary
Int	*Interpretation*
JBL	*Journal of Biblical Literature*
JETS	*Journal of the Evangelical Theological Society*
JMAT	*Journal of Ministry and Theology*
JSNTSup	Journal of the Society of the New Testament Supplement Series
JSOT	*Journal for the Study of the Old Testament*
JTI	*Journal of Theological Interpretation*
NAC	New American Commentary

Neot	*Neotestamentica*
NICNT	New International Commentary on the New Testament
NIGTC	New International Greek Testament Commentary
NovT	*Novum Testamentum*
NTS	*New Testament Studies*
PNTC	Pillar New Testament Commentary
Semeia	*Semeia*
SJT	*Scottish Journal of Theology*
STR	Southeastern Theological Review
Them	*Themelios*
TJ	*Trinity Journal*
TynBul	*Tyndale Bulletin*
VT	*Vetus Testamentum*
WBC	World Biblical Commentary
WCF	*Westminster Confession of Faith*
WTJ	*Westminster Theological Journal*
ZECNT	Zondervan Exegetical Commentary on the New Testament

Chapter 1

The Canonical Approach in Retrospect

Introduction

REVELATION PRESENTS A VARIETY of interpretative challenges for the reader, primarily due to the focus upon the climatic end of the world and the obscure imagery. As a result, it has been viewed by some as a guide to understand the current events, whereas others neglect Revelation and do not view it as relevant for today. Therefore, the reader faces several hermeneutical questions to interpret Revelation, and these questions are only multiplied due to the apocalyptic genre of the book.

In what manner should the book of Revelation be interpreted? What necessary hermeneutical boundaries must the interpreter impose upon the reading of Revelation in order to arrive at a satisfactory, proper interpretation? These are valid questions that any interpreter must ask when they begin to mine the caverns of this book.

Martin Luther doubted the inspiration and authenticity of Revelation, citing Jerome as one of the early church fathers who rejected this book.[1] After noting the lack of apostolic visions contained within the New Testament and emphasizing their contrasting clarity of speech, Luther saw similarity between Revelation and the Fourth Book of Esdras. "[Those who read Revelation] are supposed to be blessed who keep what is written in this book; and yet no one knows what that is, to say nothing of keeping it. This is just the same as if we did not have the book at all. And there are many far better books available for us to keep."[2] Luther concludes his preface by stating that he "will stick to the books which present Christ to me clearly and purely."[3]

---
[1] Martin Luther, *Luther's Works: Word and Sacrament* (Fortress Press, 1960), 35:398–399.
[2] Ibid., 35:399.
[3] Ibid.

Even John Calvin, another magisterial reformer, omitted the book from his commentary series.[4]

Despite the conclusion of Luther, Revelation contains many biblical doctrines that, as suggested by some, were provided specifically for believers in the first century who faced significant persecution by Rome. This book, then, would provide a wealth of comfort and encouragement for first-century Christians as they faced times of uncertainty. Nonetheless, Revelation ends the New Testament canon with a victory for the people of God. Those who are sealed (7:4–8) and follow the Lamb wherever he goes (14:4) will dine at the wedding feast between the bride and the Lamb (19:7). Furthermore, the unholy trinity (12–13) will be vanquished (19:20; 20:7–10), and God's dwelling place will be with man (21:3).[5] This dwelling place is in direct fulfillment to Old Testament prophecy, as are many scenes employed by the author.

Likewise, the doctrinal content and relevance of Revelation suggest that not only was the author steeped in the literature of the Old Testament but also that many themes within the book are based upon a broad understanding of the Old Testament itself. For example, the vision in 1:12–20 is related to the Son of Man vision from Dan 7:13–14, and the locusts, from the fifth trumpet in 9:1–11, bear resemblance to the plague of locusts in Exod 10:12–15.[6] In fact, Revelation contains more references to the Old Testament than any other New Testament book.[7] Thus, one can infer that the writer of Revelation believed his readers were familiar with both Old Testament theology and the imagery that he used since he does not pause and explain the images in their context as they are developed. However, alongside the multiple allusions to the Old Testament, Revelation also appears to make several connections to New Testament passages and themes. It seems that John believed his work could employ a broader understanding of the New Testament and that his reader would understand the connections.

Accordingly, after a detailed analysis of Revelation's usage of the Old Testament and possible texts based upon the Pseudepigrapha, R. H. Charles

---

4 Although no definite answer can be given regarding this striking omission, T. H. L. Parker believes Calvin simply chose to overlook Revelation once he finished preaching the Epistles. Considering Calvin's mention of Revelation some forty times in his commentary series, it does not appear this omission was due to a lack of understanding of Revelation or an agreement with Luther. See T. H. L. Parker, *Calvin's Commentaries on the New Testament*, 2nd ed. (Westminster John Knox, 1993), 116–119.

5 All Scripture translations are mine.

6 See G. K. Beale and Sean McDonough, "Revelation," in *Commentary on the New Testament Use of the Old*, ed. G. K. Beale and D. A. Carson (Baker, 2007), 1091–1093; 1114–1115.

7 See ibid., 1082, for a list of various tallied resources.

lists several passages from Revelation that suggest a dependence upon or are parallel with other earlier New Testament books.[8] This list includes passages from Matthew, Luke, 1 Thessalonians, 1 and 2 Corinthians, Colossians, Ephesians, Galatians, 1 Peter, and James. For example, John's epistolary greeting in 1:4 (χάρις ὑμῖν καὶ εἰρήνη) is identical to Col 1:2; Rom 1:7; 1 Cor 1:3; 2 Cor 1:2; Gal 1:3; Eph 1:2; Phil 1:2; 1 Thess 1:1; 2 Thess 1:2; and Phlm 3. Titus 1:4 does not contain ὑμῖν but is otherwise identical.[9] Similarity also exists in 1 Pet 1:2; 2 Pet 1:2, and Jude 2 where χάρις is substituted for ἔλεος. Matthew Y. Emerson believes that the high correlation between these examples, and those listed by Charles, suggests a reading strategy for Revelation "as the culmination of the exhortation to the churches of God."[10] This reading strategy is strengthened by the thematic connections as illustrated here and by the verbal connections between Revelation and the New Testament as a whole.

Such verbal connections provided by Charles would seem to suggest that the author of Revelation was dependent upon other New Testament texts. Furthermore, as Emerson has noted, the location of Revelation within the canon of the New Testament may be more intentional than previously suspected. Given the various connections to the rest of the New Testament, the position of Revelation at the conclusion of the New Testament canon may suggest a specific reading strategy for the book. Thus, what would this reading strategy look like considering Revelation's usage of both the Old and New Testament texts?

The argument of this book is that a canonical approach of Revelation is a neglected aspect of current New Testament studies and that such a reading will provide the ideal-reader for interpreting Revelation. This last proposal suggests itself in light of (1) the location of Revelation within the canon of Scripture; (2) the intertextual links between Revelation and the Old Testament; (3) the intertextual verbal connections Revelation shares with other New Testament texts; and (4) the allusions and themes Revelation shares with the New Testament. In order to test the assumption of this approach, one must define specifically the "canonical approach" and examine the contributions it has made to the field of biblical studies.

---

8 R. H. Charles, *A Critical and Exegetical Commentary on Revelation of St. John*, ICC (T&T Clark, 1985), 1:lxxxiii–lxxxvi.

9 Matthew Y. Emerson, *Christ and the New Creation: A Canonical Approach to the Theology of the New Testament* (Wipf and Stock, 2013), 143. Emerson further remarks that "even though 1 and 2 Timothy, out of all the Pauline Epistles, do not have some syntactical form of this phrase they do share the use of 'grace' and 'peace from God the Father' in both of their introductions (they also add 'mercy' in between 'grace' and 'peace')."

10 Ibid., 143–144.

What is the Canonical Approach?

For many years, the determinative method for interpreting the Old Testament was the historical-critical approach. Those employing this methodology sought to reconstruct the historical events behind the canonical text. The historical-critical approach became the prominent method for interpreting the Pentateuch and served as the basis for the documentary hypothesis theory proposed by J. H. Wellhausen.[11] Walter Eichrodt observed this phenomenon, noting that:

> There was no longer any unity to be found in the OT, only a collection of detached periods which were simply the reflections of as many different religions. In such circumstances, it was only a logical development that the designation 'OT Theology', which had formerly had quite a different connotation, should frequently be abandoned and the title 'History of Israelite Religion' substituted for it. Even where scholars still clung to the old name, they were neither desirous nor capable of offering anything more than an exposition of the historical process.[12] Thus, the study of the Old Testament quickly became not so much a study of the Old Testament itself, but rather of the events to which that text points.

However, the potential weakness of the historical-critical approach was the preoccupation with historical reconstructions to the neglect of the exegesis of the biblical passage. Thus, the canonical approach was formulated to offset the imbalance of the historical-critical method.[13] The canonical approach, or canonical criticism, introduces a method of Scriptural interpretation that focuses on the context of the received canon. Focusing on the received canon of Scripture frees the interpreter from the task of constructing the historical setting of the specific books of the Bible and allows the interpreter the freedom to understand the text in accordance with its surrounding context. In other words, the canonical approach examines the biblical text itself rather than allowing the text to serve as the entry point for a historical reconstruction of religious and socio-political identities.

---

11 Philemon Ibrahim, "Pentateuchal Authorship: A Critical Analysis of Existing Imaginations," AJBT 3 (2020): 179–184.

12 Walther Eichrodt, *Old Testament Theology* (Westminster Press, 1961), 1:30–31. Although this observation is regarding a coherence between the two testaments, the statement is nonetheless true even when the unity between the testaments is not considered.

13 See also Chen Xun, *Theological Exegesis in the Canonical Context: Brevard Springs Childs' Methodology of Biblical Theology* (Peter Lang, 2010), 57–110.

Brevard Childs notes the importance of what is meant by context, since there are many different contexts by which the Scripture can be interpreted.[14] Childs believes that when the "context" of Scripture is referenced, it should be understood as the environment of what is being interpreted as well as the parts that form the text.[15] Although there are other "contexts" by which Scripture can be interpreted, Childs believes that the reference to canon as a context "describes a context within which a dialectical relationship between the two Testaments is envisioned."[16]

By focusing on the Christian canon, the canonical approach requires the interpreter to consider in-depth the idea that the Scriptures are a written text, and they are theologically relevant as to content and form.[17] Thus, a canonical approach presupposes that the arrangement of the books within the broader context of Scripture informs exegesis and does the latter on that basis. An example of this broader context is the interpretation of a verse within its proper setting of paragraph-section-chapter-book.[18]

The canonical approach provides the reader with an overarching view (macro) of the Scripture as opposed to a narrow (micro) level interpretation. As a result, the canonical method explains the message of a particular passage in light of the passage's canonical section. Thus, this approach highlights the text, its canonical section, and the message that the passage relates to the canon as a whole and what the message is that is presented to the reader. As Emerson remarks, "Additionally, canonical hermeneutics seeks to show how the pieces of a particular passage (or book or corpus) fit

---

14 Brevard S. Childs, *Biblical Theology in Crisis* (Philadelphia Press, 1976), 97–114.

15 Regarding what is meant by "context" Childs remarks, "By 'context' more is meant than simply 'perspective' which focuses on the angle of vision of the interpreter. Rather, context refers to the environment of that which is being interpreted. As a literary term, context denotes the parts of a composition that constitute the texture of the narrative. To interpret a sentence 'out of context' is to disregard its place in its larger literary design. In a broader sense the term 'context' includes both the formal and the material elements of design that belong to a historical period." Ibid., 97.

16 Ibid., 111.

17 Here, I am using "Christian canon" to refer to the sixty-six traditional books of the Bible that is represented in Protestant church history. For the texts that are theologically relevant as to its content and form, see John Sailhamer, "The Canonical Approach to the OT: Its Effect on Understanding Prophecy," *JETS* 30 (1987): 307.

18 See Michael B. Shepherd, *Daniel in the Context of the Hebrew Bible* (Peter Lang, 2009). Shepherd seeks to place Daniel within the context of the Hebrew Bible by identifying the intertextual connections. "It brings to the reader a concise yet detailed commentary on the text precisely at its point of occurrence within the composition of the canon, helping the reader to appreciate the force of the book's inter-textual connections with the rest of the Hebrew Bible." Ibid., 1. It is important to note that one does need to know the history behind the text, but the canonical approach makes history serve the final form exegesis alongside the context of Scripture.

into a canonical section (whether a book, corpus, or canon), and what message that canonical whole is attempting to convey."[19] This method of interpretation is done primarily from the text the church has received throughout the centuries.[20]

Intertextuality within the Canonical Approach

When one employs the canonical approach to interpreting Scripture, other methods of exegesis are suggested by implication. Since the primary focus is upon the received canon of the Christian church, the discussion of intertextuality will appear since the received canon includes writings that reference other portions of the canon. Intertextuality, in brief, understands how a later text uses an earlier text while retaining the same meaning.[21]

To distinguish intertextuality from inner-biblical exegesis and inner-biblical allusions, Russell L. Meek draws from the 1966 essay by Julia Kristeva and provides three criteria.[22] First, texts, according to Kristeva, are a "mosaic of quotations; any text is the absorption and transformation of another. The notion of intertextuality replaces that of intersubjectivity, and poetic language is read as at least double."[23] Second, intertextuality is not concerned with the diachronic trajectory of a text's relation to another. Rather, according to Meek, intertextuality is a synchronic discussion that focuses on the relation of many texts rather than one text.

> What matters for intertextual theorists is the 'network of traces', not their origin or direction of influence. Furthermore, intertextuality is concerned

---

19 Emerson, *Christ and the New Creation*, 5.

20 "The canon of the Christian church is the most appropriate context from which to do Biblical Theology." Childs, *Biblical Theology in Crisis*, 99. This claim, of course, does not specifically address the question of which text to use for the Old Testament (Masoretic or Septuagint) or the New Testament. This issue is addressed later in the discussion of the canon.

21 John H. Sailhamer, Introduction to Old Testament Theology: A Canonical Approach (Zondervan, 1995), 95. Thus, Robert W. Wall can state that one can read the New Testament as an "intertext" of the Hebrew Bible to "listen for echoes of or allusions to the writer's own scripture." Robert W. Wall, "The Significance of a Canonical Perspective of the Church's Scripture," in The Canon Debate, ed. Lee Martin McDonald and James A. Sanders (Baker, 2002), 537.

22 Russell L. Meek, "Intertextuality, Inner-Biblical Exegesis, and Inner-Biblical Allusion: The Ethics of a Methodology," *Bib* 95 (2014): 280–291. The article by Kristeva is J. Kristeva, "Word, Dialogue, and Novel," in *Desire in Language: A Semiotic Approach to Language and Art*, ed. L. S. Roudiez, trans. T. Gora, A. Jardine, and L. S. Roudiez (Columbia, 1980), 64–91. Meek's usage of "inner-biblical exegesis" and "inner-biblical allusion" is taken from the seminal work by Michael Fishbane, Biblical Interpretation in Ancient Israel (Oxford University Press, 1985). See also Michael B. Shepherd, The Text in the Middle (Peter Lang, 2014).

23 Kristeva, "Word, Dialogue, and Novel," 66.

with 'a wide range of correspondences among texts,' and it 'examines the relations among many texts' rather than the relationship between a narrow set of texts. Thus, intertextuality is a strictly synchronic discussion of wide-ranging intertextual relationships that necessarily precludes author-centered, diachronic studies.[24]

Third, intertextuality is not concerned with establishing criteria to determine the relationship between texts since there is little concern to prove a connection between texts was intended by the author. For Meek, the dilemma of labeling this endeavor as "intertextuality" becomes problematic when the interpreter claims authorial intention and has, thereby, "entered another realm altogether, for intertextuality presupposes that the connection of texts lies solely with the reader."[25] This "other realm" becomes reader-response based interpretation rather than exegesis that seeks to discover authorial intention.[26] Thus, Meek argues that most studies on intertextuality would be more properly labeled as "inner-biblical exegesis" or "inner-biblical allusion" since these terms are more appropriate.[27]

However, for the purpose of the present volume the term "intertextuality" will be used to describe how one author of the Bible uses a text from a different source within his respective book.[28] In other words, intertextuality

---

24 Ibid., 283.

25 Meek, "Intertextuality," 284.

26 For works concerning a reader-response methodology of interpretation, see Kevin J. Vanhoozer, *Is There Meaning in This Text? The Bible, the Reader, and the Morality of Literary Knowledge* (Zondervan, 1998); Anthony C. Thiselton, *Hermeneutics: An Introduction* (Eerdmans, 2009), 306–325; Grant R. Osborne, *The Hermeneutical Spiral: A Comprehensive Introduction to Biblical Interpretation* (Baker, 2006), 465–521.

27 Meek ("Intertextuality," 284) defines "inner-biblical exegesis" as the method that attempts to "make a case that later authors are referring to a previous text in order to explicate, comment on, expand, or in some other way make it applicable to a new situation." He also notes, "If there is no diachronic relationship between texts, then there necessarily can be no inner-biblical exegesis, for in order for an author to explicate or elaborate on a text, it must have existed previously. This principle immediately distinguishes inner-biblical exegesis from intertextuality, placing the burden of proof squarely on the shoulders of the one proposing a relationship between texts." Ibid. The process of inner-biblical exegesis, then, would seek to examine how a text found in a later document utilized a text from an earlier document. He notes that inner-biblical exegesis and inner-biblical allusion are used interchangeably, but inner-biblical allusion differs because it "sets out to determine whether a receptor text has in some way referred to a source text, but the goal is not to demonstrate that the receptor text has modified the source. Rather, with inner-biblical allusion the goal is simply to demonstrate that a later text in some way references an earlier text." Ibid., 289. Meek also notes that the "later text" is synonymous with receptor language.

28 See also Paul R. Noble, "Esau, Tamar, and Joseph: Criteria for Identifying Inner-Biblical Allusions," *VT* 52 (2002): 219–252; Lyle Eslinger, "Inner-Biblical Exegesis and Inner-Biblical Allusion: The Question of Category," *VT* 42 (1992): 47–58. Here, Noble explicitly defines his work

is possible when a biblical author draws from another source outside of his book and uses the source in a way that is reflective of his context and the context of the source. An example of intertextuality is found in the way Amos utilizes the Torah in 2:9–11.[29] Here, Amos applies the story of the exodus to his hearers' present situation. In doing so, he uses the method of intertextuality. Paul Koptak notes that Prov 2–7 can be viewed as a commentary on Deut 6:7–9 and 11:19, and that Lev 25:3–7 is an explanation of Exod 23:10–11a.[30]

Shape and Its Influence Upon Interpretation

The usage of intertextuality shows the idea that the Bible should be viewed by the reader as a coherent book that has a consistent and sustained message, such that each document within it must be understood in light of the other documents, even at the level of exegesis, before doctrinal synthesis has even begun. The order of the books and their respective locations within the canon are significant for the overall theological message of the Scriptures. Thus, John Sailhamer argues, "A canonical approach recognizes as a fundamental axiom of textual studies that the very process of forming the OT canon has made itself in the textual shape of the OT."[31]

"Shape" is also another important term to consider when discussing the canonical approach, and the task of defining "shape" involves two challenges.

---

as seeking to find "inner-biblical allusions," notably in the story of Tamar and Judah and other stories within the Hebrew Bible. Yet, he also acknowledges that an inner-biblical allusion is now sometimes called "intertextuality ... used with widely divergent meanings by different scholars, depending upon their hermeneutical persuasions." Furthermore, Noble clarifies that he is using the term intertextuality "very broadly, for the interpretative relationships that pertain between texts." Noble, "Esau, Tamar, and Joseph," n1. Dane Ortlund uses the word "allusion" to "refer to a conscious though veiled literary connection with a previous text." Dane C. Ortlund, "'And Their Eyes Were Opened, and They Knew': An Inter-Canonical Note on Luke 24:31," *JETS* 53 (2010): 717n1. He distinguishes an allusion from an echo by noting that an echo is used unconsciously, citing Richard Hays's work *Echoes of Scripture in the Letters of Paul*. The problem here, though, is Ortlund's definition that refers to a "conscious though veiled" connection. Is an echo, then, not an intentional move by the author but rather a subconscious connection that he did not intend? In my work, however, I am adopting a similar method to Noble. In using the term "intertextuality" throughout this work, I am arguing that the biblical author is using the referent text in his own body of work, thus employing the image that may be found therein.

29 Taken from James A. Sanders, "Canon" in *The Anchor Bible Dictionary*, ed. David Noel Freedman (Doubleday, 1992): 1:848.

30 Paul E. Koptak, "Intertextuality" in *Dictionary for Theological Interpretation of the Bible*, ed. Kevin J. Vanhoozer (Baker, 2005), 332. In his article, Koptak uses the term "inner-biblical exegesis" interchangeably with intertextuality.

31 Sailhamer, *Old Testament Theology*, 223.

First, scholars who employ the canonical approach understand "shape" in various ways. For example, Childs understands "shape" as that which sets the boundary for the canon of Scripture.[32] The second challenge is the literary structure of the passage and how this structure affects the shape of the content.[33] Thus, for Childs, the canonical shape of Scripture establishes the boundaries of biblical interpretation more so than the giving of meaning to particular passages.

John Sailhamer disagrees with Childs and believes that the order of the Old Testament has been predetermined so that their canonical order leads to a certain hermeneutic.[34] In the canonical approach, the position of a biblical book within the canon of Scripture should influence its interpretation. "A canonical approach to OT theology focuses its attention on the shape of the OT text at the time of the formation of the Canon. A canonical approach recognizes as a fundamental axiom of textual studies that the very process of forming the OT Canon has made itself felt in the textual shape of the OT."[35] Therefore, according to Sailhamer, shape is the particular arrangement of the books within the canon of Scripture that affects the emphasis of a particular text or story within the Bible.

The relationship between canonical criticism and the canonical approach are similar, although canonical criticism does not adequately convey the various methods employed by scholars.[36] Both canonical criticism and the canonical approach seek to read Scripture within its particular shape and understand how shape affects the interpretation of the passage. Gerald T. Sheppard notes that what is clear "is that canonical criticism is less a formal 'criticism' than an approach or series of approaches that seeks to raise neglected questions about the form and function of scripture, both Jewish and

---

32 "For Childs, the canonical approach that he has developed provides the 'arena'—the canonical texts of the Old and New Testaments in which Biblical Theology should perform this task." See William Lyons, *Canon and Exegesis: Canonical Praxis and the Sodom Narrative* (Sheffield Academic Press, 2002), 40.

33 Emerson, *Christ and the New Creation*, 19.

34 Sailhamer, *Old Testament Theology*, 224. With regards to the idea of a canonical order influencing a certain hermeneutical style, Stephen Dempster writes "A particular sequence suggests hermeneutical significance." Stephen Dempster, *Dominion and Dynasty: A Theology of the Hebrew Bible* (Intervarsity, 2003), 34.

35 Sailhamer, *Old Testament Theology*, 223. David R. Nienhuis, whose efforts have primarily focused on the shaping and interpretation of the Catholic Epistles, believes that the final form of these epistles suggest a particular reading strategy and argues that James was composed in the second century to "forge together a more literarily coherent and theologically robust collection of non-Pauline letters." See David R. Nienhuis, *Not by Paul Alone: The Formation of the Catholic Epistle Collection and Christian Canon* (Baylor University Press, 2007), 13.

36 Gerald T. Sheppard, "Canonical Criticism," in *The Anchor Bible Dictionary*, ed. David Noel Freedman (Doubleday, 1992), 1:861.

Christian."[37] The desire of canonical criticism was to discover the author's "intent" apart from the historical critical method since the literal sense of Scripture was "equated with the results of historical criticism [and had] been seriously reexamined."[38] This paradigm shift occurred because the literal sense of Scripture began to be defined with the intention of the first author.[39] Where the interpreter seeks to find the literal sense of the text, the intent of the author, according to Sheppard, will only be labeled as pre-biblical, considering the fact that these authors never intended to write "biblical traditions." The writings of these authors were only so labeled in this manner at a later time "and were publically established as such when they were assigned a place within a scripture by editors."[40]

Scholars tend to define the canonical approach differently. Concerning this phenomena, Anthony Thiselton remarks that there is no single form for the canonical approach. "Just as there is no single, uniform canonical approach, "there is [no] single, uniform, 'historical-critical method.' In my judgment the term *'the* historical-critical method' should be banned from all textbooks and from students' essays."[41] Although strong similarities among canonical approaches may be found within the works of noted proponents such as Brevard Childs, John Sailhamer, Christopher Seitz, and Rolf Rendtorff, it would not be prudent to offer a single, unqualified summary of their methods. Thus, the canonical approaches of Brevard Childs and John Sailhamer will be discussed as examples of how an interpreter applies the canonical approach to the Old Testament.[42]

---

37 Ibid., 1:861.

38 Ibid.

39 Of particular note is Matthew Barrett's interaction with Luke 24:44–48, commenting that "In this resurrection narrative Jesus not only assumes the Old Testament is characterized by a canon consciousness, but teaches his disciples that the entire canon was conscious of him. That sense, *Jesus is the canon*, for all the Scriptures typologically point forward to him." See Matthew Barrett, *Canon, Covenant and Christology: Rethinking Jesus and the Scriptures of Israel* (IVP Academic, 2020), 93. See especially 41–96.

40 Sheppard, "Canonical Criticism," 1:861.

41 Anthony C. Thiselton, "Canon, Community and Theological Construction," in *Canon and Biblical Interpretation*, ed. Craig G. Bartholomew, Scott Hahn, Robin Parry, Christopher Seitz, and Al Wolters (Zondervan, 2006), 4.

42 For other proponents of the canonical approach, see Dempster, *Dominion and Dynasty*; Stephen G. Dempster, "The Prophets, the Canon, and a Canonical Approach: No Empty Word," in *Canon and Biblical Interpretation*, ed. Craig Bartholomew et al. (Zondervan, 2006), 293–322; Rolf Rendtorff, *The Canonical Hebrew Bible: A Theology of the Old Testament* (Deo Publishing, 2005); Shepherd, *The Textual World of the Bible*; Greg Goswell, "The Order of the Books in the Greek Old Testament," *JETS* 52 (2009): 449–466; Greg Goswell, "The Order of the Books in the Hebrew Bible," *JETS* 51 (2008): 673–688; Christopher Seitz, *The Goodly Fellowship of the Prophets* (Baker, 2009). The bibliography at the conclusion of each chapter in *Canon and Biblical Interpretation* also provides a plethora of works for further study.

Brevard S. Childs

Brevard Childs developed the method known as the canonical approach, specifically as a reaction against the higher criticism that had overtaken Old Testament studies. Childs noticed that the focus of historical grammatical studies shifted from the study of the Bible to an entirely different concept of biblical studies.

> I began to realize that there was something fundamentally wrong with the foundations of the biblical discipline. It was not a question of improving on a source analysis, of discovering some unrecognized new genre, or of bringing a redactional layer into sharper focus. Rather, the crucial issue turned on one's whole concept of the study of the Bible itself. I am now convinced that the relation between the historical critical study of the Bible and its theological use as religious literature within a community of faith and practice needs to be completely rethought.[43]

Furthermore, Childs preferred to use the term "canonical approach" rather than "canonical criticism" since the latter shared a connection with other higher criticisms (*Geschichten*).

> I have always objected to the term 'canoni(ical) criticism" as a suitable description of my approach. I do not envision my approach as involving a new critical methodology analogous to literary, form, or redactional criticism. Rather, the crucial issue turns on one's initial evaluation of the nature of the biblical text being studied. By defining one's tasks as an understanding of the Bible as the sacred Scriptures of the church, one establishes from the outset the context and point-of-understanding of the reader within the received tradition of a community of faith and practice.[44]

---

43 Childs, *Introduction to the Old Testament*, 15.

44 "An Interview with Brevard S. Childs (1923–2007)." Original website no longer available. Cited from Mark S. Gignilliat, *A Brief History of Old Testament Criticism: From Benedict Spinoza to Brevard Childs* (Zondervan, 2012), 155. Gerald Sheppard notes that Childs removed "criticism" after Childs's commentary on Exodus was published because Childs felt it was a "misleading label for his own approach." Sheppard, "Canonical Criticism," 1:863. Nonetheless, "canonical criticism" has continued to be used to refer to the "canonical approach." For a complete list of the published works of Childs, see *The Bible as Christian Scripture: The Work of Brevard S. Childs*, ed. Christopher R. Seitz and Kent Harold Richards (Society of Biblical Literature, 2013), xiii–xx. For a brief overview of the canonical approach contrasted to others, see Childs, *Introduction to the Old Testament*, 74–75. For an illuminating discussion on the development of Childs's academic career and his canonical methodology, see Chen, *Theological Exegesis*, 17–56.

Despite this preference, "canonical criticism" has been used to refer to the "canonical approach."[45]

Childs disagreed with what is known as the historical-critical introduction to the Old Testament in three areas. First, since this discipline was developed by Johann Gottfried Eichorn, Childs believed that the goal of the historical critical introduction was not to establish the canonical literature of the church but rather the history of development of the Hebrew literature.

> In the first place, the historical critical Introduction [sic] as it has developed since Eichorn does not have for its goal the analysis of the canonical literature of the synagogue and church, but rather it seeks to describe the history of the development of the Hebrew literature and to trace the earlier and later stages of this history. As a result, there always remains an enormous hiatus between the description of the critically reconstructed literature and the actual canonical text which has been received and used as authoritative scripture by the community.[46]

Childs, then, is more concerned with the canonical literature as the church has received it rather than the history of the Hebrew literature. This concern is significant for Childs since it not only influences his preferred method to introduce the Old Testament but also because it establishes his understanding of how the canon of the Old Testament was formed.[47]

Second, "[T]he whole dimension of resonance within the Bible which issues from a collection with fixed parameters and which affects both the language and its imagery is lost by disregarding the peculiar function of the canonical literature."[48] So, a critical introduction to the Old Testament fails to understand the various changes in the literature of Israel, its shape, and its structure. Third, the critical introduction "is constitutive of Israel's history that the literature formed the identity of the religious community which in turn shaped the literature. This fundamental dialectic which lies at the heart of the canonical process is lost when the critical Introduction [sic] assumes that a historically referential reading of the Old Testament is the key to its interpretation."[49] According to Childs, then, the critical introduction fails to

---

45 See Michael J. Kruger, *Canon Revisited: Establishing the Origins and Authority of the New Testament Books* (Crossway, 2012), 49n87.
46 Childs, *Introduction to the Old Testament*, 40.
47 See Kruger, *Canon Revisited*, 52–59.
48 Childs, *Introduction to the Old Testament*, 40.
49 "Thirdly, the usual historical critical Introduction [sic] has failed to relate the nature of the literature correctly to the community which treasured it as scripture. Childs, *Introduction to the Old Testament*, 41.

relate the literature to the community to which it was written and show how the literature influenced its shape.

The historical critical introduction assumes that a political or social factor was determinative for the biblical text rather than "the religious dynamic of the canon" so that the "issue is not whether or not an Old Testament Introduction should be historical, but the nature of the historical categories being applied."[50] According to Childs, historical critical methods have posed the wrong questions of the biblical text because the methods attempted to establish the history of the literature rather than focus upon the theological shape of the text.[51] These methods sought to "reconstruct the development of the Hebrew literature," disregard the "peculiar function of the canonical literature," and ignore "the tension between the literature's role in forming the community and the community's role in forming the literature in favor of always reading the text in terms of political, social, or economic influence."[52] Therefore, Childs focused upon the final form of the biblical text because "the final form of scripture lies in the peculiar relationship between text and people of God which is constitutive of the canon."[53] Thus, the primary method for interpreting both the Old and New Testaments is found within the canon as the Scriptures were received.[54]

Although Childs formed the canonical approach in response to the arguments of the historical critical method, he does not fully abandon this methodology. Childs employs this method when he attempts to determine the pre-history of a specific text or book, as the discussion of the Pentateuch in his *Introduction to the Old Testament as Christian Scripture* shows. He recognizes that, during his time, the vast number of introductions to the Pentateuch focus upon the documentary hypothesis theory and that the study of any canonical book cannot be divorced from the knowledge of its historical development.[55] In his commentary on Exodus, Childs does similarly to his *Introduction to the Old Testament as Christian Scripture*. He seeks to restore the best Hebrew text but also seeks "to understand how the text was heard and interpreted by later communities."[56]

---

50 Ibid.
51 G. Michael O'Neal, *Interpreting Habakkuk as Scripture: An Application of the Canonical Approach of Brevard S. Childs* (Peter Lang, 2006), 10.
52 Ibid., 9.
53 Childs, *Introduction to the Old Testament*, 75.
54 "The canonical analysis focuses its attention on the final form of the text itself." Ibid., 73.
55 See Ibid., 128.
56 Childs, *The Book of Exodus* (Westminster Press, 1974), xiv. Anthony Thiselton provides a helpful overview of Childs's commentary on Exodus and this method of determining the best text for interpretation. "Canon, Community and Theological Construction," 6–7.

Childs's *Biblical Theology in Crisis* and *The Book of Exodus* were the forerunners for his canonical approach, and he continued further to develop this method in his *Introduction to the Old Testament as Christian Scripture*.[57] Childs labels *The Book of Exodus* as "unabashedly theological," and says that it's focus was to understand Exodus "as scripture of the church."[58] For Childs, as Chen Xun correctly notes, the validity of the canonical approach is not bound on the technicality of the exegetical method but rather in the theological task itself.[59]

The canonical approach provided Childs the opportunity to study the text rather than the events behind it. This method distinguishes the canonical approach from the historical critical method, and Childs notes that a canonical approach takes the "literature which Israel transmitted as a record of God's revelation to his people along with Israel's response."[60] For Childs, the correct method of interpreting Holy Scripture is found within the Scriptures as they were received and read by Israel rather than in a history of the development of the biblical text.[61]

As previously mentioned, the shape of the Hebrew canon is significant for how Childs establishes the boundary of interpretation. The canon is the "arena" that establishes the necessary boundary of interpretation, and for Childs it is nonetheless the Old and New Testaments of the Christian Bible. Furthermore, the literary structure of a passage describes how a certain passage or book is connected to the broader section(s) of a respective book within the arena of interpretation.[62] In other words, Childs desires to understand why the writer chose his material and why it was placed in its respective position. However, "the canonical shaping serves not so much to establish a given meaning to a particular passage as to *chart the boundaries within which the exegetical task is to be carried out.*"[63] Therefore, the shape of the canon of

---

57 Childs, *Biblical Theology in Crisis*; Childs, *Exodus*. On the unity between the two Testaments, see Childs, *Biblical Theology in Crisis*, 202–209. In his *Introduction to the Old Testament*, Childs discusses his canonical approach on pp. 69–82.

58 Childs, *Exodus*, ix.

59 Xun, *Theological Exegesis*, 34.

60 Childs, *Introduction to the Old Testament as Scripture*, 73.

61 "The canonical approach to the Hebrew Bible does not make any dogmatic claims for the literature apart from the literature itself, as if these texts contained only timeless truths or communicated in a unique idiom, but rather it studies them as historically and theologically conditioned writings which were accorded a normative function in the life of this community. It also acknowledges that these texts served a religious function in close relationship to the worship and service of God whom Israel confessed to be the source of the sacred word. The witness of the text cannot be separated from the divine reality which Israel testified to have evoked the response." Ibid., 11.

62 Emerson, *Christ and the New Creation*, 19.

63 Childs, *Introduction to the Old Testament*, 83. Emphasis added.

Christian Scripture is more concerned to establish the necessary boundaries of interpretation rather than give meaning to certain passages of the Christian Scripture.[64]

In sum, Childs sought to examine the Christian Scriptures as they were received in their present form.[65] His canonical approach allows the interpreter to focus on the received text of the Christian canon rather than the events behind the text. Childs determines the pre-history of the text and how the book functions within the canon, and this determination allows him to understand the theological message of the Scriptures.[66]

JOHN SAILHAMER

John Sailhamer uses the canonical approach in a similar way to Childs, and in his writings Sailhamer primarily focuses upon the Old Testament. As previously stated, Sailhamer believes that the "canonical order ensures that the books of the OT are read in a predetermined context."[67] Sailhamer further suggests that the canonical approach views the form of the Christian canon as theologically relevant since the final shape of the Old Testament is important. This final shape, contra Childs, bears weight upon the interpretation of the Old Testament.[68]

For Sailhamer, the locus, or the primary center, of God's revelation resides solely within the text of Scripture. Since God's revelation lies within this context, Sailhamer carefully argues that a distinction must be made

---

64 Emerson notes that shaping, for Childs, is "actually a descriptive process that provides the 'launching off point' for exegesis through considering the literary structure of a passage or a book." However, this process does not include the order of the biblical books within the canon and the emphasis that derives of their unique location. So, "shaping thus provides the reader with direction," but the order of the biblical books plays no significant part in this interpretative scheme. See Emerson, *Christ and the New Creation*, 20.

65 It should also be mentioned that Childs focused more on the Masoretic Text (MT) rather than the Septuagint (LXX). He believes this focus "lies in the theological concern to preserve this common textual bond between Jews and Christians." Childs, *Old Testament Theology*, 10. The MT aids the Christian in the theological practice to relate to the Old Testament outside of the LXX since it was the LXX the Christians were utilizing to confront first-century Judaism. Thereafter, Childs reminds the reader that "a canonical approach takes the Hebrew scriptures seriously because of its confession that Israel remains the prime tradent of this witness." Ibid.

66 O'Neal, *Interpreting Habakkuk as Scripture*, 11.

67 Sailhamer, Old Testament Theology, 224.

68 "[The] canonical approach sees not only the content of the OT, but also its form, as theologically relevant. The final shape of the OT is as important as the actual course of events that are recounted in it. The message of the OT is as much a function of how it is written as of what it recounts. I do not understand the canonical approach to consist of driving a wedge between form and content; these two all-important features of the OT. It is not a matter of one or the other but of both." Sailhamer, "The Canonical Approach to the OT," 307.

between the text and the event found therein. The biblical text which describes the event that occurred is inspired, and the goal of the interpreter should be to understand the biblical text. When Scripture recounts events in the narrative, it is not "intended to direct the readers' attention outside the text but rather within the text and to the narrative world depicted there."[69] Furthermore, "Even when one clearly has in view the goal to be biblical in the textual sense of the term, that is, to get at the meaning of the text of Scripture, it is all too easy to blur the boundaries between the text and the event and to handle the text as if one were in fact dealing with the event represented in the text."[70] Therefore, Sailhamer emphasizes the text of Scripture as the locus of God's revelation in order to prioritize the text over the event of the narrative world.

To assist in clarifying between the text and the event recorded, Sailhamer draws on the categories listed by Hans W. Frei. Frei classifies scholars within the history of biblical interpretation as pre-critical, empirical, and idealistic.[71] For each classification, the locus of meaning varies: pre-critical emphasizes the Scriptures, empirical focuses upon the external historical events, and the idealistic details ideas that embody the biblical text. Frei's work recorded the shift from biblical interpretation of the text to the historicity of the Bible.

According to Michael B. Shepherd, this shift separated the Bible from itself so that the Bible's own account became questionable. As a result, the reconstruction of the events became the explanation of the text itself.[72] As an example, Shepherd notes the claim made by Longman and Dillard in their Old Testament Introduction that the exodus was God's greatest act of salvation in the Old Testament.

> This confusion between the history of ancient Israel and the text of the Hebrew Scriptures is all too common and results in a loss of meaning and significance. It can certainly be said that the original exodus from Egypt was God's greatest act of salvation in the history of ancient Israel, but the greatest act of salvation revealed in the text of the Hebrew Bible is the new exodus (e.g., Num 23:22; 24:8; Isa 11:16; 43:16–21; Hos 2:16–17 [Eng., 2:14–15]; Mic 7:15). The same can be said of the overly simplistic identification of the Hebrew Bible with the law, the old covenant, or Judaism,

---

69 Sailhamer, Old Testament Theology, 39.
70 Ibid., 57.
71 Sailhamer, Old Testament Theology, 36. Hans W. Frei, *The Eclipse of Biblical Narrative* (Yale University Press, 1974).
72 Michael B. Shepherd, *Textuality and the Bible* (Wipf and Stock, 2016), 6.

resulting in a fundamental inability to see any genuine continuity with the New Testament documents.[73]

Therefore, the "Bible's textual representation of reality was rendered irrelevant."[74] When the Bible's textual representation of reality is rendered irrelevant, the focus is now placed upon the event which the text describes.

The priority of the text over the event is crucial for Sailhamer because the recorded text of the event is what is inspired, and it is the goal of the interpreter to discuss the text of Scripture. He remarks:

> We will maintain the following discussion that while professing to be text-centered in their approach, evangelical biblical theologians sometimes treat the text of Scripture as a means of getting at what they perceive to be the real locus of God's revelation—the events in the history of Israel or the religious ideals that lie behind the text. In doing so they fail to appreciate the implications of their own orthodox view of Scripture as divine revelation.[75]

Since the Old and New Testaments are written texts, they represent the work of an author or authors who are constrained to the syntax of the language they use.[76] Furthermore, the reader cannot impose their own meaning upon the literature since the meaning of the text is given by the author. The reader must understand the "text in terms dictated by the grammatical and syntactical constraints of the language in which it is written."[77] Furthermore:

> That the bible has both a divine and a human origin does not mean that it has both a divine and a human purpose or intention. It does not mean that though the human authors may have meant one thing, God intended another. When the Bible speaks about its own origin as "inspired" Scripture (2Ti 3:16), it does not pit its human authors against its divine Author. On the contrary, its view is that the human authors were so moved by God to write that what they wrote was what God intended. As Peter puts it, "Men spoke from God as they were carried along by the Holy Spirit" (2Pe 1:21).[78]

---

73 Ibid., n16.
74 Ibid.
75 Sailhamer, Old Testament Theology, 37.
76 Ibid., 9.
77 Ibid.
78 John H. Sailhamer, *The Pentateuch as Narrative: A Biblical-Theological Commentary*

Thus, Sailhamer argues that the text of Scripture is divinely inspired.

To assist the reader in understanding what is meant by prioritizing the text over the event, Sailhamer provides the illustration of a tree that has been photographed. Sailhamer notes that the photograph is not only a simple representation of the tree but also the photograph represents the tree in a realistic and accurate fashion. The photograph captures the tree at the time of the photograph in a realistic and accurate fashion, but the photograph itself does not consist of the actual components of the tree. Although the photograph does not contain the components of the tree, the tree is still represented accurately within the bounds of the photograph. Despite the photograph lacking the components of the tree does not mean that the tree does not exist or that the photograph is an inaccurate representation since it depicts only one side of the tree. This example, Sailhamer notes, is analogous to the biblical texts because they represent the events but are not the actual corporeal events themselves.[79]

Sailhamer distinguishes between the representation of reality and the real world by discussing a still life painting of a pipe that existed in the early part of the twentieth-century.[80] This painting was done with such precision that it could be mistaken for a photograph, and under the painting the author's title read "This is a pipe." The painting and title caused such a stir among the artistic community that several groups, particularly the Dadists and Surrealists, questioned the purpose of art and their belief that art should be an expression of reality and the statement of truth. Rene Magritte, a surrealist painter, responded by painting an exact replica of the pipe and titled the painting, "This is *not* a pipe," and made his point. However realistic a painting or a photograph is, it is only a representation of the object it captured, and it is, by default, not the object.

As previously stated, Sailhamer believes that the order of the Old Testament books were predetermined and the order of these books leads to a particular hermeneutic.[81] According to Sailhamer, "a canonical order ensures that the books of the OT are read in a predetermined context."[82] While examining the "prophetic echo" of the usage of the Pentateuch within the

---

(Zondervan, 1992), 3.

79 Sailhamer, Old Testament Theology, 45–46. Furthermore, "As readers of these texts we stand before them as their authors have construed them and we look to the texts themselves for our understanding of the 'world' they depict." Ibid., 46. See a similar example employed by Sailhamer from Picasso in Sailhamer, *The Pentateuch as Narrative* 10n14.

80 Sailhamer, Old Testament Theology, 46.

81 See John H. Sailhamer, "The Canonical Approach to the OT," 307–315; "1 Chronicles 21:1—A Study in Inter-Biblical Interpretation," *TJ* 10 (1989): 33–48.

82 Sailhamer, Old Testament Theology, 252.

prophets, Sailhamer also remarks that "the location and arrangement of a text within or alongside other texts can affect how a reader understands the text."[83] Thus, in sum, for Sailhamer, the location of the Scriptures influence a hermeneutic that follows the canonical order of the Old Testament.

Canonical Approaches to the New Testament

The canonical approach has been limited primarily to the study of the Old Testament, and little has been done with using this methodology for the study of the New Testament. Perhaps the primary cause for this neglect can be found, like in Old Testament studies, in the wide application of the historical-critical method. While seeking to establish the contextual history of the New Testament, greater attention appears to have focused upon the world behind the text rather than the text itself.

Ryan Armstrong believes there is a certain reading strategy for the New Testament. He remarks, "There is a reading order within the first Testament. There is a definite reading order from the first to the second Testament. Perhaps there is also an intended development within the second Testament as one reads from Matthew to Revelation." [84] Armstrong further suggests that the reading order of the New Testament canon is an editorial feature and if, for example, Acts is read in light of the Gospels or vice versa it can affect interpretation.[85] According to Armstrong, there also exists the possibility of literary dependence across the corpus of New Testament documents, such as a possible cross-reference of Luke 10:7 and 1 Tim 5:18 as well as the possibility that James was familiar with Romans.[86]

David Trobisch argues that the New Testament, as it was received in its canonical form, "is not the result of a lengthy and complicated collecting process that lasted several centuries. The History of the New Testament is

---

83 John H. Sailhamer, *The Meaning of the Pentateuch* (IVP Academic, 2009), 14.
84 Ryan M. Armstrong, "Canonical Approaches to New Testament Theology: An Evangelical Evaluation of Childs and Trobisch" (ThM thesis., Southeastern Baptist Theological Seminary, 2007), 101.
85 Ibid., 102.
86 "In only the first chapter of James one finds several similarities to Romans. The listing of the results of suffering found in Rom 5:3–5 parallels Jas 1:2–4. The idea that sin brings death is found in both Rom 6:23 and Jas 1:15–6, which would not be significant if both passages did not follow up with a mention of the gifts of God. The contrast between the "hearers" and the "doers" in Rom 2:13 and Jas 1:22 links the New Testament together even if one takes them both as coming from Matt 7:26. Even the editors of the Novum Testamentum Graece, 27th edition note numerous cross references to Romans in the margins throughout the book of James." Armstrong, "Canonical Approaches to New Testament Theology," 104. See also pp 102–105. In the NA28, the editors kept many of the references Armstrong cites.

a history of an edition, a book that has been published and edited by a specific group of editors, at a specific place, and at a specific time."[87] He further argues that there is enough evidence for a canonical edition of the New Testament and that this evidence is found within the earliest manuscripts, ones that were not available to previous scholars. "The arrangement and number of New Testament writings in the oldest extant manuscripts of the Christian Bible provide the most important evidence for describing the history of the canon."[88] Trobisch carefully examines the various textual evidence for this canonical formation, but does not thoroughly examine a reading strategy for the New Testament canon, save a few pages at the conclusion of his work.[89]

For Childs, approaching the New Testament canonically is relatively simple. He believes that a canonical approach is present within a book's structure and the author's intent, since the author normally states the purpose of his book in the beginning.[90] The canon, then, was shaped not so much as pertaining to sociological matters but rather "toward engendering faith and did not lie inert as a deposit of uninterpreted [sic] data from a past age."[91]

Childs notes that the controversy between the canonical approach and the historical critical method begins to emerge at this point. The canonical approach recognizes the existing tension when the historical critical scholar historicizes the material of the New Testament. The result of this historicizing leads to the understanding that if one has a better historical focus one has a better method of interpretation.[92] Whenever new information is introduced, the text is often silenced in favor of the historical background. Thus, "the critic presumes to stand above the text, outside the circle of tradition, and from this detached vantage point adjudicate the truth and error of the New Testament's time-conditionality."[93] Contrasted to this, the canonical interpreter focuses upon the text received, the received tradition, and strives to interpret the Scripture.[94] Furthermore, the canonical interpreter focuses upon the

---

[87] David Trobisch, *The First Edition of the New Testament* (Oxford University Press, 2000), 6. See also *Paul's Letter Collection* (Quiet Waters Publication, 2001), 52–54.

[88] Ibid., 21.

[89] Trobisch, *The First Edition of the New Testament*, 78–101.

[90] Brevard Childs, *The New Testament as Canon: An Introduction* (Fortress Press, 1984), 49. Childs, primarily trained in the field of Old Testament Studies, spent five years in research in order to master the field of New Testament studies. He noticed, after a conversation with a New Testament colleague from Yale, that the canonical approach had "touched on few issues which were of real interest to a New Testament scholar." Ibid., xvi.

[91] Ibid., 51. He lists five hits in perspective in the formation of the New Testament canon as compared to that of the Old Testament. See ibid., 12–15.

[92] Ibid.

[93] Ibid.

[94] Ibid., 51–52.

shape of the canonical collection and the influence it has on its respective parts, such as Gospels, Pauline, and the Catholic Epistles.[95] Childs concludes his canonical approach to the New Testament by noting that this approach is not a shortcut to exegesis nor does it offer an interpretation for each passage within the New Testament.

> Rather, it seeks to sketch a different vision of the biblical text which profoundly affects one's concept of the enterprise, but which also makes room for the continuing activity of exegesis as a discipline of the church. It is likely that future scholars who work seriously with the implications of the canon will arrive at different interpretations of individual passages and indeed of the entire books. Such correction is all to the good. However, the nature of the debate will be vastly different among those who share a canonical vision of interpreting the New Testament as sacred scripture of the church. One test of continuity between generations of readers will be to determine the extent of a genuine family resemblance which reflects both diversity and individuality within the discipline.[96]

Like Childs, Robert Wall believes that a book of the Christian canon was intended for a particular religious community and the literal or plain sense of the Scripture has value "only in relationship to a more holistic end."[97] Approaching the New Testament canonically provides the interpreter the opportunity to examine the biblical text in its privileged role in Christian formation. As a result, the aim of biblical interpretation is to understand the text theologically.[98]

Furthermore, to approach the New Testament canonically means that one should allow the shape and final form of the canon to influence interpretation of the biblical text.[99] Much like Sailhamer argued that the Old Testament canonical order was predetermined and that determination leads to a particular hermeneutic, so the reader who approaches the New Testament

---

95 Ibid., 52–53.
96 Childs, *The New Testament as Canon* ,53.
97 Robert W. Wall, "The Function of the Pastoral Letters Within the Pauline Canon of the New Testament: A Canonical Approach," in *The Pauline Canon*, ed. Stanley E. Porter (Brill, 2004), 14. See Brevard S. Childs, *Biblical Theology of the Old and New Testaments* (Fortress Press, 1992), 719–727. For five reasons why Wall believes the canonical approach is the preferred hermeneutic, see Robert W. Wall, "The Canonical Approach," in *Biblical Hermeneutics: Five Views*, ed. Beth Stovell and Stanley E Porter (InterVarsity Press, 2012), 111–130.
98 Robert W. Wall, "The Significance of a Canonical Perspective of the Church's Scriptures," in *The Canon Debate*, ed. Lee Martin McDonald and James A. Sanders (Hendrickson, 2002), 528.
99 Michael B. Shepherd, *The Textual World of the Bible* (Peter Lang, 2013), 87–88.

canonically must do so as well.¹⁰⁰ For example, David R. Nienhus believes that the form of the Catholic Epistles is intentional and, with Wall, the "markers of canonical shaping ... recommend a reading strategy that considers intertextual allusions within the collection as instances of theological magnification."¹⁰¹ Nienhuis writes:

> First, the sequence 'James-Peter-John' does not make sense according to stichoi length and appears designed to echo Paul's listing of the 'Pillars' of the Jerusalem church in Galatians 2:9. Second, since the collection begins with a letter from 'James, a servant of God and the Lord Jesus Christ,' and ends with one from 'Jude, a servant of Jesus Christ and brother of James,' one might easily conclude that the collection as a whole is delivered in the 'embrace' of letters from Jesus' brothers according to the flesh. From there it is not too great a stretch to posit that the outward shape of the collection was intended to signify the letter group as a literary witness to the Jerusalem apostolate.¹⁰²

---

100 Employing the contextuality of John Sailhamer, Emerson argues that the order of the New Testament books suggests a reading strategy that points to Jesus Christ as the fulfillment "of the Old Testament's eschatological messianic hope through inaugurating the new creation in his life, death, resurrection, ascension, and Pentecost and consummating it at his return." See Emerson, *Christ and the New Creation*, ix. Emerson further comments, "New creation is not a theme that arises only with the advent of Christ in the New Testament. It is a well-attested theme in the Old Testament and one that is prominent throughout the whole of Scripture." For Sailhamer's discussion of contextuality see Sailhamer, *Old Testament Theology*, 213–215.

101 David R. Nienhuis and Robert W. Wall, *Reading the Epistles of James, Peter, John and Jude as Scripture: The Shaping and Shape of a Canonical Collection* (Eerdmans, 2013), 68. See the critique by Darian Lockett, "Not Whether, but What Kind of Canonical Approach: A Review Essay," *JTI* 9 (2015): 127–136. For the Pauline Epistles, see Childs, *The Church's Guide for Reading Paul*, he interacts with the shape of the Pauline corpus by examining Romans and the Pastoral Epistles, respectively, and provides a helpful overview of Paul's programmatic epistle (Romans) and the concluding words of his corpus.

102 Nienhuis, *Not by Paul Alone*, 7. See also 29–97. A certain difficulty arises when both Nienhuis and Wall contend for "canonization" over composition as the true point of the origin of Scripture. They argue that the original meaning of Scripture lies not in the composition of the biblical text itself but rather when the text was canonized. This "shift from a text's point of composition to its points of canonization, with its various ancillary claims of canonical rather than authorial intent and textual meaning, follows the epistemology of modernity's defense of a text's 'original meaning." Nienhuis and Wall, *Reading the Epistles of James, Peter, John, and Jude as Scripture*, 12. This suggestion of original meaning seems to remove any authorial intention in composition and prioritizes the canonization process as that which gives meaning. The canonization process becomes more significant than the composition of the biblical work in their understanding. Thus, there is an apparent disconnect between author and book and a greater emphasis lies upon the reader interpreting the biblical text within the context of the canon. This is an unfortunate conclusion by Nienhuis and Wall, and the result isolates composition of the biblical text within the first received community. See the helpful critique by Darian R. Lockett, "Not Whether; but What Kind of Canonical Approach: A Review Essay," *JTI* 9 (2015): 127–136.

Darian R. Lockett believes there are connections between James and Jude in the way both epistles begin and end. For example, neither James nor Jude highlight their familial connection with Jesus, nor do they draw attention to their apostleship.[103] Furthermore, Lockett believes that the conclusions of each letter stress not only the restoration of a lost brother but also "mercy triumphing over judgment [as] integral to both letters."[104] Therefore, for Lockett, the Catholic Epistles should not be read in isolation to one another, but maintain a balance between the history and the theology of the Catholic Epistles.[105] This balance would primarily include reading the Catholic Epistles as a whole, examining the thematic connections that show the collection of the Catholic Epistles as intentional.[106]

But the canonical approach can also be used to examine the entirety of the New Testament canon itself, as attested by Matthew Emerson, in order to form a coherent New Testament theology.[107] Emerson applies the canonical method to the New Testament, and argues that this approach shows that "Jesus Christ is the fulfillment of the Old Testament's eschatological messianic hope through inaugurating the new creation in his life, death, resurrection, ascension, and Pentecost and consummating it at his return."[108] According to Emerson, not only is a canonical hermeneutic supported by theological foundations that are provided in the history of interpretation and "reflect a coherent understanding of bibliology, pneumatology, and Christology," but also that a canonical hermeneutic is textual; that is, "the locus of revelation, and therefore of interpretation, is in the text."[109] Emerson's research, besides that of Childs, is one of the few works that focuses upon the New Testament canon as a whole. His attempts to trace a coherent argument based upon the order of the books of the New Testament is refreshing in light of atomistic and fragmented historical-critical readings.[110]

---

103 Darian R. Lockett, *Letters from the Pillar Apostles: The Formation of the Catholic Epistles as a Canonical Collection*. (Wipf & Stock, 2017), 189–190.

104 Ibid., 193.

105 Darian R. Lockett, "Are the Catholic Epistles a Canonically Significant Collection? A Status Quaestionis," *CBR* 14.1 (2015): 79.

106 Lockett, *Letters from the Pillar Apostles*, 196–230.

107 Christ and the New Creation: A Canonical Approach to the Theology of the New Testament is a revised edition of Emerson's doctoral dissertation, *"Christ and the New Creation: A Canonical Approach to the Theology of the New Testament"* (PhD diss., Southeastern Baptist Theological Seminary, 2011). For a helpful overview of the order of the New Testament books influences interpretation, see Greg Goswell, "The Order of the Books of the New Testament," *JETS* 53 (2010): 225–241.

108 Emerson, *Christ and the New Creation*, ix.

109 Ibid., 2, 12. Emerson provides five tenets of a canonical hermeneutic, with "textual" as the final. See 6–13. See also Shepherd, *The Textual World of the Bible*, 89–90.

110 See also Greg Goswell, "Two Testaments in Parallel: The Influence of the Old Testa-

Critiques of the Canonical Approach

Perhaps the most common critique of the canonical approach is that the approach does not favor the historical setting of the biblical text and is deemed anti-historical.[111] Jeffrey Niehaus suggests that the canonical approach cannot attest to the Bible's veracity in the matters of history, theology, and praxis since the proponents of the canonical approach have accepted the conclusions of higher criticism.[112] "Put another way, canonical criticism of that sort is, at its root, nothing more than a stratagem or tactic by which someone who does not believe that the Bible records true history or actual acts of God in history can still take the Bible's contents as a viable basis for doing theology."[113] He provides a reference to the work by John F.A. Sawyer, who holds to the canonical method but rejects Mosaic authorship, as an example of how the canonical method leads to ahistorical interpretation.[114] Niehaus is correct to

---

ment on the Structuring of the New Testament Canon," *JETS* 56 (2013): 459–474. Goswell compares the New Testament structure to that of the Old Testament canon and notes possible parallels, which might suggest the location of the respective section of the New Testament. He acknowledges that the Pauline corpus is arranged, in its present sequence, by length, but that Romans also serves as a guide for the conclusion of Acts since Romans is viewed as Paul's most robust theological work. Goswell concludes his article by noting that although location influences reading, the books of the New Testament canon are organized by size, genre, and common authorship. Trobisch disagrees. After noting traditional arrangement of adding new letters to older works, he notes that "The letters of Paul are arranged according to their addresses into two parts: the letters to congregations and the letters to individuals." Trobisch, *Pauline Letter Collections*, 52.

111 There are, of course, several others. For a critique of Childs see R. W. L. Moberly, "Theology of the Old Testament," in *The Face of Old Testament Studies*, ed. David W. Baker and Bill T. Arnold (Baker, 1999), 467–472. Moberly also mentions the work of J. Barton, *Reading the Old Testament: Method in Biblical Studies* (Westminster, 1984); James Barr, *Holy Scripture: Canon, Authority, Criticism* (Westminster, 1983); and M. Brett, *Biblical Criticism in Crisis? The Impact of the Canonical Approach on Old Testament Studies* (Cambridge University Press, 1991). See the defense by Christopher R. Seitz, *The Character of Christian Scripture: The Significance* of a *Two-Testament Bible* (Baker, 2011), 27–92.

112 "Such an affirmation can be distinguished from a canonical approach that accepts the conclusions of higher criticism of Gunkelian form criticism (e.g., of Genesis) on the one hand and yet, on the other hand, affirms a canonical unity of Genesis or of the Bible. Scholars who do so then proceed to do theology on the basis of that canonical, overarching unity. Such canonical criticism is simply a way for those who accept a disintegrative analysis of the Bible to write theology as though the Bible were, in fact, an organic whole." Jeffrey J. Niehaus, *Biblical Theology Volume 1: The Common Grace Covenants* (Weaver, 2014), 22.

113 Ibid., 23.

114 Sawyer notes, "'The Mosaic authorship of the Pentateuch' is only one of many examples where we must approach Old Testament tradition at two levels; usually in the development of Christianity and Judaism, the level of the meaning of the text as it stands has been far more influential than the reconstructed original, and must therefore in the context of the study of religion be treated sympathetically.... *In other words it is the meaning of the text that is important, whether or not it is historically true*. It is what the author wants to get across to his

make this connection for, in its purest form, the canonical approach is not concerned with the historicity of the events of the Scripture. What is important for a pure canonical criticism is how the text influenced the community in which it was shaped, whether or not the event actually occurred.[115] Niehaus also cites Childs, who would reject the historicity of the biblical text if he deemed necessary, as further proof that one cannot use a canonical method for interpreting the Scripture.[116]

James Barr's critique of Childs's *Introduction to the Old Testament as Scripture* focuses upon the suppressed anti-historical nature of Childs's work and the development and inclusion of the biblical text within the canon of Scripture. "The effect of Childs' principles is that it does not much matter—for theological reading—what went on in Old Testament times. Authority is concentrated in the canonical text, and not in the people or events out of which that text came."[117] Furthermore, according to Barr, Childs "reads into the minds of the redactors and canonizers his own passionate hermeneutical interest."[118] Thus, there is not a canonical hermeneutics of sorts but rather Childs's anachronistic reading of the biblical canon. Barr concedes the possibility of a "canonizer" including a Deutero-Isaiah within Isaiah, but the person who establishes the biblical canon of Samuel and omits "the important text elements known from LXX and Qumran, was not doing anything hermeneutic: rather, he was saying, 'here we are, this is the text and this is the end; sense or no sense, this is what we have.'"[119]

This critique by Barr is a fair and necessary assessment of Child's methodology. Childs responds to Barr and argues that the "issue at stake is the nature of the Bible's historicality and the search for a historical approach,

---

readers or listeners that should be the Conner of every teacher of the Old Testament." Ibid., 23 n34. See also John F. A. Sawyer, *From Moses to Patmos* (SPCK, 1977), 9–10. Emphasis added

115 Frank W. Spina, "Canonical Criticism: Childs Versus Sanders," in *Interpreting God's Word for Today*, ed. Wayne McCown and James Earl Massey (Warner, 1982), 179.

116 "The canonical approach to the Hebrew Bible does not make any dogmatic claims for the literature apart from the literature itself, as if these texts contained only timeless truths or communicated in a unique idiom, but rather it studies them as historically and theologically conditioned writings which were accorded a normative function in the life of this community. It also acknowledges that the texts served a religious function in closest relationship to the worship and service of God whom Israel confessed to be the source of the sacred word. The witness of the text cannot be separated from the divine reality which Israel testified to have evoked the response." Childs, *Introduction to the Old Testament*, 73.

117 James Barr, "Childs' Introduction to the Old Testament as Scripture," *JSOT* 16 (1980): 16. See also the critique of Jeffrey Niehaus in *Biblical Theology Volume 1*, 22.

118 Ibid., 17.

119 Barr, "Childs Introduction," 17. See the critique of Barr's critique of Childs in Christopher R. Seitz, *The Character of Christian Scripture: The Significance of a Two-Testament Bible* (Baker, 2011), 44–48.

which is commensurate with it. The whole point of emphasizing the canon is to stress the historical nature of the biblical witness. There is no 'revelation' apart from the experience of historical Israel."[120] The issue, then, is not the historical reality that the events of Scripture describe. The focus for those who are proponents of the canonical approach is the event, as described within the biblical passage. The text itself is the primary center of study and does not simply serve as a source to the historical event. Therefore, under the canonical approach, the Scriptures are a witness to the history of Israel rather than its sources.[121]

Despite the claim by Niehaus, his argument that a canonical method cannot be used to interpret the Scriptures suggests that all who subscribe to a canonical hermeneutic are guilty of what Sawyer or Childs suggest and have therefore accepted the conclusions of Gunkelian form criticism. Evangelicals, such as Sailhamer, have rejected the areas which affect the inspiration of Scripture and the truthfulness of the history of the biblical text. These scholars do understand that the Scriptures are one organic whole that have been integrated, through the guidance of the Holy Spirit, in order to point to the Messiah.[122] As Sailhamer remarks, "A text-oriented approach to the OT would insist that the locus of God's special revelation is in the Scriptures themselves, i.e., in the text."[123]

Although Sawyer, and others like him, may deny the historicity of the biblical text, it is unwise to suggest that all would do likewise who use a canonical approach. Rather, the Scriptures provide the appropriate "arena" or "location" for interpreting the correct history of Israel and, for that matter, any other event found within the biblical canon. The Scriptures themselves provide the most appropriate and trustworthy lens for which to gleam and understand the historical background that inhabits the biblical world. In other words, the Scriptures bear witness to unique events that have special significance for the Christian life.[124]

---

120 Childs, *Introduction to the Old Testament*, 71. It should be noted that Childs does not mean the word "historicality" in the same way an evangelical would. What Childs means here is the fact that the community who received the text has their own method of interpretation and since they believed it to be true, this plays in part to the historicality of the Scripture.

121 See also Seitz, *The Character of Christian Scripture*, 28–36.

122 The canonical approach as presented in this work is concerned with this connection. It would perhaps be unwise to say that any person who holds to a canonical approach would agree with this statement, for each scholar uses the term in their own respective fashion.

123 Sailhamer, *Old Testament Theology*, 56.

124 For example, the crucifixion of Jesus was only one of many Roman executions; yet, if God had not spoken of it in the Scriptures, the reader would have never known of its salvific effect. See J. I. Packer, *God Speaks to Man, Revelation and the Bible* (Westminster, 1965), 51–52.

Although Childs may have pioneered the canonical approach, the notion that the received community gives the biblical event the historical reality is rejected within this volume. From an historically orthodox standpoint, the reality and historical veracity of the biblical events do matter; to hold otherwise would imply that the Bible has no inherit value for salvation and becomes nothing more than a book that simply contains moral philosophy. Therefore, it is my opinion that the recorded historical events of the text are of great importance, and the present writer affirms the biblical history of Israel and all of the biblical events as recorded in the text of Scripture.

The canonical approach should focus the reader upon three areas of significance that distinguishes it from other hermeneutical methods. First, the biblical text is prioritized as the focal point of interpretation rather than the historical background. The interpreter does not have to, necessarily, reconstruct the historical background of the text in view, but should rather focus upon the written text. This focus provides the primary distinction between a historical-critical method and a canonical approach. Second, Scripture is viewed as a coherent piece through intertextuality. The reader is afforded the opportunity to see how, for example, the Book of the Twelve incorporates the theme of the "day of the Lord" to interpret a specific day of judgment for the recipients of these books as well as look forward to the future eschatological day of judgment.

> Strong evidence indicates that the book has been carefully crafted to link the various chapters into an overall unity, beginning with Hosea and ending with Malachi, linking the various chapters into an overall unity. For example, a prophetic saying about the Lord roaring from Zion closes the prophecy of Joel (3:16 [MT 4:16]) and opens the following prophecy of Amos (1:2). Obadiah succeeds Amos and deals with Edom, which features in the last chapter of Amos 9:12. Jonah treats the repentance and salvation of Nineveh, Micah predicts the judgment of a proud Assyria, and Nahum consists of a series of oracles describing the fall of an unrepented and incorrigible Nineveh.[125]

Both the prophets, the Book of the Twelve, and the New Testament authors assumed that readers of the Bible would be familiar with other texts of Scripture.[126]

---

125 Dempster, *Dominion and Dynasty*, 183.
126 Sailhamer, *Old Testament Theology*, 213; Shepherd, *The Twelve Prophets in the New Testament*.

Third, the reader examines how shape affects emphasis within interpretation, and the book of Ruth provides an example of this emphasis. In the Masoretic Text and the LXX, Ruth is located in two separate places. In the Masoretic Text, Ruth is placed in the Writings section of the threefold division of Law-Prophets-Writings, and Ruth follows the book of Proverbs. Proverbs concludes with a celebration of the excellent wife and provides numerous examples of how this excellent wife might act. Her actions are contrasted with the strange and foreign woman of chapters 5–7, and she is the "human reflex of Woman Wisdom herself."[127] The chapter and book of Proverbs concludes with the statement in v. 31 that this woman's work will praise her in the gates. In Ruth 3:11, the reader is told that Boaz praises Ruth for being a "worthy woman," and this event occurs at the city gates.[128]

In the LXX, Ruth is placed within the historical books, preceding 1 Samuel and following the book of Judges. The author of Ruth places the context of this story within the time frame of the judges (Ruth 1:1) and, as the reader will remember, during this time "everyone did what was right in his own eyes" (Judg 17:6; 21:25). The main theme of Judges is the unfaithfulness of Israel, and this theme is seen whenever the Israelites turn to idols until they are redeemed by a judge who was appointed by God. Once the judge dies, the pattern is repeated.

Ruth is the story of a gentile woman who acts in a godly manner and is redeemed by a man who serves as her kinsman redeemer (גאל). The two themes are similar in that the contrasting nature of Israel-Ruth (unfaithful/faithful) and the redeeming nature of God-Boaz stand in parallel to one another. Furthermore, Ruth ends on the foreshadowing event that it is through Ruth that one will come who is the son of Jesse, named David. The emphasis upon David cannot be missed, for the author mentions him in 4:17 and 4:22. Furthermore, the placement of Ruth before 1 Samuel emphasizes the importance of David even before he is met in 1 Sam 17. As Emerson notes, "Continuing with the theme of deliverance that began in Judges and continued in Ruth through the kinsman redeemer, God uses David to deliver His people from the great enemy, the Philistines, in 1 Samuel 17."[129]

The differing order of a book's location within the Masoretic Text or the LXX provides an example of how placement within the canon may affect the

---

127 Tremper Longman III, *Proverbs* (Baker, 2006), 540.
128 "That this poem concludes the book helps explain why, in the Hebrew canon, Proverbs is followed by Ruth (who herself is called a 'noble woman' in Ruth 3:11), and then by the Song of Songs, a book in which the woman is the main speaker and initiates the relationship." Ibid.
129 Emerson, *Christ and the New Creation*, 34.

emphasis of the material. However, the location a book has within the canon does not neglect key themes that appear within the work. Despite the location of Ruth, one is still able to understand Ruth as the virtuous woman in the LXX or the theme of God's deliverance in the Masoretic Text, for those themes are present within the book. It does suggest, however, that the order of the books naturally provides a method of interpretation that emphasizes certain themes above others.

A Need for the Canonical Approach to Revelation

The shape of the New Testament is significant because, as previously discussed, the location of a book within the canon does affect the degree of emphasis upon interpretation placed upon the biblical text. In other words, the canonical order may suggest a certain reading strategy for how the New Testament should be read and understood. The New Testament begins with the four Gospels that describe, in narrative, the life and ministry of Jesus from their respective viewpoints. The Gospels serve as background for the rest of the New Testament, since what follows the Gospels focuses primarily upon Jesus.[130] Acts continues the narrative genre and is not only joined together to Luke by the introduction in 1:1–3 but also provides the furtherance of the gospel message as the gospel moves throughout Jerusalem, Judea, Samaria, and the ends of the earth (Acts 1:8).[131] This record fulfills the commission given to the disciples by Jesus in Matt 28:19–20. The epistolary section of the New Testament begins after the narratives of the Gospels and Acts, starting with the Pauline corpus (Romans—Hebrews), and the Catholic Epistles (James—Jude).[132]

Revelation concludes not only the New Testament canon, but also the entirety of Scripture. It is clear that Revelation depends upon the Old Testament for several themes and allusions, and much has been written on this subject.[133] How the author uses intertextuality to various Old Testament stories suggests

---

130 Robert W. Wall, "The Significance of a Canonical Perspective of the Church's Scripture," 536.

131 Sinaiticus (01 א) lists the Pauline corpus after the Gospels, and places Acts with the General Epistles.

132 However, Vaticanus (B 03) begins with the General Epistles rather than the Pauline corpus. David Trobisch notes that the book of Hebrews was categorized into the Pauline corpus. See Trobisch, *The First Edition of the New Testament*, 59. Hebrews was also included in the Pauline corpus in the Muratonian canon. Bruce M. Metzger, *The Canon of the New Testament: Its Origin, Development, and Significance* (Clarendon, 1997), 197. See also Ched Spellman, *Toward a Canon-Conscious Reading of the Bible*, 222–223.

133 See G. K. Beale, *John's Use of the Old Testament in Revelation*, ed. Stanley E. Porter, JSNTSup 166 (Sheffield Academic Press, 1998), 60–128. See also the extensive bibliography in

a familiarity of the Old Testament for the author, but also for his intended audience as well. For example, Dempster notes that the

> choice of the book of Revelation to conclude the Christian Bible makes the New Testament a mirror image of the revised Old Testament canon with history (Gospel and Acts) followed by the present (Pauline and General Epistles) concluded with a look to the future (Apocalypse). The ending vision of the prophetic Revelation resonates with the beginning of the Torah, but it explodes those constraints.[134]

Thus, if the New Testament ends on a note that looks to the fulfillment of the visions within the New Testament and those from the Old Testament, then perhaps the reading strategy for Revelation is found by considering both Testaments. That is to say, the ideal-reader of Revelation is one who is familiar with both the Old and New Testament.

Neither the canonical approach for interpreting Revelation, nor the verbal connections provided by Charles, have been pursued in detail.[135] Rather, the typical default interpretation for Revelation has been a historical-grammatical hermeneutic in which the interpreter attempts to set Revelation within its appropriate historical background. Although placing Revelation in this background is a valid interpretive method, doing so exclusively neglects the location of Revelation within the canon, the verbal connections it serves with other New Testament books, the allusion to New Testament themes, and how those connections signify an implied reading strategy for the conclusion of the canon.

Revelation concludes the Christian canon for a specific reason, and this can be seen from the eschatological overtones that compose most the book's content. Goswell notes that the future orientation which Revelation depicts is perhaps a reason it concludes the canon.[136] Likewise, Wayne Grudem suggests that because of its contents, Revelation must be placed last in the canon.[137] Although Goswell's and Grudem's observations are perhaps true, nonetheless the markers of the author employing various New Testament verbal connections and allusions also suggests that the ideal-reader of the Apocalypse is familiar with the entirety of Scripture.

Johannine Writings and Apocalyptic: An Annotated Bibliography, ed. Stanley E. Porter and Andrew K. Gabriel (Brill, 2014), 258–261; 286–298.

134 Dempster, "The Prophets, the Canon and a Canonical Approach: No Empty Word," 313.

135 Spellman examines a few verbal connections. Spellman, *Toward a Canon-Conscious Reading of the Bible*, 174–178.

136 See Goswell, "The Order of the Books of the New Testament," 240.

137 Wayne Grudem, *Systematic Theology* (Zondervan, 2000), 65.

This work seeks to examine the New Testament verbal connections and allusions provided by Charles and argue that the canonical approach, or the canonical reading of Revelation, is the ideal-reader perspective for interpreting Revelation. The canonical approach incorporates both Testaments of the Christian canon in order to present the overall message of Revelation: Jesus the slain and resurrected Lamb is coming again as the eschatological King and Judge.[138]

---

138 Andreas J. Köstenberger, L. Scott Kellum, and Charles L. Quarles, *The Cradle, the Cross and the Crown: An Introduction to the New Testament*, 2nd ed. (B&H Academic, 2016), 928.

Chapter 2

The Problem of Interpreting Revelation

Introduction

Revelation presents the reader with substantial interpretive challenges. Even a cursory glance through the published works on Revelation shows a wide range of opinions as to its nature, purpose, and theological emphases.[1] For instance, Jerome argued that the Arians and "other heretics might fulfill prophecies concerning God and Magog (Rev 20:7–8), while barbarian invasions showed that the Antichrist was near."[2] John Wycliffe "decided the papal institution irredeemably was corrupt and declared the papacy to be the Antichrist."[3] It is easy to see the ideology of the Reformers as they sought to recover significant doctrines that had been suppressed by the papal institution, yet more critical ideological readings of Revelation continue to persist even to this day. A modern-day ideological reading of the biblical text will tend to focus on the positive aspects of themes of liberation, while critiquing the repressive themes. For example, a feminist reading of Gen 1:26 will celebrate the fact that all people are created in God's image, but critique a reading of 1 Cor 11:17 where Paul says that a woman is the glory of man.[4] The latter's reading is patriarchal and oppressive, while the

---

1 Regarding the history of interpretation for Revelation, see Gerald Stevens, *Revelation: The Past and Future of John's Apocalypse* (Pickwick, 2014), 3–142; Alan S. Bandy, *Reading Revelation with the Church* (forthcoming); Craig R. Koester, *Revelation* (Yale University Press, 2014), 29–64.

2 Koester, *Revelation*, 38.

3 Stevens, *Revelation: The Past and the Future of John's Apocalypse*, 55. Wycliffe's claim of the papacy is reflected in the Westminster Confession of Faith as this document declares the Pope of Rome to be the Antichrist. "There is no other head of the Church but the Lord Jesus Christ. Nor can the Pope of Rome, in any sense, be head thereof; but is that Antichrist, that man of sin, and son of perdition, that exalts himself, in the Church, against Christ and all that is called God." *WCF* 25.6.

4 Robin Parry, "Ideological Criticism," in *Dictionary for Theological Interpretation of the*

former is liberating. It is possible to read into Revelation similar motifs and themes, as depicted by feminist readings; yet, this ideological reading, like others, convolutes the intended message of Revelation.[5]

Traditionally, the tendency of scholars has been to use four views in their interpretation of Revelation.[6] First, the historicist approach was popular because it sought to apply the prophecies, events, and symbolism of Revelation to specific events of history, though this view has since been all but abandoned.[7] Second, the preterist approach divides into two subordinate schools of thought. One school views the book of Revelation as a message of judgment against an apostate Israel, whereas the other considers the Roman Empire and Christians to be the subject of John's prophecy.[8] The fulfillment of the prophecies happened previously and, therefore, Revelation is only focused upon past events. Third, the idealist view understands the prophecies not in so much an historical understanding but on the struggle of good versus evil.[9] These prophecies are nothing more than an exposition of spiritual truths as to what is good and what constitutes the great dangers of evil.[10] The

---

Bible, ed. Kevin J. Vanhoozer (Baker, 2005), 314. Parry argues that ideological readings of the biblical text "function as 'glasses behind the eyes,' shaping the way reality is perceived and guiding behavior." Ibid.

5 For some feminist readings of Revelation, see Tina Pippin, *Apocalyptic Bodies: The Biblical End of the World in Text and Image* (Routledge, 1999); *Death and Desire: The Rhetoric of Gender in the Apocalypse* (Westminster John Knox, 1992); Hanna Stenström, "They Have Not Defiled Themselves with Women: Christian Identity According to the Book of Revelation," in *A Feminist Companion to the Apocalypse of John*, ed. Amy-Jill Levine (T&T Clark, 2009). Grant Osborne notes that feminist scholarship on Revelation has gone "virtually unnoticed in the major works." Grant R. Osborne, "Recent Trends in the Study of the Apocalypse," in *The Face of New Testament Studies: A Survey of Recent Research* ed. Scot McKnight and Grant R. Osborne (Baker, 2004), 486.

6 For a helpful overview of these approaches see Cory M. Marsh, "Kingdom Hermeneutics and the Apocalypse: A Promotion of Consistent Literal Methodology," *JMAT* 20 (2016): 85–102.

7 For example, the Franciscans sought to connect the number 666 to Pope Benedict XI and the magisterial reformers regarded John's harlot of Babylon as a stand-in for the Vatican, because of the latter's antipathy to the true church and its people. For other examples, see Andreas Köstenberger, Scott Kellum, and Charles L. Quarles, *The Cradle, the Cross, and the Crown*, 1st ed. (Broadman and Holman, 2009), 968. See also Grant Osborne, *Revelation*, BECNT (Baker, 2002), 18; Stevens, *Revelation: The Past and Future of John's Apocalypse*, 55–63.

8 For the view of Revelation as a judgment against the apostate Israel, see Kenneth L. Gentry, *Before Jerusalem Fell: Dating the Book of Revelation* (American Vision, 1998); Kenneth L. Gentry, "A Preterist View of Revelation," in *Four Views on the Book of Revelation*, ed. Stanley N. Gundry and C. Marvin Pate (Zondervan, 1998), 37–92. For the view that Revelation considers the Roman Empire and Christian's as the subject of John's prophecy see G. K. Beale, *The Book of Revelation: A Commentary on the Greek Text*, NIGTC (Eerdmans, 1994), 44–45; Osborne, *Revelation*, 19–20.

9 Osborne, *Revelation*, 20.

10 Revelation, then, teaches "the action of great principles and not special incidents" as it portrays the victory of God over Satan. William Milligan, *Revelation of St. John* (Macmillan, 1887), 153.

fourth view, and perhaps the most well-known, is the futurist view, which contends that the events detailed in Rev 4–22 find their fulfillment in the future, during the last days of humanity.[11]

Since each view has its own respective weakness, most interpreters follow an eclectic approach, working elements of two or more methods into their own frameworks. For example, very few would fully endorse a true historicist approach to Revelation, but some might view the world today as if it were currently fulfilling the prophecies of the book. Scholars such as G. K. Beale, Grant Osborne, Leon Morris, and Robert Mounce manage in some way to incorporate multiple schools of thought into their interpretative methods.[12] If one can safely combine the methods as they do, the result is a welcome degree of exegetical flexibility. The interpreter is free to accept and/or reject this or that view based on its merits in dealing with specific passages and larger sections of material. This combination allows the interpreter both to accept and/or reject the respective strengths and weaknesses of each position.[13]

The dating of Revelation also bears significant interpretative weight, and the scholarly opinion is consistently divided between an early date under Nero's reign (64–69) or a later date under the Domitian rule (95–96).[14] Some, such as David E. Aune, opt for a middle date which sets the beginning of the composition somewhere in the 60s and its completion in the late 90s.[15] This

---

[11] The works of C. I. Scofield and Lewis Sperry Chafer propelled the futurist view into mainstream Christianity, and it was the study Bible produced by Scofield that translated this view into laymen's terms. The futurist view is associated with both classical and progressive dispensationalism, and two factors that separate these positions are the questions as to how much room the interpreter should leave for figurative language, particularly in reference to Revelation's measurements of time and space, as well as the relationship between Israel and the Church. For the progressive view, see Pate, "A Progressive Dispensational View of Revelation," in *Four Views on the Book of Revelation*, 133–176. For the classical view, see Robert L. Thomas, "A Classical Dispensational View of Revelation," in *Four Views of the Book of Revelation*, 177–230. The key textbook for Progressive Dispensationalism is C. A. Blaising and D. L. Bock, *Progressive Dispensationalism* (Baker, 1993).

[12] G. K. Beale, *Revelation*; Grant Osborne, *Revelation*; Leon Morris, *Revelation* (IVP Academic, 2009); Robert Mounce, *The Book of Revelation, Revised NICNT* (Eerdmans, 1998). See also Carson and Moo, *Introduction to the New Testament*, 720, though they ascribe to the futurist position.

[13] This concept is most evident in the interpretation of the symbols in Revelation. For a brief and helpful overview see Osborne, "Recent Trends in the Study of the Apocalypse," 490–491.

[14] For the view of the time of Nero see Epiphanius, *Pan.* 51.12; Gentry, *Before Jerusalem Fell*; Barclay Newman, "The Fallacy of the Domitian Hypothesis," *NTS* 10 (1963): 133–139; Albert A. Bell, "Date of John's Apocalypse: The Evidence of Some Roman Historians Reconsidered," *NTS* 25 (1978): 93–102. Many view Gentry's work as the primary defense for a Neronic date. For the Domitian view see Irenaeus, *Haer.* 5.30.3; Jerome, *Vir. ill.*, 9; Mark L. Hitchcock, "A Defense of the Domitianic Date of the Book of Revelation" (PhD diss., Dallas Theological Seminary, 2005). Most scholars affirm a Domitian reign.

[15] David E. Aune, *Revelation 1—5*, WBC (Thomas Nelson, 1997), lxix—lxx. Aune presents

discussion of the date of Revelation leads to a greater focus upon the social setting and the level of persecution that the seven churches of Asia Minor faced. Thus, the interpreter will likely seek to understand Revelation in the light of either Domitian or Neronian persecution. Therefore, the view that an interpreter holds will affect their interpretation of Revelation. Likewise, how one understands the date of composition also affects the social setting and specific persecutions that the churches faced. As shown, this social setting plays a fundamental role in how various scholars have approached and interpreted Revelation.

Conceptual Background for Interpreting Revelation

In what manner, then, should one understand these four views? Are they "methods of interpretation" or conclusions drawn from the interpreter's hermeneutic? A cursory glance of some major commentaries and New Testament Introductions shows that under the "methods of interpretation" section for both commentaries and New Testament Introductions, both focus primarily upon these four views.[16] Despite their inclusion in the "methods of interpretation" section of commentaries, these four views are derived from the interpreter's hermeneutic that is based primarily upon the date and background of Revelation. The interpreter views Revelation through a chosen hermeneutical lens and draws conclusion based on this process. The majority of scholars interpret Revelation by employing some aspect of the historical-critical method.[17]

---

an astute summary of each position which is divided into nine explanations. He further remarks, "The position taken in this commentary is that *both* views contain aspects of the correct solution, since it appears that while the final edition of Revelation was completed toward the end of the reign of Domitian (or, more likely, during the early part of the reign of Trajan), the first edition of the book was composed as much as a generation earlier based on written and oral apocalyptic traditions that reach back into the decade of the A.D. 60s, if not somewhat earlier." Ibid., lviii.

16 Paige Patterson, *Revelation*, NAC (Broadman and Holman, 2012), 26–30; Carson and Moo, *New Testament Introduction*, 719–720; Osborne, *Revelation*, 18–22; Mounce, *Revelation*, 24–30; Beale, *Revelation*, 44–49.

17 This hermeneutic seeks to identify the time and place from which Revelation arose, viewing this background as decisive when combined with appropriate grammatical methods. According to Craig L. Blomberg, "The historical-critical/grammatical approach is one way of referring to the method of interpreting the Scriptures … that seeks to recover an author's meaning as disclosed in a text or utterance designed for a specific audience or audiences. It is historical because it prioritizes acquiring as much information as possible, from both inside and outside of the text, about the historical and cultural circumstances in which the text was composed. It is critical in the sense of being analytical, not in the sense of criticizing." Craig L. Blomberg, "The Historical-Critical/Grammatical View," in *Biblical Hermeneutics: Five Views*, ed. Stanley E. Porter and Beth M. Stovell (IVP Academic, 2012), 46. See also the helpful discussion

David Aune believes that the natural starting-point of historical-critical exegesis is the Greco-Roman world, with the challenge then being to identify the powers that be as headed either by Nero or Domitian.[18] Aune's three volume commentary on Revelation argues that the theological agenda of John was to remodel Jewish apocalypticism for his community.[19] In other words, John sought to present his own eschatological understanding for the seven churches of Asia Minor.[20] His exegesis of Rev 4 provides a good example of how the Greco-Roman traditions might lead to a historical understanding within Revelation that is consistent with its background. Aune notes that Rev 4 "bears such a striking resemblance to the ceremonial of the imperial court and cult that the latter can only be a parody of the former."[21] He notes that the primary role of a Roman emperor was to distribute justice, which may cause the Roman emperor to be compared to the mythical gods Zeus and Jupiter who were "guarantors of justice and that they provided sanctions supporting the maintenance of the laws and customs of men."[22] Since the emperor was able to fulfill these legal demands, this action made the emperor an equal with the gods and, possibly, stand in contrast to God sitting upon his throne.[23]

---

in Grant R. Osborne, *The Hermeneutical Spiral: A Comprehensive Introduction to Biblical Interpretation*, rev. ed. (IVP Academic, 2006), 37–108.

18 See also the work by Adela Yarbro Collins, *Crisis and Catharsis: The Power of the Apocalypse* (Westminster, 1984); "Reading the Book of Revelation in the Twentieth Century," *Int* 40:3 (1986): 229–242. Collins believes that Revelation should be interpreted in light of a proper understanding of social radicalism, which is simply a "social, political, and economic withdrawal from life." Collins, *Crisis and Catharsis*, 107. Thus, Rev 13:16–17 is not about a future mark required to buy and sell material goods but rather John's directive for his readers not to use Roman currency and the 144,000 from Rev 14:1–5 are not exalted believers who stand with the Lamb upon Mount Zion but are those who are encouraged to continue their pursuit of the Christian life. See ibid., 124–131.

19 David E. Aune, *Revelation 1–5*; *Revelation 6–16*, WBC (Thomas Nelson, 1998); *Revelation 17–22*, WBC (Thomas Nelson, 1998).

20 He rejects traditional Johannine authorship and believes the author was a Palestinian Jew who was equally familiar with the Hebrew and Greek texts of the Old Testament. "While the final author-editor of Revelation was named 'John,' it is not possible to identify him with any other early Christian figures of the same name, including John the son of Zebedee or the shadowy figure of John the Elder." Ibid., lvi.

21 David Aune, "The Influence of Roman Imperial Court Ceremonial on the Apocalypse of John," *BR* (1983): 5.

22 Aune, "The Influence of Roman Imperial Court," 8.

23 Aune further elaborates on this potential comparison by noting that the emperor and the principal governors, who were his lesser counterparts, "were surrounded by friends (amici) and advisors (consilium) whose task it was to aid [the emperor] in his role of dispensing justice. Further, emperors were, like consuls, accompanied by lictors bearing fasces, and by other apparitores (public servants), and sat between the consuls on their bench." Ibid. See also Aune, *Revelation 1–5*, 287–292. The comparison between the emperor and the heavenly courtroom scene can be seen, but the comparison with the biblical text is not perfect. In John's vision in Rev 4, the one who is seated upon the throne (ἐπὶ τὸν θρόνον καθήμενος) takes no counsel

In contrast, G. K. Beale views the Jewish background of Revelation as dispositive, while retaining some concern for the latter's Greco-Roman setting.[24] The interpretative key, then, is to read Revelation through the lens of the Old Testament. He notes that "there is a general acknowledgment that the Apocalypse contains more Old Testament references than any other New Testament book.[25] This claim is significant because it constitutes Beale's basis for his method of relying heavily upon the Old Testament. Therefore, there are two presuppositions that justify Beale's extensive reference to the Old Testament: first, Revelation contains multiple references and allusions to the Old Testament, and, second, Revelation is properly interpreted in light of the Old Testament.[26] Beale argues that the biblical allusions used by John are not to be read in such a way that one finds John to have departed from the Old Testament context. "A large number of references to the same OT texts, whether specific verses or larger segments, strongly suggests that the writer was absorbed with these texts and had probably mediated on them and enhances the probability that he was familiar with the meaning or, at least, was attempting to interpret that OT text (e.g., the use of Daniel and Ezekiel in Revelation 4–5)."[27] John's usage of these Old Testament texts suggests his familiarity with these texts, their original meaning within the context of the Old Testament itself, and his usage further implies that his readers understand these Old Testament texts.

Some, such as Richard Bauckham, have partially downplayed the historical-critical method, for the sake of emphasis on Revelation's theological content. He examines the theology of Revelation primarily through his

---

from those who surround him, whether the four living creatures who fly around his throne or the elders who are seated before him. Rather, the one who is seated upon the throne receives worship from those in his presence (4:8, 11). Furthermore, in no instance in Revelation does God, presumably the Father in Rev 4, receive counsel from anyone; rather, God acts upon the goodness of his own judgment and wisdom and rules as he desires (cf. Isa 40:13; Rom 11:34). This account of Aune's exegesis illustrates the extent of his reliance upon the Greco-Roman background in understanding Revelation. Because of his belief that Revelation is a product of redaction criticism and that there are two editions of Revelation, Aune traces the visions of Revelation back to more than one author. It is only from the work of the redactors that Revelation can be viewed as a composite work. Nonetheless, his contribution to studies of Revelation is seen as significant because he shows how John possibly interacts with the Greco-Roman themes in order to reveal to his readers a basis for hope in the midst of intense persecution.

24 Beale, *The Book of Revelation; John's Use of the Old Testament in Revelation* (Sheffield Academic Press, 1998); *The Use of Daniel in Jewish Apocalyptic Literature and in Revelation of St. John* (University Press of America, 1984). See also the bibliography in *The Book of Revelation*, xxx—xxxi.
25 Beale, *John's Use of the Old Testament*, 60.
26 Beale, *The Book of Revelation*, xix, 76–99.
27 Ibid., 83–84.

understanding of the book's genre: prophecy, apocalypse, and letter.[28] Bauckham argues that in ancient books, the beginning typically identifies its nature or genre, such that this genre signals how it should be interpreted. Thus, when John pens the word ἀποκάλυψις in the first verse he intends for Revelation to be interpreted in the genre of an apocalypse.[29] However, John also states in verse 3 that the one who reads and hears the words of the prophecy (τῆς προφητείας) are blessed, which indicates a prophetic genre for the book. The claim that Revelation is a prophecy is confirmed by the former's epilogue.[30] Yet, there remains a third category which suggests that Revelation should also be interpreted as a letter/epistle. In verses 4–5, the reader finds the normal epistolary greeting, as seen in other epistles of the New Testament (cf. Gal 1:3; Eph 1:2; etc.), and this greeting may suggest that Revelation was to serve as a circular letter to the seven churches in Asia, as determined by the content found in chapters 2–3.[31] Thus, Bauckham argues that Revelation should be interpreted in light of its three-fold genre and that each category should inform or, at least, suggest a particular hermeneutic.[32]

THE ROLE OF HISTORICAL BACKGROUND INFORMATION

The difference between a canonical approach to Revelation and the previous approaches is determined by the interpreter's choice of emphasis. In other words, the canonical approach has as its main focus the written text of Scripture rather than understanding that the biblical passage is a testimony to the cultural setting. However, when the emphasis is placed upon the historical context over the biblical text, the biblical text becomes nothing more than a tool used to understand the historical matters in the time of writing. The narrative components of Revelation are not meant to direct "the readers' attention outside the text but rather within the text and to the narrative world depicted there."[33] It is within the biblical text that God's revelation resides, not the historical event it describes.

---

28 Richard Bauckham, *The Theology of the Book of Revelation* (Cambridge University Press, 1993).
29 Bauckham, *The Theology of the Book of Revelation*, 1.
30 Ibid.
31 Ibid., 2. See also Colin Hemer, The Letters to the Seven Churches of Asia in their Local Setting (Sheffield Academic Press, 1989), 1–2, 20–25.
32 Bauckham does not neglect the historical background of Revelation and the apparent emphasis this background may suggest for its interpretation. For example, Bauckham notes that the question of who God is for the reader of Revelation is closely tied to the world of John's readers. He believes, much like Aune, that the vision of God in Rev 4 parallels the political context in which John was writing. See Bauckham, *The Theology of the Book of Revelation*, 31–35.
33 John Sailhamer, *Introduction to Old Testament Theology: A Canonical Approach*

If one argues that God's revelation is found within the biblical text, the argument does not negate any historical event that may be described as either false or depicted inaccurately. The Bible records specific historical events and then informs the reader of their significance. When the argument is made that the locus of God's revelation is within the biblical text, this argument should not mean that the historical events described are false or depicted incorrectly. Furthermore, this argument does not mean that the historical events recorded in Scripture are unimportant or fictitious. Rather, to suggest that God's revelation is found in the locus of Scripture forces the interpreter to distinguish between what is meant by the biblical text and the event the text describes. Sailhamer aptly notes that, for evangelicals, the decision to choose between whether the text has meaning within itself or serves as a witness to God's self-revelation that the text records is a difficult choice to make.

> The choice between these two alternatives is not a happy one. [An evangelical's] desire and inclination is to remain open to both options. Recognizing the importance of the inspired text of Scripture, they want to affirm that an interpretation of the OT, or the Pentateuch, should look to the text itself as its source. However, wanting also to affirm the importance of history and God's revelation of his will in historical events, they do not wish to minimize the importance of the historical events recounted in Scripture.[34]

Yet, this dichotomy between choosing either history or Scripture is unnecessary since evangelicals should affirm both realities. The question is not whether God has acted in history; rather, the focus should be upon how God has revealed himself through holy Scripture and the emphasis an interpreter has upon this special revelation.[35] He further argues that divine revelation should be thought of as lying within the narrative itself in order to provide the meaning of the events.[36]

(Zondervan, 1995), 39.

34 John Sailhamer, *The Pentateuch as Narrative: A Biblical-Theological Commentary* (Zondervan, 1992), 7.

35 "In fact, as evangelicals, we do not have to choose between Scripture and history. Evangelicals should and do affirm the absolute importance of both. For an evangelical, the question should not be whether God has acted in history. The historical basis of biblical faith is fundamentally important and will always remain so. The real issue is our commitment to an inspired *written* Word of God as the locus of God's special revelation." Ibid.

36 "Thus divine revelation may be thought of as lying within the narrative text of Scripture as a function of the meaning of the events in their depiction." Sailhamer, *Old Testament Theology*, 39. He continues, "What we are really saying is that the Bible does its job of recounting events so well that the chain of historical events it depicts in its narratives, rather than their

The discussion by Sailhamer is focused upon the study of Old Testament theology, and it is his response to the tendency of interpreters to focus on the event of the text rather than the text itself. Although Sailhamer is not opposed to the historical study of the biblical world, he "recognized correctly that they do not replace the text as the object of the study."[37] Within New Testament studies, the tendency is to elevate historical background studies over the biblical text. The recent commentary on Colossians by Old Testament scholar Christopher Seitz provides a helpful case-study of foregrounding the text within the New Testament.

Case-Study in Colossians

Christopher R. Seitz, a student of Childs, utilized the canonical approach on Colossians that foregrounded the text rather than the historical background of Colossae.[38] His commentary works under three presuppositions, but the third presupposition is the most significant. "Paul's letters come to us in a given canonical form. That form foregrounds certain things and lets other things fall out of specific focus or priority."[39] Thus, the introduction to Seitz's work affords the reader a glimpse into how his canonical method will affect not just introductory matters related to the book of Colossians but also other interpretive issues that the canonical method naturally foregrounds.

Seitz does not desire to read Colossians by itself; rather, he places Colossians within the context of the Pauline canon.[40] He argues that both a positive and negative result exists when the commentator focuses upon a single book of Paul and neglects the other volumes contained within the Pauline canon. The positive result in reading Colossians by itself is that the commentator focuses upon matters such as authorship, setting, and so forth; yet, the

---

depiction, becomes the proper object of study in OT theology. In reading, the text as such is not the focus of the reader's attention. The reader focuses on the events recorded as if they were the real thing right before one's eyes. One is thus led to focus on a holy history (*Heilsgeschichte*) behind the text in place of a holy history within Scripture itself." Ibid.

37 Robert L. Cole, "Preface," in *Text and Canon: Essays in Honor of John Sailhamer*, ed. Robert L. Cole and Paul J. Kissling (Wipf and Stock, 2017), vii.

38 Christopher R. Seitz, *Colossians* (Brazos Press, 2014). See also Christopher R. Seitz *Prophecy and Hermeneutics: Toward a New Introduction to the Prophets* (Baker, 2007), 24–51.

39 Seitz, *Colossians*, 20. This desire to foreground certain things and allow others to fall by the side is what Seitz means by his "canonical presentation," for this presentation "guards against imbalances emerging at periods in the history of interpretation, when certain questions have been hyperextended or no longer gain interest or lose their capacity for resolution or assent. The canonical presentation offers a commentary on how history and God's abiding voice are inextricably related. It seeks to maintain a balance in what is worthy of comment and what is less decisive." Ibid.

40 Ibid., 21–27.

negative result flows from the positive since it abandons a Pauline unity within his works.

While matters such as authorship and setting are an important focus of a commentary, Seitz argues that these matters bear relatively little on the interpretation of the text itself.[41] Furthermore, Seitz is more concerned with the literary collection of the Pauline works and a coherent message that may exist between them rather than foregrounding certain questions about authorship.[42] Thus, Seitz's commentary on Colossians is a work on a single letter, but the commentary seeks "to read the letter without the modern assumptions attending [a] single-letter commentary, where a certain species of particularity and independence is prized as the goal of interpretation."[43] It is unfortunate that Seitz concludes authorship, and various other introductory matters, bear little on interpretation; yet, his point is well made when one considers the focus of modern day commentaries and their isolation of books from a set of works.[44]

An important discussion within Colossians is the identity of the false teachers that have infiltrated the church, which is often labeled as the "Colossian heresy."[45] The teachings of this heresy are hinted at within Colossians, but Paul focuses his attention more specifically in chapter 2, where his discussion covers possible issues of their teaching.[46] In contrast, Seitz does not address the possible identity of this group when he discusses the Colossian heresy. He believes that this refusal is not based on his canonical methodology alone, but rather it is within the bounds of the history of interpretation. Since the identity of the false teachers has been notoriously difficult, Seitz chooses to allow only the book of Colossians to address their teachings rather than attempting to identify them. He cites Douglas J. Moo's argument that what exactly the false teachers were saying is only ascertained by analyzing the discussion of Paul against the known background of the world of

---

41 Ibid., 21–22. "Much of the modern preoccupation with particularity—whatever its strength—has meant a forfeit or even disqualification of reading the letters in the light of one another." Ibid., 22.

42 "Ours is not here a question of historicity (did Paul in fact author Colossians, or Ephesians?) but is rather an observation about the naturalness of a more integrative reading when these questions have not been foregrounded, due to the existence of a literary collection that orients them toward one another as a totality." Seitz, *Colossians*, 22–23.

43 Ibid., 23.

44 Concerning authorship, see the critique by Joel White in *Them* 40 (2015): 133–134.

45 Although James Dunn disagrees. See J. D. G. Dunn, *The Epistles to the Colossians and to Philemon*, NIGTC (Eerdmans, 1996), 25.

46 Ian Smith suggests four possible groups and concludes the group is a form of Jewish mysticism. Ian Smith, *Heavenly Perspective: A Study of the Apostle Paul's Response to a Jewish Mystical Movement at Colossae* (T&T Clark, 2006). See Col 2:8–9, 11, 13, 16, 18, 20–21, 23.

Colossae. However, this process is "a very inexact and uncertain one."[47] Moo admits that identifying the false teaching at Colossae is not possible, but their fundamental beliefs can be described. Seitz remarks:

> This comment tracks well not only with the implications of canonical interpretation in respect of historical contextualizing, but also suggests that the final form of the letter, as it now exists (where the solution precedes the problem: cure before diagnosis) properly belongs to the interpretative intention of the letter—whatever we might say about success in bringing precision to the false teaching Paul is addressing (from afar and secondhand).[48]

Thus, when Seitz discusses the Colossian heresy in his commentary, his chapter is entitled "The So-Called Conflict at Colossae." He argues that since no specification is given for the identity of the group, the Colossians appear to be at least familiar with their teachings. "He either assumes the Colossians know what this relationship is, or he speaks as he does in order to be comprehensive and to allow his audience to make connections on their own side."[49]

In his review of Seitz's book, Joel White highlights the absence of the "Colossian heresy" discussion by Seitz. Those who are familiar with "modern Colossians commentaries will be shocked to discover that, whether in the introduction or in his treatment of the relevant texts, Seitz almost completely dispenses with any discussion of the so-called 'Colossian Heresy.'"[50] White correctly notes that Seitz does not believe there was a single body of teaching that might be labeled as this heresy, but he also disagrees with the either/or approach Seitz presents; that is, either they are identified by the author or, if they are not identified, the interpreter cannot know their identity and must refrain from labeling the group.[51] Rather, White prefers to have a balance between historical-critical exegesis and the canonical approach since these methods of interpretation are complementary.[52]

---

47 Seitz, *Colossians*, 26. See Douglas J. Moo, *The Letter to the Colossians and to Philemon*, PNTC (Eerdmans, 2008), 49.

48 Seitz, *Colossians*, 27.

49 Ibid., 121.

50 White in Them 40 (2015): 134.

51 "If this either/or approach is a necessary consequence of canonical interpretation (it is certainly not a necessary consequence of the theological interpretation of Scripture; commentators going back to the 4th century discussed the nature of the heresy), I do not regard it as a salutary one." White, *Them*, 134.

52 Ibid., 134–135.

However, this critique by White, that an identity of the "Colossian Heresy" should be attempted despite the silence of Paul, is the problem that the canonical approach avoids. Since Paul chooses to describe the false teaching in general terms, the interpreter should also seek to understand the teaching in these general terms. Paul is utilizing a strategic selection in his inclusion and exclusion of certain elements, and the interpreter should remain bound to his device of selectivity.[53] In other words, where the text of Scripture is silent as to the identity of this group, the interpreter should likewise remain silent (cf. 2 Cor 10–13).

In his review, White himself does not identify the heresy despite arguing that one cannot learn everything about the Colossians by reading it in light of the other Pauline epistles, which is the claim of Seitz. Yet, White relies on the historical context to determine this heresy and, ultimately, the interpretation of Colossians as a whole. But as Seitz has shown by his interaction with Moo, if Colossians is set within its historical context, the book still does not answer the question of the identity of the heresy nor those who the proponents of this heresy are.[54]

Conclusion

We have summarized various approaches that have been used to interpret Revelation. The four schools of interpretation were determined to be conclusions that explain how an interpreter understands Revelation based upon his hermeneutics. The four approaches view Revelation through a chosen hermeneutical lens and, as a result, the interpreter understands Revelation from this process of interpretation.

In the history of religions approach, the interpreter primarily views Revelation based upon the Greco-Roman world. The interpreter will conduct historical background research to gather the necessary information and interpret Revelation, at times, in light of the findings from the Greco-Roman world. Those who employ a hermeneutic more focused with the Hebrew Bible will do background studies as well, but their focus is derivative on how John employed Old Testament imagery and texts. In a similar fashion, a theological interpretation of Revelation utilizes sources from both interpretative methods, and a theological conclusion is emphasized.

---

53 "The historian must select events to include and exclude. That selection determines the message his story will convey." John Sailhamer, *First and Second Chronicles* (Moody Press, 1983), 10.

54 See also Ched Spellman, "Colossians: A Review Article," *JETS* 58 (2015): 655–658.

A canonical approach to Revelation, while affirming the historicity of the events described in the text, would foreground the text over the historical background. The biblical text is the locus of God's special revelation and, as such, should be foregrounded over the historical background. The example by Christopher Seitz provided a case-study as to what this work may entail for a New Testament book. In order to interpret Revelation in a canonical approach, like that of Seitz, the canon of the New Testament must first be established. By examining what "canon" entails and the location of Revelation within the canon, only then is a canonical interpretation of Revelation feasible.

CHAPTER 3

REVELATION IN THE CONTEXT OF THE NEW TESTAMENT CANON

INTRODUCTION

Thus far, this work has argued for the importance of the canon as a dimension of biblical interpretation. The sixty-six books of the Christian Bible provide the appropriate context for conducting not only Biblical Theology, as Brevard Childs has noted, but also for performing the exegetical task.[1] The canon of the Christian Bible binds the interpreter to its realm so that those who employ the canonical approach focus not only on the order of the material within the book, but also its location within the canon.[2]

The question of canon is significant to the interpretive task, given that the establishment of the canon provides the necessary definition and framework for this hermeneutical method. If one is unable to establish the canon, then a canonical hermeneutic is unattainable. Therefore, this chapter will discuss several aspects of the New Testament canon in the following order.[3]

First, the canon is defined, and the question of canon is then explored in accordance with its multifaceted dimensions. Second, the New Testament

---

[1] Brevard Childs, *Biblical Theology in Crisis* (Westminster Press, 1976), 99.

[2] John Sailhamer labels this method as "con-textuality." It "is the notion of the effect on meaning of the relative position of a biblical book within a prescribed order of reading." John Sailhamer, *Introduction to Old Testament Theology: A Canonical Approach* (Zondervan, 1995), 213.

[3] For a discussion on the Old Testament canon, see Stephen Dempster, "Canons to the Rights and Canons to the Left: Finding a Resolution in the Canon Debate," *JETS* 52 (2009): 47–77; Ian Provan, "Canons to the Left of Him: Brevard Childs, His Critics and the Future of Old Testament Theology," *SJT* 50 (1997): 1–38; Brevard S. Childs, *Introduction to the Old Testament as Scripture* (Fortress Press, 1979), 46–108; Brevard S. Childs, "The Canon in Recent Biblical Studies: Reflections on an Era," in *Canon and Biblical Interpretation*, ed. Craig G. Bartholomew, Scott Hahn, Robin Parry, Christopher Seitz, and Al Wolters (Zondervan, 2006), 33–57; A. C. Sundberg Jr., "'The Old Testament:' A Christian Canon," *CBQ* 30 (1968): 143–155.

canon will be examined, and its sequence will be established with particular emphasis upon the location of Revelation. Third, an analysis of the structure and content of Revelation is provided. Last, a brief examination of how one would approach Revelation in the canonical method is discussed, with mention of the verbal connections Revelation has with the rest of the New Testament.

The Concept of Canon

Of significant importance in the discussion of "canon" is its proper definition of the term, since there has been much confusion over this term. Childs once lamented, "Much of the present confusion over the problem of canon turns on the failure to reach an agreement regarding the terminology."[4] Lee Martin McDonald notes the importance of arriving at a proper definition of "canon," because "canons (i.e., laws, regulations, patterns, models) were quite common in many spheres of life in the ancient world long before Jews and Christians began to focus on closed Scripture canons."[5] Thus, in order to arrive at a satisfactory understanding of "canon" one must focus on the narrowness of its aspect.

Concerning the semantic domain of κανών, Hermann Wolfgang Beyer notes that, in its secular usage, the term related to a reed and indicated a "straight rod or staff."[6] Over time, the word tended to reflect the "norm, whether the perfect form and therefore the goal to be sought on the one hand, or the infallible criterion (κριτήριον) by which things are to be measured on the other."[7] Bruce M. Metzger remarks that κανών conveys a "kaleidoscopic variety of senses" and "very broadly, a κανών provides one with a *criterion* or *standard* (Latin *norma*) by reference to which the rectitude of opinion or actions may be determined."[8]

When κανών occurs in the New Testament it has the sense of a measure of

---

[4] Childs, *Introduction to the Old Testament as Scripture*, 51. Lee Martin McDonald provides an interesting overview of the term. See Lee Martin McDonald, *The Biblical Canon: Its Origin, Transmission, and Authority* (Baker, 2006), 39–48.

[5] Ibid., 47.

[6] Hermann Wolfgang Beyer, "κανών," *Theological Dictionary of the New Testament* Eerdmans, 1964–1985), 3:596. See also BDAG, s.v. "κανών;" Harry Y. Gamble, "Canon," *The Anchor Bible Dictionary*, 6 vols., ed. David Noel Freeman (Doubleday, 1992), 1:838–861. See also Eugene Ulrich, "The Notion and Definition of Canon," in *The Canon Debate*, ed. Lee Martin McDonald and James A. Sanders (Baker, 2002), 21–35.

[7] Beyer, "κανών," 3:597. His discussion is especially helpful as Beyer traces the data until the time of the New Testament.

[8] Bruce M. Metzger, *The Canon of the New Testament* (Oxford University Press, 1997), 289. See also Eugene Ulrich, "The Notion and Definition of Canon," in The Canon Debate, Lee Martin McDonald and James A. Sanders (Baker, 2019), 22–23.

assessment that signifies the norm or the standard of rule. For example, Paul uses κανών in Gal 6:16, in the discussion of whether or not one is bound by the Old Testament law of circumcision in order to obtain salvation. The apostle Paul writes, "And as many who walk according to this rule (τῷ κανόνι τούτῳ), [may] peace and mercy be upon them, and upon the Israel of God." As Ched Spellman notes, Paul's usage of κανών parallels that of *1 Clement* as Clement "commends his readers for teaching the young women 'to abide by the rule of obedience' (τῷ κανόνι τῆς ὑποταγῆς)."[9] Furthermore, Spellman writes, "later in the second century, Clement of Alexandria admonishes his readers to live according to the 'rule of faith' (ὁ κανών τῆς πίστεως)."[10] Thus, it is clear that Paul uses κανών to describe a standard of rule and, as Beyer argues, Gal 6:16 summarizes the entire content of not only Galatians but also "the whole doctrine of true Christian behaviour."[11]

The term κανών is used three other times in the New Testament. With reference to 2 Cor 10:13–16, Metzger notes:

> Much disputed is the import of the word in this exegetically difficult passage of 2 Cor. x. 13–16, where it occurs thrice in connection with the field or sphere that God has allotted to Paul for his work as a missionary. This God-given κανών ('province') refers, it seems, not so much to the nature and orientation of the work laid on Paul, but rather to the circumscribed, geographical area in which he is to labour.[12]

Beyer, in like manner, comments that Paul's usage of κανών in 2 Cor 10:13–16 is less problematic than the usage in Gal 6:16. However, he concedes that Paul's usage of this term is consistent with the defense of his apostolic authority at Corinth, since there were some who attempted to remove Paul from leadership. Paul argues that the claim by the opponents—i.e., that he is weak in appearance but weighty in his letters—is boastful, but his boast is not self-centered; rather it is κατὰ τὸ μέτρον τοῦ κανόνος οὗ ἐμέρισεν ἡμῖν ὁ θεὸς μέτρου. Beyer summarizes:

> He thus has a canon or standard for his work and for the associated claim to apostolic validity which he has not conferred on himself but received from God. In what does this canon consist? Its content is indicated by the ἐφικέσθαι ἄχρι καὶ ὑμῶν, which is dependent on ἐμέρισεν μέτρον. He is given

---

9 Ched Spellman, *Toward a Canon-Conscious Reading of the Bible: Exploring the History and Hermeneutics of the Canon* (Phoenix: Sheffield, 2014), 15.
10 Ibid., 15–16.
11 Beyer, "κανών," 3:598.
12 Metzger, *The Canon of the New Testament*, 290.

the standard that he needs by the fact that it was given to him to press forward to Corinth and to establish the community there.[13]

Thus, Paul does not misuse κανών in discussing his apostolic commission to the Corinthian church.

The notion that κανών is the "standard" or "rule of faith" was the primary understanding of κανών in the first and second centuries.[14] However, McDonald notes that during the second century the New Testament writings were not classified as Scripture (γραφή) even though numerous writers identified certain writings as such.[15] It was not until the fourth century that an emphasis was placed upon determining a standard of writings for books that were considered to be authoritative. "Thus, someone writing in 400 CE could use the phrase 'Canon of the New Testament' (κανών τῆς καινῆς διαθήκης) without qualification or expansion."[16] This sentiment is echoed by Daniel Driver as he remarks that "today there is a near-consensus that the fourth century is the proper terminus."[17] David Trobisch believes the formation of the canon was completed in three parts. "During the first phase numerous Christian writings emerged, each with a distinct claim to be authoritative. In the second phase, which took place during the second and third century, Christian writings were combined into various collections. The third and last phase, the actual canonization, took place in the fourth century, when the church finally established normative lists."[18] With the broad spectrum of application for the term κανών, Metzger is not surprised that "eventually the word came also to be applied to the list of books regarded as authoritative for Christians."[19] Having shown that κανών has been determined to mean a collection of books that are regarded as authoritative for Christians, we may now establish the canon of the New Testament.[20]

---

13 Beyer, "κανών," 3:599.

14 Spellman, *Canon-Conscious*, 16. Furthermore, "The initial sense of κανών is well established long before it is applied to the collection of authoritative biblical writings and its initial sense lingers in new applications of the term." Ibid., 17.

15 L. M. McDonald, "Canon" in *The Dictionary of the Later New Testament and Its Developments*, ed. Ralph P. Martin and Peter H. Davids (IVP, 1997), 135. See the helpful overview by Metzger, *The Canon of the New Testament*, 290–292. Harry Y. Gamble, "The New Testament Canon: Recent Research and the Status Quaestionis," in The Canon Debate, ed. Lee Martin McDonald and James A. Sanders (Baker, 2019), 268–294.

16 Spellman, *Canon-Conscious*, 20.

17 Daniel R. Driver, *Brevard Childs: Biblical Theologian for the Church's One Bible* (Baker, 2010), 22.

18 David Trobisch, *The First Edition of the New Testament* (Oxford University Press, 2000), 4. See also Kurt Aland, *The Problem of the New Testament Canon* (A. R. Mowbray and Co., 1962), 8.

19 Metzger, *The Canon of the New Testament*, 292.

20 The extensive discussion of the formation and development of the New Testament

The Development of a Canonical List

The most comprehensive list of New Testament books is found in the Muratorian Canon, which, based upon internal evidence of the canon itself, is dated to the second century.[21] The Muratorian Canon, also known as the Muratorian Fragment, "consists of only 85 lines; the beginning and probably the end are missing, for the Fragment commences in the midst of a sentence and ends abruptly."[22] Although the fragment is damaged both at the beginning and end, Brooke Westscott believes that, withstanding these defects, the fragment is still of great importance.[23] This discovery, uncovered by Lodovico Antonio Muratoria (1672–1750), describes a catalog of texts that confirms "the scriptural status of twenty-two of the twenty-seven New Testament books."[24]

However, the Muratorian Canon is not simply a list of accepted and rejected texts made by early church councils; rather, the Canon provides a helpful discussion of the books and "appends historical information and theological reflections as well."[25] Furthermore, "these comments allow [one] to draw conclusions as to the author's understanding of the motives and norms lying behind the formation of the New Testament Canon."[26] The Muratorian

---

and various letters is beyond the scope of this work. For a helpful discussion see Bruce M. Metzger, *The Early Versions of the New Testament: Their Origin, Transmission and Limitations* (Oxford University Press, 2001); Metzger, *The Canon of the New Testament*, 39–190; William R. Farmer and Denis M. Farkasfalvy, *The Formation of the New Testament Canon: An Ecumenical Approach* (Paulist Press, 1983); Alford von Harnack, *The Origin of the New Testament and the Most Important Consequences of the New Creation* (Williams and Norgate, 1925); Robert F. Hull Jr., *The Story of the New Testament Text: Movers, Materials, Motives, Methods, and Models* (Society of Biblical Literature, 2010).

21 David DeSilva, *An Introduction to the New Testament: Contexts, Methods and Ministry Formation* (InterVarsity Press, 2004), 33; Metzger, *Canon of the New Testament*, 191; Michael J. Kruger, *The Question of Canon: Challenging the Status Quo in the New Testament Debate* (IVP Academic, 2013), 162–167. For the fourth century, see A. C. Sundberg Jr., "Canon Muratori: A Fourth Century List," *HTR* 66 (1973): 1–41; Gamble, "Canon, New Testament," 1:852–861; Geoffrey Mark Hahneman, *The Muratorian Fragment and the Development of the Canon* (Clarendon Press, 1992).

22 Ibid., 5. Athanasius was the first to list the twenty-seven books that are commonly identified today as the New Testament. See Athanasius, *Festal Letter*, 39.

23 "It is mutilated both at the beginning and end; and is disfigured throughout by remarkable barbarisms, due in part to the ignorance of the transcriber, and in part to the translator of the original text; for there can be little doubt that it is a version from the Greek. But notwithstanding these defects it is of the greatest interest and importance. Enough remains to indicate the limits which its author assigned to the Canon; and the general sense is sufficiently clear to shew [sic] the authority which he claimed for it." Brooke Foss Westscott, *A General Survey of the History of the Canon of the New Testament* (Macmillan and Co., 1889), 211–212.

24 Kruger, The Question of Canon, 162. See especially 162–164.

25 Metzger, *Canon of the New Testament*, 194. Metzger also helpfully comments that the Muratorian Canon is not a canon in "the narrow sense of the word, that is, a bare list of titles, but is a kind of introduction to the New Testament."

26 Ibid., 194–195.

Canon includes the four Gospels, Acts, thirteen epistles of Paul, the epistle of Jude, two Epistles of John, the Wisdom of Solomon, Revelation, and the *Apocalypse of Peter*.[27]

It is important to note several intricacies contained within the content of the Muratorian Canon for the purposes of this study. First, the Muratorian Canon lists the four Gospels in the same order as Sinaiticus (01 ℵ), Alexandrinus (A 02), Vaticanus (B 03), and Ephraemi Rescriptus (C 04).[28] Second, the author of the Canon believed that Paul wrote to seven churches, and followed the example of his predecessor John.[29] This remark is undoubtedly a reference to John writing to the seven churches in Asia Minor (Rev 2–3), and it is perhaps the reason why the author places Revelation before the Pauline Epistles instead of at the end of the Canon. Third, there is an awareness of non-canonical works such as the *Shepherd* of Hermas and the *Apocalypse of Peter*.[30] Fourth, several heretical books are rejected by the early church.[31]

---

27 Ibid., 194–198; Hahneman, *The Muratorian Fragment*, 88–90; Westscott, *A General Survey of the History of the Canon of the New Testament*, 215–220. Edgar J. Goodspeed does not provide a collected list of the Muratorian Canon; rather, he scatters his discussion of its content throughout his work. See Edgar J. Goodspeed, *The Formation of the New Testament* (The University of Chicago Press, 1926), 27, 29, 31, 70, 76–78, 112, 159, 160, 188. Hahneman remarks, "These distinctions in form are particularly useful in differentiating the implications of the context and nature of sources when comparing different canonical listings. They also hint at the development of the Canon. The movement from comments to collections to catalogues is instructive in the formation of the Christian Bible. The boundaries of the elements of the canon are fixed gradually just as the boundaries of these categories are gradually defined. Comments generally precede collections in the formation of the Christian canon, just as collections precede catalogues." Ibid., 89.

28 See the list provided by Spellman, *Canon-Conscious*, 222–223; Metzger, *The Canon of the New Testament*, 295–300; Lee Martin McDonald, "Lists and Catalogues of New Testament Collections," in *The Canon Debate* ed. Lee Martin McDonald and James A. Sanders (Baker, 2002), 591–597.

29 "*Cum ipse beatus apostolus paulus sequens prodecessoris sui Iohannis ordine nonnisi* (c) *nomenati semptae eccles*(e)*iis*." Taken from Hahenman, *The Muratorian Fragment*, 7.

30 Metzger remarks, "One detects an interesting development involving three stages. At the first stage there are three apocalypses (those of John, Peter, and Hermas); at the second, there are only two (John and Peter); finally, only John is apostolic. The first position has already been passed; despite the author's sympathy that he feels for Hermas, he accepts the solution of only two apocalypses. One sees a hint of the third stage when the author mentions those who accept only John's apocalypse. Although he does not share this point of view, he does not discuss the grounds for rejecting it. In fact, he seems to have lacked any precise criterion for solving the problem." Metzger, *The Canon of the New Testament*, 198. DeSilva remarks, "It also specifically mentions the Wisdom of Solomon (usually thought of as being included in the Old Testament) and the *Apocalypse of Peter* among the received books. Although the author acknowledges that the public reading of the latter in church is a matter of dispute." DeSilva, *An Introduction to the New Testament*, 33. Edmon L. Gallagher and John D. Meade note that the Shepherd of Hermas was rejected for public reading but encouraged for private reading. Edmon L. Gallagher and John D. Meade, The Biblical Canon Lists from Early Christianity: Texts and Analysis (Oxford University Press, 2017), 177.

31 "But we accept nothing whatever of Arsinous or Valentinus or Miltiades, who also com-

Another significant work is that of Eusebius of Caesarea in his *Ecclesiastical History*. For his category of *homolegumena* (ὁμολεγούμενα) twenty-two books are listed: the four Gospels, Acts, Paul's epistles including Hebrews, 1 Peter, and 1 John.[32] The second category Eusebius labeled as the antilegomena (ἀντιλεγόμενα), the disputed books, and includes the Epistle of James, Jude, 2 Peter, and 2 and 3 John. His rejected or illegitimate (νόθα) books are the *Acts of Paul*, the *Shepherd of Hermas*, the *Apocalypse of Peter*, the *Epistle of Barnabas*, the *Teachings of the Apostles*, the *Gospel according to the Hebrews*, and Revelation.[33]

Thus, one can surmise that both the Muratorian Canon and the collection provided by Eusebius show an awareness of a list of authoritative and illegitimate, or rejected, works that were recognized prior to the fourth century. Spellman recognizes this pattern and provides the following classification for a canonical awareness. After the initial composition of the biblical material, there is the period of "gradual canonization where these initial compositions are gathered into groupings and associated with other documents ... [and] there is a move to consolidate and formalize the order and content of the biblical material."[34] This grouping and subsequent association with other documents is reflected in the various canonical orders of the books of the Bible as provided in various Greek uncial codex manuscripts of the fourth and fifth century.[35]

The Canonical Order of the New Testament

Rather than using scrolls as their primary writing material, the New Testament was initially written on a codex. The codices were able to hold more texts than a scroll, it reduced costs of production and publication, and it allowed that no smaller writing would be omitted.[36] The books of the New

posed a new book of psalms for Marcion, together with Basilides, the Asian founder of the Cataphrygians." Ibid., 182.

32 The following lists are compiled by Metzger, *The Canon of the New Testament*, 202–204; Hahneman, *The Muratorian Fragment*, 134, 138–140. See also Goodspeed, *The Formation of the New Testament*, 98–105.

33 Hahneman notes, "In one place Eusebius appeared to identify the author of Revelation as John the apostle and evangelist (*HE* 3.18.1), while in another place he acknowledged that if it was not the apostle, it was probably the presbyter John who saw the Apocalypse (*HE* 3.39.5–6). In his own list Eusebius enumerated Revelation among the *homologoumena*, but with the qualifier, 'if it really seems proper' (*HE* 3.25.4). In the previous chapter, Eusbeius had noted that the opinions of most were still divided (*HE* 3.24.18). Eusebius' comments may reflect a hesitancy introduced by the remarks of Dionysius of Alexandria." Ibid., 24.

34 Spellman, *Canon-Conscious*, 39.

35 Gamble, "The New Testament Canon," 291–294.

36 David Trobisch, *The First Edition of the New Testament* (Oxford University Press, 2000),

Testament were circulated within their respective codices before they were dispersed to various churches and/or people. As David Trobisch remarks, "from the very beginning, New Testament manuscripts were codices and not scrolls."[37] Thus, the recipients of these codices would have been read together alongside one another, and this reading would have provided a comparison between the manuscripts.

Metzger remarks that early in the second century the codes, which were a leaf form of a book, came into church use. The codices were made of one or more sheets of papyrus that were sewed together in the middle.[38] Writing the material on a codex afforded several benefits for the circulation of these books over a roll.[39] Furthermore, compared to non-Christian literary texts, the New Testament "has been passed on to us almost exclusively in codex form; the oldest extant fragments reach back to the second century."[40] Trobisch cites the research of C.H. Roberts and T.C. Skeat who evaluated 172 Greek manuscripts and fragments from the Scriptures that date back to the first four centuries and discovered that 158 originated from codices while fourteen were from scrolls.[41] The binding of the documents in a codex is practical, for Constantine suggested that Eusebius "produce and send him for use in Constantinople fifty copies of the sacred Scripture" since he considered them viable for the Christian church.[42] Also, it appears that the idea of a canon already contained a certain number of "sacred texts [that were] already

---

76. Trobisch also provided a helpful overview of both scrolls and codices, their production, and why the canon was eventually composed on codices. See ibid., 69–77.

37 Trobisch, *The First Edition of the New Testament*, 19.

38 Bruce M. Metzger and Bart D. Ehrman, *The Text of the New Testament: Its Transmission, Corruption, and Restoration* (Oxford University Press, 2005), 12.

39 Metzger and Ehrman note, "(1) it permitted all four Gospels or all the Epistles of Paul to be bound into one book, a format that was impossible so long as the roll was used; (2) it facilitated the consultation of proof texts; and (3) it was better adapted to receiving writing on both sides of the page, thus keeping the cost of production down." Ibid., 12–13. They further remark, "Other scholars have maintained that the codex became popular among Christians because of the influence exerted on the entire tradition by some particularly authoritative sacred text or texts—either the Gospel of Mark, the four Gospels together, or the epistles of Paul."

40 Trobisch, *The First Edition of the New Testament*, 20.

41 Ibid., 20. The source is Colin Henderson Roberts and T. C. Skeat, *The Birth of the Codex* (Oxford University Press, 1983), 38–44. See the contrasting view by Peter M. Head, 'Graham Stanton and the Four-Gospel Codex: Reconsidering the Manuscript Evidence,' in *Jesus, Matthew's Gospel and Early Christianity*, ed. Daniel Gurtner, Joel Willitts, and Richard A. Burridge (T&T Clark, 2011), 93–101; Graham N. Stanton, 'The Fourfold Gospel,' *NTS* 43 (1997): 317–346. Head also critiques Skeat's position in Peter M. Head, "Is P4, P64 and P67 the Oldest Manuscript of the Four Gospels? A Response to T. C. Skeat," *NTS 51* (2005): 450–457.

42 Dimitris J. Kyrtatas, "Historical Aspects of the Formation of the New Testament Canon," in *Canon and Canonicity: The Formation and Use of Scripture*, ed. Einar Thomassen (Museum Tusculanum Press, 2010), 30.

fully developed and strongly advocated by at least some church leaders."[43] If the idea of canon contained a number of sacred texts, then it would suggest that the early church already formed an understanding of canon and what remained within its boundaries.

The canonical order of the New Testament varied through the early circulation of the collections within the codices; however, the location of the books of the New Testament remained fairly consistent.[44] Two complete editions that are dated to the fourth century are Codex Sinaiticus (01 ℵ) and Codex Vaticanus (B 03).[45] The comparison between the two codices is as follows.[46]

Sinaiticus (01 ℵ)	Vaticanus (B 03)
Matthew	Matthew
Mark	Mark
Luke	Luke
John	John
Romans	Acts
1 Corinthians	James
2 Corinthians	1 Peter
Galatians	2 Peter
Ephesians	1 John
Philippians	2 John
Colossians	3 John
1 Thessalonians	Jude
2 Thessalonians	
Hebrews	Romans
1 Timothy	1 Corinthians
2 Timothy	2 Corinthians
Titus	Galatians
Philemon	Ephesians

---

43 Ibid. Kyrtatas draws this conclusion primarily from the work of Eusebius collecting the various documents for Constantine. He also cites two of these texts as Codex Vaticanus (B) and Codex Sinaiticus (ℵ).

44 For the purposes of this book, "location" references the physical location of a book/epistle in relation to other surrounding books/epistles of the canon.

45 Metzger and Ehrman, *The Text of the New Testament*, 62–67.

46 List gathered for Sinaiticus, Vaticanus, Alexandrinus, and Ephraemi Rescriptus are taken from Metzger, *The Canon of the New Testament*, 295–300; Trobisch, *The First Edition of the New Testament*, 24–25; Spellman, *Canon-Conscious*, 222–223. The spacing is used to indicate a division between the different groupings of the text. See also McDonald, "Lists and Catalogues of New Testament Collections," 591–597.

	Philippians
Acts	Colossians
James	1 Thessalonians
1 Peter	2 Thessalonians
2 Peter	Hebrews
1 John	
2 John	
3 John	
Jude	
Revelation	
Barnabas	
Herm	

Figure 3.1: Sinaiticus and Vaticanus Canon List

Our comparison between Sinaiticus and Vaticanus reveals several key differences. First, the Gospels are placed at the beginning of both codices and are in the same order. The location of the four Gospels serves to introduce the reader to the main subject of the New Testament, which is Jesus Christ.[47] Jonathan Pennington argues that the Holy Spirit was active in the church and guided the church to accept these four books into the canon. If one accepts this confessional argument, "then clearly the fourfold Gospel book has always stood, consistently and significantly, at the head of the New Testament canon, providing the linchpin between the Testaments."[48] C.E. Hill examines the contribution made by Irenaeus in the second century and remarks that Irenaeus:

> argued that there are, and can only be, four legitimate Gospels—because they alone teach the truth about Jesus and because they alone had been handed down in the church from the time of the apostles—Irenaeus lies like a fallen Redwood in the path of those who would see the choice of the four Gospels as a late and politically motivated manoeuvre of the fourth century.[49]

---

47 Thus, Βίβλος γενέσεως Ἰησοῦ Χριστοῦ serves not only to introduce the Gospel of Matthew but the entire New Testament.

48 Jonathan Pennington, *Reading the Gospels Wisely: A Narrative and Theological Introduction* (Baker, 2012), 246. In pages 229–258, Pennington argues that the Gospels serve as an archway to the canon of Scripture.

49 C. E. Hill, *Who Chose the Gospels?* (Oxford University Press, 2010), 41.

Second, in Sinaiticus, the Pauline corpus, including Hebrews, immediately follows the Gospel narratives; whereas, in Vaticanus, Acts follows the Gospels followed by the Catholic Epistles. Third, the final section of Sinaiticus begins with Acts, followed by the Catholic Epistles, Jude, Revelation, and the two early writings of the *Letter of Barnabas* and the *Shepherd of Hermas*.[50] Vaticanus, however, concludes with some of the Pauline corpus that, like Sinaiticus, includes Hebrews; yet, the codex ends abruptly with Hebrews and does not include several works.[51] Trobisch observes:

> The arrangement of the writing varies from the Codex Sinaiticus in that the Praxapostolos is placed between the Tetraeuangelion and the Corpus Paulinum. The manuscript breaks off in the middle for the Letter to the Hebrews (Heb 9:14), which follows 2 Thessalonians. The pastorals [sic], the Letter to Philemon, and Revelation of John are missing, due to the loss of the last part of this manuscript.[52]

Sinaiticus is also the only manuscript that contains all the books of the New Testament.[53] Thus, we can surmise that these two complete editions were intentionally shaped and that they retained groups of works together in order to provide a cohesive unit. Furthermore, both manuscripts conclude with Revelation, which further suggests the compilers recognized its apocalyptic genre and positioned it at the end.

Two other complete codices that have survived are Alexandrinus (A 02) and Ephraemi Rescriptus (C 04) and are dated to the fifth century.

Alexandrinus (A 02)	Ephraemi Rescriptus (C 04)
Matthew	Matthew
Mark	Mark
Luke	Luke

---

50 Peter Michael Hansell, "Why was the Shepherd of Hermas left out of the New Testament Canon? A Contextual Study in Church History and its Contemporary Relevance," *BTF* 34.2 (2002): 38–57.

51 "1 Timothy, 2 Timothy, Titus, and Philemon are missing from the end of the manuscript. [Alexandrinus, Sinaiticus, Vaticanus, and Ephraemi Rescriptus] were written independently; that is to say, none of them is a copy of any of the others." Daniel Trobisch, *Paul's Letter Collections* (Quiet Waters Publication, 2001), 7.

52 Trobisch, *The First Edition of the New Testament*, 24–25.

53 Sinaiticus was "discovered in 1844 in the library of the monastery of St. Catherine at Mount Sinai and brought to Russia in 1869. In 1933 the Russian government sold it to the British Museum, where it is kept today as one of the great treasures of the museum." Trobisch, *Paul's Letter Collections*, 7.

John	John
	Acts
Acts	
James	Romans
1 Peter	1 Corinthians
2 Peter	2 Corinthians
1 John	Galatians
2 John	Ephesians
3 John	Philippians
Jude	Colossians
	1 Thessalonians
Romans	2 Thessalonians
1 Corinthians	1 Timothy
2 Corinthians	2 Timothy
Galatians	Titus
Ephesians	Philemon
Philippians	Hebrews
Colossians	
1 Thessalonians	James
2 Thessalonians	1 Peter
Hebrews	2 Peter
1 Timothy	1 John
2 Timothy	2 John
Titus	3 John
Philemon	Jude
Revelation	Revelation
1 Clement	
2 Clement	

Figure 3.2: Alexandrinus and Ephraemi Rescriptus Canon List

These final two codices also warrant further scrutiny. First, as with Sinaiticus and Vaticanus, the Gospels lead the New Testament in Alexandrinus and Ephraemi Rescriptus. Second, Acts follows the Gospels in both Alexandrinus and Ephraemi Rescriptus. Third, both codices include all of the traditional Pauline collection. Fourth, all of the Catholic Epistles are included, although Alexandrinus places this group at the beginning of the collection and

Ephraemi Rescriptus at the end. Last, Alexandrinus include two traditional Christian letters, whereas Ephraemi Rescriptus concludes with Revelation.

Although the reasons for the various differences in the way the earliest manuscripts order the New Testament books is beyond the scope of this study, a brief overview will shed some light on why Revelation is the *terminus ad quem* of the New Testament canon. First, Matthew Emerson remarks that the reversal of the Pauline and Catholic Epistles, as reflected in Alexandrinus and Vaticanus, were moved to their location in Sinaiticus and Ephraemi Rescriptus. This movement would reflect what is seen in the English Bibles of today, and Emerson believes it is possible that this shift occurred with the publication of Jerome's translation of the Bible into the Latin.[54] Second, there is also the possibility that the New Testament canon is intended to mirror the LXX. Greg Goswell argues for this position when he writes, "The suggestion has been made that the familiar canonical order parallels that of the Greek OT (exemplified by Vaticanus), so that the Gospels correspond to the Pentateuch, Acts to the Historical Books, the letters to the Poetic Books, and Revelation to the Prophetic Books."[55] Third, Arthur G. Patizia provides a helpful list of early and later canonical orderings of the New Testament canon, and his index appears to note that the Council of Carthage was the first occurrence where Paul's letters appeared before the General epistles.[56]

Revelation in the Context of the Canon

Thus far it has been shown that in the four collated lists of Sinaiticus, Vaticanus, Alexandrinus, and Ephraemi Rescriptus, as well as within the Muratorian Fragment, Revelation has appeared at the end of the canonical lists.[57] There is access to reliable information about the early New Testament canon and this information shows that, with regard to Revelation, the compilers believed that this book appropriately concluded the New Testament or, in

---

54 "At some point (possibly with Jerome's translation of the Bible into Latin) the General epistles were shifted to come after Paul's letters and Hebrews was moved from the middle (usually between 2 Thessalonians and 1 Timothy) to the end, to reflect the order we see today in our English Bibles." Matthew Emerson, "Victory, Atonement, Restoration, and Response: The Shape of the New Testament Canon and the Holistic Gospel Message," *STR* 3 (2012): 179–180 n7.

55 See Greg Goswell, "The Order of the Books of the New Testament," *JETS* 53 (2010): 225–226. Trobisch believes arranging the "New Testament writings according to genre may very well reflect the organizing principle used in the Old Testament. The editors created a unified user interface for both parts of the edition." Trobisch, *The First Edition of the New Testament*, 64.

56 See Arthur G. Patzia, *The Making of the New Testament: Origin, Collection, Text, and Canon* (InterVaristy Press, 1995), 155–156.

57 See Garrick V. Allen, "The Apocalypse in Codex Alexandrinus: Exegetical Reasoning and Singular Readings in New Testament Greek Manuscripts," *JBL* 135 (2016): 859–880.

the instance of Alexandrinus and Sinaiticus, belonged at the end of the canon. Due to the content and scope of Revelation, one would expect it to be placed at the end of the canon. Revelation involves the overall theme of God, working through the arrival of the Son, to make all things new once more. It is at the end of the days that a new creation is established, and the inhabitants of this new heaven and new earth will no longer deal with the curse of sin.[58]

Revelation not only concludes the New Testament canon but concludes the entire biblical canon as such.[59] This conclusion is both locative and theological, as the *inclusio* in Rev 21–22 corresponds to Gen 1–3. That is, Genesis begins with the creation of the heavens and the earth, and Revelation concludes with the re-creation of the new heaven and the new earth.[60] Thus, Revelation can be seen as "a work of Christian prophecy that understands itself to be the culmination of the whole biblical tradition."[61] Likewise, James Hamilton concludes, "The Apocalypse of John is like an exclamation point at the end of the long sentence that is the Bible."[62] As Thomas R. Schreiner remarks, "Revelation is a fitting conclusion to the canon of Scripture. God's kingdom is established in and through Jesus Christ. Jesus, as the lion and the lamb, won the victory over the dragon, the ancient serpent (see Gen. 3:15) by virtue of his cross and resurrection."[63] Therefore, Revelation does not simply end the New Testament canon but the entire biblical canon with the victory of God and of his people.

However, the theme of God making all things new again is not initially determined in the beginning of the work but is developed as the narrator composes what he is witnessing firsthand. Therefore, it is pertinent to examine the structure and content of Revelation in order to (1) interpret Revelation in a canonical method, and (2) determine how Revelation incorporates the New Testament through intertextual exegesis.

---

[58] Isaac Watts captures this new-creation theme in "Joy to the World" when he writes, "No more let sins and sorrows grown, nor thorns infest the ground. He comes to make his blessings flow, far as the curse is found."

[59] T. Desmond Alexander, *From Eden to the New Jerusalem: An Introduction to Biblical Theology* (Kregel Academic, 2006), 171–187.

[60] "In particular, through a network of intertextual allusions to the Pentateuchal narratives of Genesis 1–3, John creates in Revelation 21–22 a macrostrctural inclusio for the biblical canon and storyline." Spellman, *Canon-Conscious*, 225.

[61] Richard Bauckham, *The Theology of the Book of Revelation* (Cambridge University Press, 1993), 144.

[62] James M. Hamilton Jr., *God's Glory in Salvation Through Judgment: A Biblical Theology* (Crossway, 2010), 541.

[63] Thomas R. Schreiner, *The King in His Beauty: A Biblical Theology of the Old and New Testaments* (Baker, 2013), 629.

Approaching Revelation Canonically

When the reader approaches Revelation canonically, it allows the reader to interpret some "canonical signals" the author has left in his work.[64] First, the reader is introduced to the common name "John," and given no clue as to the identity of this author. This ambiguity, as previously mentioned, has presented several possible identities of this "John." However, if one approaches Revelation in a canonical manner, the identity of this John is understood to be the author of the Fourth Gospel and 1–3 John. Similarities between Revelation and the other Johannine writings, such as the openings of John 1:6–7, 1 John 1:1–2 and Rev 1:1–2, the identity of Jesus as the Word of God (John 1:1, 14; 1 John 1:1; Rev 19:13), and the "I am" statements suggest the same author (cf. John 6:35; Rev 1:8).[65]

Second, the reader of the New Testament should also expect Revelation to function in a similar manner to that of the Gospel of John. In other words, the Gospel of John is distinct in both form and, at times, content of the Synoptic Gospels. This difference has led some to conclude that the Gospel of John may function as a theological commentary on the life of Jesus rather than a historical biography.[66] If one accepts this premise, then Revelation could also be understood in the same way. Revelation, approached canonically, is an interpretation of the events that will soon take place (Rev 1:1), and they are interpreted through the lens of the Christian Bible.

The Structure of Revelation

The narrative of Revelation progresses urgently from one scene to the next. Scenes of judgment are depicted and then followed by an interlude until the narrative returns to the scene of judgment. For example, this narrative shift is seen in the opening of the seven seals. In 6:1–17, the Lamb opens the sixth seal, but this narrative is interrupted by the sealing of the 144,000 and the vision of a great multitude (7:1–17). The seal narrative then concludes in 8:1–4.

---

64 David R. Nienhus, *A Concise Guide to Reading the New Testament: A Canonical Introduction* (Baker, 2018), 155.

65 For a full list, see ibid., 156.

66 This "theological commentary on the life of Jesus" can be proposed in several different ways. See Matthew Y. Emerson, *Christ and the New Creation: A Canonical Approach to the Theology of the New Testament* (Wipf and Stock, 2013), 55–60; Andreas J. Köstenberger, *A Theology of John's Gospel and Letters: The Word, the Christ, and the Son of God* (Zondervan, 2009), 336–354; Nienhuis, *A Concise Guide*, 11; Richard B. Hays, *Reading Backwards: Figural Christology and the Fourfold Gospel Witness* (Baylor University Press, 2014), 75–92.

Because the narrative changes abruptly, scholars have proposed various structures for Revelation. Adela Yarbro Collins proposes a seven-fold structure:[67]

1. Prologue (1:1–8)
2. The Seven Messages (1:9–3:22)
3. The Seven Seals (4:1–8:5)
4. The Seven Trumpets (8:2–11:19)
5. Seven Unnumbered Visions (12:1–15:4)
6. The Seven Bowls (15:1–16:21)
    a. Babylon Appendix (17:1–19:10)
7. Seven Unnumbered Visions (19:11–21:8)
    a. Jerusalem Appendix (21:9–22:5)
8. Epilogue (22:6–21)

Collins's structure focuses primarily upon the main narrative movements within Revelation, as is visible by her emphasis upon the number "seven." This structure recognizes the prominence of the number within the book and it also suggests that the way in which Revelation is best understood is through these specific events. Unfortunately, her structure is overly simplistic, since certain sections of Revelation fall out of the category of "seven." For example, Collins arranges 4:1–8:5 under the narrative of the seven seals, but chapter four has nothing to do with the seven seals. Rather, chapter four is focused upon the heavenly vision of God seated upon the throne. The scroll is not mentioned until 5:1, and there the emphasis is not upon the scroll as it is upon the one who is worthy to take the scroll and to open its seals. This same line of argument can also be made for chapter seven, where the two visions received by John are not dependent upon the opening of the seven seals. Despite these weaknesses, the structure proposed by Collins is a helpful outline that attempts to find a central theme which runs through the book as a whole.

Elisabeth Schüssler Fiorenza understands Revelation to have a chiastic structure that is patterned after an epistolary framework.[68]

A Prologue (1:1–8)
B   Inaugural Vision and Letter Septet (1:9–3:22)

---

[67] Adele Yarbro Collins, *The Combat Myth in the Book of Revelation* (Scholar Press, 1976), 13–29.

[68] Elisabeth Schüssler Fiorenza, *The Book of Revelation: Justice and Judgment* (Fortress Press, 1985), 175–176. Compare the chiastic structures of Hamilton, *God's Glory in Salvation Through Judgment*, 544; Kellum, Köstenberger, Quarles, *The Cradle, Cross, Crown*, 957–958.

C   Seven-Sealed Scroll Vision (4:1–9:21; 11:15–19)
D   Small Prophetic Scroll (10:1–15:4)
C¹ Seven-Sealed Scroll Vision, Continued (15:1, 5–19:10)
B¹ Visions of Judgment and Salvation (19:11–22:9)
A¹ Epilogue (22:10–22:21)

Her argument is convincing, and if one were to accept a chiastic structure of Revelation, the former would suggest that an author or editor intended to parallel several themes with one another. For Schüssler Fiorenza, "the main function of Rev. is the prophetic interpretation of the situation of the community," and this prophetic interpretation would be made evident in this epistolary framework.[69] However, a chiastic structure is not needed to determine that the primary function of Revelation is to interpret the situation of the community. Furthermore, this structure breaks the narrative into separate groups, such as C and C¹, and it disrupts the flow of the narrative. Although Schüssler Fiorenza's proposed outline is helpful, her chiastic structure appears forced.[70]

W. R. Kempson surveyed numerous proposed structures for Revelation and believes that a new attempt is needed. Kempson includes a keyphrase approach, incorporating "in the Spirit" and "sign" with major themes that appear in the book. In turn, this approach divides the book into four visions.[71]

1. Prologue (1:1–8)
2. Vision I (1:9–3:22)
3. Vision II (4:1–16:21)
   A. Introduction: Revealing Heaven's Purpose (4:2–5:14)
   B. The Scroll Unsealed (6:1–8:1)
   C. The Scroll Heralded and Summarized (8:2–11:19)
   D. The Scroll Opened and Executed
      i. The Woman and the Dragon (12:1–14:20)
      ii. The Seven Bowls of God's Wrath (15:1–16:21)
4. Vision III (17:1–21:8)
   A. The Harlot and the Beast (17:3–18)

---

69 Schüssler Fiorenza, *The Book of Revelation*, 175.

70 Hamilton's chiastic structure of Revelation is a helpful outline of the work and appears to be the strongest example of a chiasm provided. See Hamilton, *God's Glory in Salvation Through Judgment*, 544.

71 W. R. Kempson, "Theology in the Revelation of John" (PhD diss., Southern Baptist Theological Seminary, 1982). See the helpful summary by Christopher R. Smith, "The Structure of the Book of Revelation in Light of Apocalyptic Literary Conventions" *NT* 36 (1994): 373–375. The outline of Kempson's suggestions is taken from this article. Also, see the structure based off the four visions in Terry L. Wilder, J. Daryl Charles, and Kendell Easley, *Faithful to the End: An Introduction to Hebrews Through Revelation* (B&H Academic, 2007), 281.

    B. The Dirge Over Babylon (18:1–19:10)
    C. The Final Victory (19:11–21:8)
5. Vision IV (21:9–22:5)
6. Epilogue (22:6–21)

The difficulty of Revelation's structure is compounded by the abrupt changes in the narrative of Revelation and the complexities of the visions which were seen by John.

If one interprets Revelation from a canonical perspective, its structure emerges from developments of its wider narrative. A key division marker is ἐν πνεύματι, and in each instance (1:10; 4:2; 17:3; 21:10) John receives a vision that is distinct from the previous vision.[72] This outline, then, would refrain from an unnecessary grouping or separation of material that does not fit into a specific category (i.e., Schüssler Fiorenza).[73]

1. Prologue (1:1–8)
2. The Vision of Christ (1:9–3:22)
3. The Vision of Heaven (4:1–16:21)
4. The Vision of the Wilderness (17:1–21:8)
5. The Vision of the Mountain (21:9–22:5)
6. Epilogue (22:6–21)

This outline emphasizes the narrative of the book as it unfolds. Furthermore, as shown below, it encourages the reader to interpret the book following a canonical approach with an emphasis upon the four major visions.

THE CONTENT OF REVELATION

For the purposes of this work, and in order to examine verbal connections that Revelation may share with other texts of the New Testament, the content of Revelation must first be outlined. This brief overview of Revelation is developed from a canonical vantage-point and, therefore, several aspects of John's usage of the Old Testament are highlighted as well as other New Testament themes. The New Testament themes that overlap within Revelation

---

    72 For a helpful discussion, see Alan S. Bandy, "The Prophetic Lawsuit in the Book of Revelation: An Analysis of the Lawsuit Motif in Revelation with Reference to the Use of the Old Testament," PhD diss. (Southeastern Baptist Theological Seminary, 2006), 152–155.

    73 This is the proposed outline in Kellum, Köstenberger, Quarles, *The Cradle, Cross, Crown*, 965. However, I believe the phrase ἐν πνεύματι is important for Revelation and that this structural marker appears to divide the book more naturally, as opposed to the other suggestions.

and various books in the New Testament, along with the possible verbal connections of Revelation, strengthen the thesis of this work; namely, that the ideal reader of Revelation is one who is familiar with both the Old and New Testament canonical books.

The Prologue (1:1–8)

The prologue informs the reader of Revelation that it is an apocalyptic work, one that describes a vision of Jesus given to his servant John.[74] John is viewed as an eyewitness to the events of the book, which makes him a prophetic witness.[75] The reader of this book, both the initial recipients of the seven churches (1:4) and those who are "reading aloud and hearing the words of this prophecy and keeping what is written in it" (1:3), are declared blessed. Reading aloud Revelation does not bring forth the blessing; rather, it is both hearing and keeping (τηροῦντες) what is written.

After John promises a blessing on all who read aloud, hear, and keep the words of this book, a similar greeting comparable to ones used by the apostle Paul (χάρις ὑμῖν καὶ εἰρήνη) sounds forth from the Trinity and introduces Jesus as the Danielic Son of Man who "comes upon the clouds" (1:7a; Dan 7:13). The prologue concludes by noting the eternality of the Father as "the [one] who is and the one who was and the one who is to come, the Almighty One" (1:8).

The Vision of Christ (1:9–3:22)

In Rev 1:9–20, John describes the inaugural vision he receives of the resurrected Savior. John uses the first person ἐγώ to begin the work in an autobiographical format, which parallels both the Old Testament prophets and his Gospel (cf. John 19:35; 21:24).[76] John, exiled to the island of Patmos because of

---

74 The phrase Ἀποκάλυψις Ἰησοῦ Χριστοῦ introduces the book as a whole, and the genitive Ἰησοῦ Χριστοῦ is more likely both objective and subjective. Thus, the letter is both "from Jesus Christ" and "about Jesus Christ." See Daniel B. Wallace, *Greek Grammar Beyond the Basics: An Exegetical Syntax of the New Testament* (Zondervan, 1996), 112–119.

75 "In Rev 1:1, John testifies (μαρτύρησεν) as an eyewitness to the veracity of the message directly handed down to him by God. The forensic sense of μαρτύρησεν retains its full force, as if in a lawcourt, he solemnly swears 'to tell the whole truth and nothing but the truth.' This usage corresponds with other occurrences of μαρτυρέω in the NT asserting the official and eyewitness nature of giving testimony (cf. 1 John 1:1–3). In the other two-self-designations, it is as if John states his name for the record (Rev 1:4a, 9a cf. 22:8a). What is more, Jesus (Ἐγὼ Ἰησοῦς) also states his name for the record at the end of the vision to verify John's testimony (Rev 22:16; cf. 22:8–9). As such, John fulfills the role of a witness to Christ and to the churches by submitting his testimony in writing, which consists of all that he has seen (ὅσα εἶδεν)." Bandy, "The Prophetic Lawsuit," 178–179.

76 John uses the first person throughout the work. See 1:10, 12, 17a; 4:1–2; 5:1–2, 4, 6, 11, 3;

the Word of God (διὰ τὸν λόγον τοῦ θεοῦ), hears a voice, as that of a loud trumpet (φωνὴν μεγάλην ὡς σάλπιγγος), commanding him to write his visions and send them to the seven churches in Asia. "His prophetic authority is enforced by the description of the voice that he heard as 'a great voice as a trumpet,' evoking the same voice that Moses heard when Yahweh revealed himself to [Moses] on Mount Sinai (Exod 19:16, 19–20)."[77] As John turns to see the voice that speaks to him, he sees only the resurrected and glorified Jesus Christ. Here, John draws heavily from Old Testament language to convey his vision to the reader.[78] Overwhelmed at the experience, John falls down before Jesus as if he were a dead man (cf. Isa 6:5; Dan 8:17). However, Jesus assures John not to fear and explains the meaning of the seven lampstands and the seven stars which he previously witnessed.[79]

Chapters 2–3 provide instruction for the seven churches in Asia Minor from the resurrected Lord himself, and each letter begins in a similar way.[80] In the greetings, John addresses the angel of each respective church and provides a description of the resurrected Christ. The message officially begins with the usage of οἶδά, and either an admonishment to continue to persevere in the good (cf. 2:2–3) or for a call to repentance (2:14–16, 20) follows. The brief address concludes with a call to listen to what the Spirit says (2:7a, 11a, 17a, 29; 3:6, 13, 22) and with a promise of deliverance for the one who conquers (Τῷ νικῶντι; 2:7b, 11b, 17b, 26; 3:5, 12, 21).

The Vision of Heaven (4:1–16:21)

Chapter four begins the second vision and the main narrative of the book. John is transferred from Patmos to heaven through a "door standing open in heaven" (4:1), and this event "also constitutes a thematic transition from

---

6:1–3, 5–8, 12; 7:1–2, 4, 9, 14; 8:2, 13; 9:1, 13, 16–17; 10:1, 4–5, 8–11; 11:1, 3; 12:10; 13:1, 11; 14:1–2, 6, 13–14; 15:1–2, 5; 16:1, 5, 7, 13; 17:3, 6; 18:1, 4; 19:1, 6, 10–11, 17, 19; 20:1, 4, 11–12; 21:1–3, 22; 22:7–8. Although in John 19:35 and 21:24 the examples are not in the first person, the focus is upon the testimony John himself.

77 G. K. Beale and Sean M. McDonough, "Revelation" in *Commentary on the New Testament Use of the Old Testament* (Baker, 2007), 1091.

78 See Robert M. Mounce, *Revelation*, NICNT (Eerdmans, 1997), 57–60.

79 The identity of the seven angels is highly contested. See the helpful overview in Grant R. Osborne, *Revelation* (Baker, 2006), 98–99. Perhaps an amalgamation of points two and four provide the best explanation.

80 The phrase Τῷ ἀγγέλῳ τῆς ἐν [region] ἐκκλησίας γράψον is found in each address. Schreiner remarks, "One of the striking characteristics of Revelation is that the book is addressed to churches (Rev. 1:4, 11; 2:1–3:22). Each church in particular is named in the introduction to the various letters (Rev. 2:1, 8, 12, 18; 3:1, 7, 14), and yet the letters intended for a specific church are also specifically said to be for all the churches (Rev. 2:7, 11, 17, 29; 3:6, 13, 22)." Thomas R. Schreiner, *New Testament Theology: Magnifying God in Christ* (Baker, 2008), 749.

a juridical investigation of the churches to an investigation of the nations."[81] John, upon his transference to heaven, beholds the throne of God with God seated upon it. To describe this vision, John draws from the prophet Ezekiel (Ezek 1:5, 10, 18, 22, 27) and records the heavenly song of both the four living creatures (cf. Isa 6:3) and the twenty-four elders (4:11).

However, the scene dramatically changes from heavenly worship to sorrow, as none are found worthy to take the scroll from the hand of the one who sits upon the throne. While John weeps, one elder commands John to stop weeping because the Lion of the tribe of Judah, the Root of David has conquered (ἐνίκησεν ὁ λέων ὁ ἐκ τῆς φυλῆς Ἰούδα, ἡ ῥίζα Δαυίδ, ἀνοῖξαι). Upon turning to gaze upon this strong Lion, John beholds a slaughtered Lamb who stands as though it has been slain, and this lamb is deemed worthy to take the scroll and open the seals.[82] Thus, the Lamb is worthy to judge the nations.

Since the Lamb is worthy to judge the nations, he begins to open the seven seals of the scroll that was in the hand of the Father.[83] When each seal is opened, judgment is brought forth upon the earth. The first judgment effected is through the four horsemen of the Apocalypse (6:1–8).[84] These horsemen are released upon the earth at the opening of the first four seals, and they bring conquest, war, famine, and death. The fifth seal is opened to reveal the persecuted church under the altar of souls. These Christians were slain for the word of God, and they cry out that their blood might be avenged. "He has not forgotten those being martyred. It is not a question *if* the righteous will be vindicated and the wicked will be punished, but *when* (6:9–11)."[85] The judgments progress to the culmination of the sixth seal as the earth-dwellers attempt to hide themselves from God and from the wrath of the Lamb, "because the great day of their wrath has come, and who is able to stand?" (6:17).[86]

---

81 Kellum, Köstenberger, Quarles, *The Cradle, Cross, Crown*, 975. Cf. Rev 1:1–8.

82 For the Old Testament imagery of these allusions, see David E. Aune, *Revelation 1–5*, WBC (Thomas Nelson, 1997), 349–353; Beale and McDonough, "Revelation," 1101–1102; Bandy, "The Prophetic Lawsuit," 252–253.

83 Hamilton rightly mentions that "God inaugurates the new exodus with the death and resurrection of Jesus, and he *consummates* it with the plagues of the trumpets and bowls in Revelation." Hamilton, *God's Glory in Salvation Through Judgment*, 548. Thus, the theme of God removing his people from this "new Egypt" and transferring them to a "new Promise Land" can be traced throughout Revelation.

84 For the Old Testament background for the horsemen, see G. K. Beale, *The Book of Revelation*, NIGTC (Eerdmans, 1999), 372–374; R. H. Charles, *Revelation* (T&T Clark, 1985), 1:168–169.

85 Schreiner, *The King in His Beauty*, 622.

86 As Osborne, I am using "earth-dwellers" to refer to those who have not sided with the Lamb and are inhabitants of the earthly kingdom that wages war with the heavenly kingdom

The question posed by the earth-dwellers leads naturally into the first interlude where the scene changes from judgment to protection, and John sees an angel ascend from the sun to seal the 144,000 of Israel.[87] The earth-dwellers question of who is able to stand is answered in the second unit, as this section focuses on God's salvation upon those who are "standing before the throne and before the Lamb" (ἑστῶτες ἐνώπιον τοῦ θρόνου καὶ ἐνώπιον τοῦ ἀρνίου). This interlude concludes with a description of things to come whereby God's people will one day be fully satisfied in his presence when the Lamb serves as their shepherd and God wipes away all tears.

The opening of the seventh seal brings about total silence in heaven for half an hour, and then seven angels are given seven trumpets to blow.[88] The sounding of the first four trumpets bring forth judgment upon the earth, and each judgment causes devastation to a third of its own respective category: a third of earth's vegetation is burned, a third of saltwater turns to blood, a third of the freshwater becomes bitter, and a third of the stars, sun, and moon becomes dark.[89] The final three trumpets are directed specifically at the earth-dwellers. The fifth trumpet releases an army of demon locusts that inflict those who have not been sealed, and the sixth trumpet releases a cavalry of horses prepared for battle. Yet, these earth-dwellers still refuse to repent (cf. 6:16; Exod 20:13–15).

throughout Revelation.

87 Some take the 144,000 as a literal reference to the tribes of Israel while others interpret it symbolically as the believers who have come out of the great tribulation. For a summary of the respective views, see Beale, *Revelation*, 416–423. For the view that the 144,000 are ethnic Israel, see Robert L. Thomas, *Revelation 1–7: An Exegetical Commentary* (Moody, 1992), 475–483. For the symbolic view, see Osborne, *Revelation*, 302–303; Craig L. Blomberg, *From Pentecost to Patmos: An Introduction Through Revelation* (B&H Academic, 2006), 529–530. However, the 144,000 are best understood as a representative of the whole church of God. Canonically, the church is viewed as a renewed Israel sent out to fulfill what the old Israel was unable to do. In Matt 19:28, Jesus tells his disciples that one day they will judge the twelve tribes of Israel as they sit upon their twelve thrones. In Rom 2:29 Paul says that the believer who professes faith in Christ is the true Jew because being a Jew is an issue of the heart and not of obligation to the act of circumcision. In Gal 6:16 Paul calls the church the Israel of God, and James begins his book as addressing the twelve tribes in the Dispersion (1:1), which means Christians are exiles from their homeland of heaven. Peter calls Christians, and subsequently the church, a royal priesthood and a holy nation, which is explicitly taken from both Isa 43:20 and Exod 19, and he applies it to the church. Furthermore, in Gal 3:27–29 Paul himself says again that there is neither Jew nor Greek, for all are all in Christ. Thus, the 144,000 are the church of God, the new and better Israel.

88 "The trumpets in Revelation … are eschatological trumpets. They herald the day of God's wrath. Zeph 1:14–16 describes the great day of the Lord as 'a day of wrath … a day of distress and anguish … a day of trumpet and battle cry.'" Mounce, *Revelation*, 173.

89 There are parallels between the trumpets and the seals. See ibid., 177. For the comparison between the trumpets and the seven bowls, see David E. Aune, *Revelation 6–16*, WBC (Thomas Nelson, 1998), 497–498. Aune also discusses the trumpets in light of the Exodus plague tradition. See ibid., 499–506.

The portion of 10:1–11:19 contains the second interlude of Revelation, as the narrative is interrupted with the vision of two main subjects that will appear throughout the work. In 10:1–11:19, the reader is introduced to the theme of God's people who serve as a prophetic witness to the earth-dwellers. The first unit (10:1–11) finds John receiving of the divine message that he must give to the nations, and he is told to seal up what the seven thunders told him and consume the scroll (cf. Ezek 3:1–3).[90] The second unit (11:1–14) depicts the ministry of two prophetic witnesses to the nations.[91] "These sections are inextricably bound together because they pertain to the fulfillment of a prophetic ministry to the nations. John's prophetic commission is ultimately completed in the ministry of the faithful witnesses."[92] When the days are completed for the witnesses to declare their message, the beast rises from the bottomless pit, makes war upon them, and kills them (11:7). This event does not just anticipate the arrival of the beast in Revelation, but it also introduces the completion of the message of the witnesses to the world. The final time of judgment has arrived, as indicated in the blowing of the seventh trumpet in 11:15–19.[93] This final trumpet signals the second interlude to Revelation that will bring the end of God's wrath upon the earth, because the bowls that will be poured out in 16:1–21 are intended to destroy the earth.

In 12:1–15:1, the narrative divides into two main sections, with an interlude in 14:1–20.[94] The first main section describes the holy war upon the earth (12:1–17), as the dragon attempts to consume the newborn child and Satan is cast down to the earth.[95] Once Satan is cast down, he goes forth to make war with the offspring of the woman (12:17a), and the war transfers from heaven

---

90 "The injunction to eat the scroll represents a clear allusion to Ezek 3:1–3. The broader context of Ezek 3:1–11 confirms the fact that the contents of the scroll relate to a message of judgment intended for an obstinate audience." Bandy, "The Prophetic Lawsuit in the Book of Revelation," 294.

91 This prophetic ministry to the nations is clearly seen in 11:9a, καὶ βλέπουσιν ἐκ τῶν λαῶν καὶ φυλῶν καὶ γλωσσῶν καὶ ἐθνῶν τὸ πτῶμα αὐτῶν ἡμέρας τρεῖς καὶ ἥμισυ καὶ τὰ πτώματα αὐτῶν. The identity of the two witnesses range from Moses and Elijah, Enoch and Elijah, and the church. See Beale, *Revelation* 572 n293 for various options. See also Aune, Revelation 6–16, 598–603. Likely, one should equate the witnesses with the faithful members of Smyrna and Philadelphia. See Charles H. Giblin, "Revelation 11.1–13: Its Form, Function and Contextual Integration," *NTS* 30 (1984): 443.

92 Kellum, Köstenberger, Quarles, *The Cradle, Cross, Crown*, 978.

93 On the importance of 10:1–11:18 for Revelation, see Mark Seaborn Hall, "The Hook Interlocking Structure of Revelation: The Most Important Verses in the Book and How They May Unify Its Structure," *NovT* 44 (2002): 278–296.

94 In 14:1–20, the narrative of war upon the believers is interrupted to show God's protection for his people and the beginning of the final judgment upon the earth.

95 The woman here is Israel. See Osborne, *Revelation*, 455–458; Craig Keener, *Revelation* (Zondervan, 1999), 314; Mounce, *Revelation*, 236; Collins, *Combat Myth*, 106–107.

to earth in the second main section. Satan is the first member of the unholy Trinity, and 13:1–18 provides an introduction for the other two members. The first beast is depicted in similar language to the Son, and the second beast functions similarly to the Holy Spirit.[96]

In the midst of the spiritual and physical conflict, John provides three sections of encouragement. First, in 12:10–12 John reminds his readers that the accuser of the brothers (ὁ κατήγωρ τῶν ἀδελφῶν) has been conquered by the blood of the Lamb (cf. 5:6). Second, 13:9–10 calls for the endurance of the saints amidst the intense persecution from the unholy Trinity.[97] Third, 14:1–20 serves to remind the reader that the believers will ultimately be vindicated: they have been redeemed as first fruits for God and the Lamb (14:4; cf. 2 Thess 2:13; Jas 1:18), and the smoke of their tormenters will go up forever (14:11; cf. Gen 19:24).

15:1–8 provides an introduction to the final sign, as seven angels with seven plagues appear and the wrath of God is finished (15:1). As the angels pour out the bowls upon the earth (16:1–21), those who have the mark of the beast and worship him are afflicted by the judgments of God.[98] The first bowl results in painful sores, the second turns the sea into blood (cf. 8:8–9), and the third does the same for fresh water. The fourth bowl increases the power of the sun and it scorches the earth-dwellers. Both the fifth and sixth bowls affect the kingdom of the beast, and the seventh brings forth the realization that God's punishment has ended.[99]

---

96 The parallels between the second beast and the Son are striking. As the Father gives the authority and power to Jesus (5:6–7), the first beast (Satan) grants his "power and his throne and great authority" (13:2). One head of the beast appeared (ἐσφαγμένην) to have a mortal wound, but the wound had been healed (cf. 1:18), and the earth-dwellers worship the beast (13:4; cf. 5:8–14). For ἐσφαγμένην used in the sense of deception, see BDAG, σφάζω. Bandy believes the first beast in 13:1–8 represents "the brute force of the political and military power of Rome." Bandy, "The Prophetic Lawsuit," 306–307. This view is also taken by Richard Bauckham, *The Climax of Prophecy: Studies in the Book of Revelation* (T&T Clark, 1993), 343.

97 "The unjust and merciless onslaught against believers may tempt them to either retaliate or conform, but John encourages them to remain faithful as they patiently endure captivity and execution (cf. Jer 15:2). By responding to this oppression with patient endurance, they place the judgment of their enemies in the hands of God and the Lamb (cf. Rev 6:10)." Bandy, "The Prophetic Lawsuit," 310. Schreiner notes that the New Testament clarifies that when a believer's faith works, "it has a transforming effect. Hence, John writes to summon believers to endure even if they are destined for imprisonment or death (Rev. 13:9–10)." Schreiner, *New Testament Theology*, 613.

98 "The seal judgments impacted a fourth of the earth and its population, the trumpets a third, but the bowls release the full fury of God's wrath in its entirety." Kellum, Köstenberger, Quarles, *The Cradle, Cross, Crown*, 980. For a comparison of the trumpets and bowls, see Beale, *Revelation*, 808–812.

99 Ibid., 823–846.

The Vision of the Wilderness (17:1–21:8)

The third vision begins with a transition in 17:1–2 when one of the seven angels beckons John to come and see the judgment of the great prostitute who has seduced the kings of the earth.[100] He is carried away in the Spirit (ἐν πνεύματι; cf. 1:10; 4:2; 21:10) where he sees a prostitute upon the back of the beast, drunk with the blood of believers (17:3–6). This woman "represents the blasphemous religion that seduces the nations and the economic system that draws them into its earthly luxury."[101] This prostitute may be a personification of Rome, and as she sits upon the back of the beast she is portrayed as dependent upon Satan's kingdom for her survival.[102] However, the ten horns will rise up against Babylon and destroy her from within.[103]

This destruction is vividly recounted in 18:1–24, where the promise of the angel in 17:1 comes to fruition. The emphasis in 18:1–24 is placed upon the idolatry found within Babylon and the worldwide judgment that will ensue. The description of Babylon's fall is filled with many Old Testament references as God judges the city in accordance with sexual immorality, wealth, and political power.[104] The kings, merchants, and the shipmasters express disbelief, as the once "great city" (ἡ πόλις ἡ μεγάλη) has now been destroyed. This destruction brings forth praise from heaven (19:1–4; cf. 6:10; Deut 32:43) as the marriage supper of the Lamb has begun.

From this rejoicing God brings forth judgment as the one who is called "Faithful and True" (19:11) sits upon a white horse (cf. 6:20) and arrives as the Divine Warrior who is clothed with a robe dipped in blood.[105] He returns to

---

100 "Since the fall of Babylon takes place already in 16.19, it appears that Rev. 17.1–18.24 serves as a parenthetical expansion to describe and explain the Babylon theme in more detail." Jan Fekkes, *Isaiah and the Prophetic Traditions in the Book of Revelation: Visionary Antecedents and their Development* (Sheffield Academic Press, 1994), 88–89.

101 Osborne, *Revelation*, 610.

102 Here, I agree with Paul Hoskins that the reference to the seven mountains is unlikely intended only for a specific geographical reference. Paul Hoskins, "Another Possible Interpretation of the Seven Heads of the Beast and the Eighth King (Revelation 17:9–11)," *BBR* 30 (2020): 91–94.

103 "The drying up of the Euphrates' waters in 16:12 is a picture of how the multitudes of Babylon's religious and economic adherents throughout the world (also portrayed as 'waters' here in 17:15) become disloyal to it. 'The kings of the earth' (vv. 16–18) dissuade Babylon's innumerable economic-religious followers from remaining loyal to her. The disenchantment with Babylon is a prelude to her judgment by the kings (described in v. 16) and the final judgment itself. Likewise, in 16:12 the invasion of kings follows the drying up of the waters." Beale, *Revelation*, 883.

104 For a discussion of the Old Testament references, see Beale and McDonough, "Revelation," 1140–1142.

105 Bauckham suggests that "John has taken from the Jewish apocalyptic tradition the notion of a temporary messianic reign on earth before the last judgment and the new creation

make war against Babylon, and the description of Jesus by John provides the theme of this judgment as finally realized.[106] The beast and the false prophet are captured and thrown alive into the lake of fire, and the remaining earth-dwellers are killed by the "sword of the one who sat upon the horse which came forth from his mouth" (19:21). The dragon is subsequently captured and sealed for a thousand years, and those who were killed on account of the word of God are resurrected and rewarded (20:4–6; cf. Dan 7:9–10, 22–27). The second resurrection (20:11–15) is the individual judgment of all people, and the books that are utilized contain every act committed by mankind.

The Vision of the Mountain (21:9–22:5)

After the scenes of judgment conclude, the narrative changes to a focus upon salvation, as God renews his creation and the New Jerusalem (21:2) arrives.[107] God has rid the earth of evil, his dwelling place is with man (21:3), and now a new creation has been established.

> Therefore, what begins in Gen. 1–3 and is developed throughout the rest of the biblical canon finds its climax in Rev. 21:1–22:5, which recapitulates Gen. 1–3 and portrays the goal that the last Adam and his people have finally attained. Thus … the biblical material between the poles of creation and new creation is to be read not only in the light finally of its origins in Gen. 1–3 but also in view of its goal in Revelation.[108]

This New Jerusalem, then, is fully depicted as a new and better Eden.[109] Its walls have twelve foundations (cf. Ezek 48) and written on these walls are the twelves names of the twelve apostles of the Lamb (cf. Rev 7:1–8).[110]

(cf. 2 Bar. 40:3; 4 Ezra 7:28–29; b.Sanh. 99a), but he has characteristically made something different of it. He has used it to depict an essential aspect of his concept of the victory of the martyrs over the beast. He has given the image of the millennium a very specific function." Bauckham, *The Theology of the Book of Revelation*, 108. Also, the arrival of Jesus to redeem his people brings the realized "new exodus" to the "new Promise Land" as "the hope of a new conquest of the land is fulfilled in Revelation 19 when Jesus comes as a conquering new Joshua." Hamilton, *God's Glory in Salvation Through Judgment*, 548.

106   Aune notes that the white horse was a common Roman symbol for triumphing over enemies. See David E. Aune, *Revelation 17–22* (Thomas Nelson, 1998), 1050–1051.

107   The New Jerusalem stands in contrast to the harlot city of Babylon. See Osborne, *Revelation*, 745–767.

108   G. K. Beale, *A New Testament Biblical Theology: The Unfolding of the Old Testament in the New* (Baker, 2011), 176–177.

109   Osborne, *Revelation*, 768–776.

110   In Ezek 48, Ezekiel gives his description of the city. There are places made available where the tribes would go to their respective land; but here, the point is that of the entrance.

Epilogue (22:6–22:21)

John concludes his work with several testimonies in order to provide evidence of his truthfulness to the churches. First, John remarks that his record is eyewitness testimony (22:8). Second, Jesus avows that he will return soon, reward the righteous, and punish the wicked (22:12–16). After stating his warning that no one must add or take away from the contents of this book, John concludes Revelation with a plea that Jesus Christ would come soon.

Conclusion

Thus far, in order to interpret Revelation in the canonical approach, several factors were addressed. First, "canon" was determined to be the "standard," "rule," or "norm," and this emphasis was placed upon a standard writing of books that were considered to be authoritative. Second, the development of the canon was examined, focusing primarily upon the fragments which contained a completed list of the authoritative books. The Muratorian Canon provided the most comprehensive list of the church's Scripture and it marked the necessary boundaries of what was considered authoritative and non-authoritative books. Furthermore, Sinaiticus, Alexandrinus, Vaticanus, and Ephraemi Rescriptus also provided lists of canonical works. Third, most pertinent to the focus of this study, the location of Revelation within each list was noted. Of the five lists provided, only Vaticanus omits Revelation. Nevertheless, each codex and the Muratorian Canon contains Revelation and places it towards the conclusion of the work. Fourth the need to examine both the structure and the content of Revelation in order to interpret the work has been defended.

However, another important facet for interpreting Revelation in a canonical approach is the apparent New Testament verbal connections that the author of Revelation employs.[111] These verbal connections were proposed by R. H. Charles, and they may suggest a dependence of the author of Revelation upon other New Testament texts. The author appears to use these verbal connections in order to provide the reader with reminders to certain

---

Perhaps we should see in the New Jerusalem and the many points of entry as the abundant possibility of entrance here for God's people, for those whose name has been written in the Book of Life.

111 This work assumes Johannine authorship of Revelation. For a defense, see Vern Poythress, "Johannine Authorship and the Use of Intersentence Conjunction in the Book of Revelation, WTJ 47 (1985): 329–336; Osborne, *Revelation*, 2–6 esp. 5. For a thorough summary of both positions, see Hugh A. Cotro, "Could the Author of Revelation step forward, please?" DaLog 14 (2015): 71–89.

portions of the New Testament and, at times, similar contexts are found in these references.

Furthermore, as Emerson has noted, the location of Revelation within the canon of the New Testament may be more intentional than previously suspected.[112] Given the various connections with other works of the New Testament, the position of Revelation at the conclusion of the New Testament canon may also suggest a specific reading strategy for the book. Thus, what would this reading strategy look like considering Revelation's usage of both the Old and New Testament texts?

---

112 Emerson, *Christ and the New Creation*, 142–144.

CHAPTER 4

REVELATION'S USAGE OF THE SYNOPTIC GOSPELS AND ACTS

INTRODUCTION

IN ORDER TO EXAMINE AND ESTABLISH the verbal connections of the New Testament within Revelation, one must determine the criteria that validates a possible textual connection. For example, as previously stated, G. K. Beale argues that in order to interpret properly the content of Revelation, the reader must understand and read Revelation in light of the Old Testament. After all, "there is a general acknowledgment that the Apocalypse contains more Old Testament references than any other New Testament book."[1] Furthermore, since Beale understands how the Old Testament is utilized throughout Revelation, he argues for three degrees of allusion: clear, probable, and possible. A clear allusion mirrors the Old Testament source exactly, a probable allusion includes the idea or wording of the Old Testament source, and a possible allusion is the most difficult to prove since it may faintly mirror the prospective source in either word or concept.[2]

The categories proposed by Beale are helpful for determining the strength of possible verbal connections that R. H. Charles observed in his commentary on Revelation.[3] Charles argues that "it follows quite decidedly that our author had the Gospels of Matthew and Luke before him, 1 Thessalonians, 1 and 2 Corinthians, Colossians (or else the lost [Epistle] to the Laodiceans, which presumably was of a kindred character), Ephesians, and possibly Galatians,

---

[1] G. K. Beale, *John's Use of the Old Testament in Revelation* (Sheffield Academic Press, 1998), 60.

[2] G. K. Beale, *The Book of Revelation*, NIGTC (Eerdmans, 1999), 78–79. See Chapter 2 for a full description and explanation of Beale's categories.

[3] R. H. Charles, *A Critical and Exegetical Commentary on Revelation of St. John*, ICC (T&T Clark, 1985), 1:lxxxiii—lxxxvi.

1 Peter, and James. Our author shows no acquaintance with St. Mark."[4] Furthermore, Charles also believes that it is possible the author of Revelation "had one or more other books of the N.T."[5] Although this claim is impossible to prove, Charles provides forty-four examples that suggest the author of Revelation may have been familiar with certain biblical texts.[6]

As evidenced by the many Old Testament allusions that are not explained, the author of Revelation appeared to believe that his writers were familiar with the Old Testament and various theological subjects. However, if the author also includes several New Testament verbal connections to various New Testament texts and themes, then Revelation would require a specific reading pattern.

The following two chapters seek to examine the possible connections Revelation has with other New Testament texts as presented by R. H. Charles by utilizing the model of Beale. Thus, the categories of clear, probable, and possible, are used in examining these verbal connections. A fourth category is also included, that of unlikely or no verbal connection. The context of both Revelation and the New Testament text will be examined as well in order to determine any possible overlap in contextual pattern. Chapter four will examine Revelation's usage of the Gospels and Acts, and chapter five will examine both the Pauline and Catholic Epistles.[7]

The Gospels and Acts

The Gospels and Acts constitute the largest number of verbal connections

---

4 Ibid., lxv–lxvi.

5 Ibid., lxxxiii.

6 This total is calculated per the division of possible verbal connections rather than an individual sum. Charles also lists Rev 6:2–7:1 as paralleling Matt 26:6–7, 9a, 29; Luke 21:8–12a, 25–26. The present work excludes this reference because of imagery rather than intertextual connections.

7 Before one proceeds to discuss these various connections of the New Testament in Revelation, it is necessary to answer the charge of anachronism. After all, to say that Revelation incorporates various New Testament texts throughout its work presupposes that the New Testament canon was established before Revelation. This presumption is not the case. Even though most scholars differ in the dating of Revelation between 64–69 and 95–96, both groups would agree that the canon of the New Testament, as it appears today, was not established. Thus, it is perhaps false to argue that one can suggest that Revelation used the New Testament during its compositional stage. To counter this claim of anachronism, one can argue for a distinction by what is meant by "canon." Ched Spellman argues that the term "canon," in its historical usage, was used in two senses: Canon 1, the canon as norm, and Canon 2, the canon as list. He argues that "canon" was a term of ambiguity that was intentionally utilized because of a development dialectic between "rule" and "list" within the early church. Therefore, the canon appears to have a particular usefulness for describing the contents of the New Testament in view of its varied meanings. See Ched Spellman, *Toward a Canon-Conscious Reading of the Bible: Exploring the History and Hermeneutics of the Canon* (Sheffield, 2014), 33–41.

Revelation utilizes for the narrative, totaling thirty-six references. Revelation uses Matthew fifteen times, Mark twice, Luke sixteen times, and Acts three times.[8] In some instances, there are overlaps of Gospel accounts with the Pauline and Catholic Epistles (Matt 24:30 and 2 Cor 1:20; Matt 24:43 and 1 Thess 5:2; Matt 10:32, Luke 12:8, and 1 Cor 16:9; Luke 4:25 and Jas 5:17) as outlined by Charles. Both the overlapping materials and the examples by Charles are discussed below in their appearance in Revelation.

REVELATION 1:1; MATTHEW 24:6; LUKE 21:9

(1:1) Ἀποκάλυψις Ἰησοῦ Χριστοῦ ἣν ἔδωκεν αὐτῷ ὁ θεὸς δεῖξαι τοῖς δούλοις αὐτοῦ ἃ δεῖ γενέσθαι ἐν τάχει, καὶ ἐσήμανεν ἀποστείλας διὰ τοῦ ἀγγέλου αὐτοῦ τῷ δούλῳ αὐτοῦ Ἰωάννῃ,	(Matt 24:6) μελλήσετε δὲ ἀκούειν πολέμους καὶ ἀκοὰς πολέμων· ὁρᾶτε μὴ θροεῖσθε· δεῖ γὰρ γενέσθαι, ἀλλ᾽ οὔπω ἐστὶν τὸ τέλος.
	(Luke 21:9) ὅταν δὲ ἀκούσητε πολέμους καὶ ἀκαταστασίας, μὴ πτοηθῆτε· δεῖ γὰρ ταῦτα γενέσθαι πρῶτον, ἀλλ᾽ οὐκ εὐθέως τὸ τέλος.

Revelation 1:1 begins the book of Revelation by identifying the subject (Ἀποκάλυψις Ἰησοῦ Χριστοῦ), the recipient (τῷ δούλῳ αὐτοῦ Ἰωάννῃ) and the audience (δεῖξαι τοῖς δούλοις αὐτοῦ) of this vision that must soon take place (δεῖ γενέσθαι). This vision is revealed to John only by the assistance of an angel who was sent from God (ἐσήμανεν ἀποστείλας διὰ τοῦ ἀγγέλου αὐτοῦ), and the vision is not the only instance within Revelation that an angel reveals something to John.

The phrase δεῖ γενέσθαι is viewed by Charles to have an intertextual connection with both Matt 24:6 and Luke 21:9. In Matt 24:6 the content is focused upon the signs of the end of the age and the results that follow the consummation of the end of the age. Similarly, in Luke 21:9, Jesus foretells the destruction of the temple, but not necessarily the end of all things. Here, the emphasis is upon warning the people not to be concerned when they hear of wars and tumults, for these things must occur first (δεῖ γὰρ ταῦτα γενέσθαι). In both Matt 24:6 and Luke 21:9, the emphasis is placed upon an event that will take place in the future which will usher the coming of God's kingdom and bring about the end of the world.

The usage of δεῖ γενέσθαι in Rev 1:1 appears to play upon this theme of bringing about the fulfillment of the end, since it is this book that not only captures the end of the world but also foretells it. The emphatic nature of

---

[8] This total excludes the references listed in n6.

δεῖ combined with γενέσθαι stresses an urgency of the times for the reader of Matthew and Luke and "is not to curb enthusiasm for the Lord's return but to warn against false claimants and an expectation of a premature return based on misconstrued signs."[9] Δεῖ γενέσθαι does not occur outside of the Gospels and Revelation, and it appears that John uses this phrase in order to signify to his readers that what was predicted by Christ is the same as that which was given to him by the angel.[10] Based upon the rarity of the word usage and the combined similar contexts, this allusion is clear.

Revelation 1:3; Luke 11:28

(1:3) **Μακάριος ὁ ἀναγινώσκων καὶ οἱ ἀκούοντες τοὺς λόγους τῆς προφητείας καὶ τηροῦντες τὰ ἐν αὐτῇ γεγραμμένα, ὁ γὰρ καιρὸς ἐγγύς.**	(Luke 11:28) αὐτὸς δὲ εἶπεν· μενοῦν μακάριοι οἱ ἀκούοντες τὸν λόγον τοῦ θεοῦ καὶ φυλάσσοντες.

Revelation 1:3 introduces the theme of blessedness to those who hear the word of the prophecy and keep it, and this verse is viewed as the first beatitude of Revelation.[11] The hearer of the word is described by two participles, οἱ ἀκούοντες and τηροῦντες, and both are substantival participles, as the subject is retained by the participles themselves.[12] The emphasis is upon the actions of ὁ ἀναγινώσκων, for it is not simply the reading of Revelation that is to garner a blessing, but the hearing and keeping of its content (cf. Deut 4:6; Jas 1:22–25).

Luke 11:28 ends a broader section within Luke's Gospel which shows Jesus casting out a demon from a mute man (11:14) and then teaching those who claim that he casts out demons by Beelzebul (11:17–26). Tension is embedded within this narrative as some reject him and request that Jesus perform

---

9 D. A. Carson, "Matthew," in *The Expositor's Bible Commentary*, ed. Frank E. Gaebelein (Zondervan, 1984), 498. For the emphatic nature of δεῖ γενέσθαι, see Charles L. Quarles, *Matthew, EGGNT* (B&H Academic, 2017), 282.

10 The phrase also occurs in Mark 13:7, Rev 4:1, and 22:6. David E. Aune notes the inclusio of 1:1 and 22:6 with this phrase. See David E. Aune, *Revelation 1–5*, WBC (Thomas Nelson, 1997), 13–15. It also occurs three times in Dan 2:28–29 LXX. Craig R. Koester, *Revelation* (Yale University Press, 2014), 126–132, 213.

11 Grant Osborne, *Revelation*, BECNT (Baker, 2002), 57. Μακάριος is also found in 14:13; 16:15; 19:9; 20:6; 22:7, 14.

12 See Daniel B. Wallace, *Greek Grammar Beyond the Basics: An Exegetical Syntax of the New Testament* (Zondervan, 1996), 619–620. For the aspectual usage of participles, see Buist M. Fanning, *Verbal Aspect in New Testament Greek* (Clarendon Press, 1990), 406–419; Stanley E. Porter, *Verbal Aspect in the Greek of the New Testament, with Reference to Tense and Mood* (Peter Lang, 1993), 366–391; Constantine R. Campbell, *Verbal Aspect and Non-Indicative Verbs: Further Soundings in the Greek of the New Testament* (Peter Lang, 2008), 13–48.

a sign for their belief (11:16). Yet, in Luke 11:27 a woman offers a note of praise (μακαρία) for the mother of Jesus, thus showing that some are, at least, receptive to his teaching and ministry.[13] In response, Jesus offers his own beatitude (μακάριοι) specifically upon those who not simply hear but keep it (cf. Luke 8:21).[14]

The overlap between the two sections is clear upon examination of their context. Where John asserts that any who hear the words of the prophecy and keep it are blessed, Jesus teaches in like manner. The parallel suggests that John understood his words of prophecy (τῆς προφητείας) to be the words of God himself, as it is the words of God that provide the blessing in the Christian's life. Furthermore, what guarantees membership in the family of God is not ancestry but obeying the word of God, which is a prominent theme in both Revelation and Luke. Jesus identifies his family as those who keep the word of God.[15]

Although Revelation uses τηροῦντες and Luke φυλάσσοντες to describe keeping or guarding the word, there is not much semantic difference between the two. Both words, in their respective context, carry the emphasis that to keep God's word is to do or act upon God's word.[16]

It is possible that John could be drawing on this story from the life of Jesus and, rather than using φυλάσσω he instead uses τηρέω which frequently occurs in his Gospel and epistles in the same manner. However, a stronger connection between Rev 1:3 and Luke 11:28 would be made by using the same word for "keeping." The words are similar, but the idea is the same: those who hear and keep the Word of God are considered blessed. It is perhaps wise to conclude that the connection between Rev 1:3 and Luke 11:28 is a probable verbal connection since the words are different, but the overall theme is present.

---

13 Darrell L. Bock, *Luke 9:51–24:3*, BECNT (Baker, 2008), 1094.

14 "Jesus' response ... amends her beatitude because more needs to be said. His mother is not blessed because of the fertility of her womb and the milk in her breasts, but because she listened to God's word, believed it, and acts on it. Jesus' correction reasserts that blessedness is open to all who hear and obey 'the word of God' and is not based on kinship." David E. Garland, *Luke*, ZECNT (Zondervan, 2011), 485.

15 Darrell L. Bock, *A Theology of Luke and Acts: God's Promised Program, Realized for All the Nations* (Zondervan, 2012), 106. See also 347 and 443.

16 See BDAG, s.v., "τηρέω;" Ibid., "φυλάσσω;" Harald Riesenfeld, "τηρέω," *Theological Dictionary of the New Testament* (Eerdmans, 1972), 8:144–146; Georg Bertram, "φυλάσσω," *Theological Dictionary of the New Testament* (Eerdmans, 1974), 9:239–240. The usage of τηρέω in Revelation is also similar to John's usage of it in his Gospel and epistles.

Revelation 1:3; Matthew 26:18

(1:3) Μακάριος ὁ ἀναγινώσκων καὶ οἱ ἀκούοντες τοὺς λόγους τῆς προφητείας καὶ τηροῦντες τὰ ἐν αὐτῇ γεγραμμένα, ὁ γὰρ καιρὸς ἐγγύς.	(Matt 26:18) ὁ δὲ εἶπεν· ὑπάγετε εἰς τὴν πόλιν πρὸς τὸν δεῖνα καὶ εἴπατε αὐτῷ· ὁ διδάσκαλος λέγει· ὁ καιρός μου ἐγγύς ἐστιν, πρὸς σὲ ποιῶ τὸ πάσχα μετὰ τῶν μαθητῶν μου.

The second verbal connection Rev 1:3 shares is found in Matt 26:18. John concludes his prologue by mentioning that the time is near (ὁ γὰρ καιρὸς ἐγγύς), and in connection with the rest of v 3, it should be understood that the words of this prophecy are close to their fulfillment. Charles notes, "These words relate to the blessedness of those who are faithful in the present evil time; for they will not have long to wait; the season of their deliverance is at hand."[17]

Similar wording is found in Matt 26:18, but the context is entirely different. There, Jesus is preparing to eat the Passover meal with his disciples. He gives his disciples instructions to enter into a town and tell a certain man of his plans, but the disciples must tell the man that "The Teacher says, 'My time is at hand (ὁ καιρός μου ἐγγύς ἐστιν).'" Contextually, the time that Jesus is concerned with is not his return or the fulfillment of a specific prophecy, but rather his death, since he is arrested shortly after taking the meal with his disciples (26:47–56). As Quarles notes, "The [construct] ὁ καιρός μου means 'the time of my death.'"[18] Thus, this verbal connection does not correspond to any of Beale's categories and is unlikely to be intentional.

Revelation 1:7; Matthew 24:30; 2 Corinthians 1:20

(1:7) Ἰδοὺ ἔρχεται μετὰ τῶν νεφελῶν, καὶ ὄψεται αὐτὸν πᾶς ὀφθαλμὸς καὶ οἵτινες αὐτὸν ἐξεκέντησαν, καὶ κόψονται ἐπ᾽ αὐτὸν πᾶσαι αἱ φυλαὶ τῆς γῆς. ναί, ἀμήν.	(Matt 24:30) καὶ τότε φανήσεται τὸ σημεῖον τοῦ υἱοῦ τοῦ ἀνθρώπου ἐν οὐρανῷ, καὶ τότε κόψονται πᾶσαι αἱ φυλαὶ τῆς γῆς καὶ ὄψονται τὸν υἱὸν τοῦ ἀνθρώπου ἐρχόμενον ἐπὶ τῶν νεφελῶν τοῦ οὐρανοῦ μετὰ δυνάμεως καὶ δόξης πολλῆς·

---

17 Charles, *A Critical and Exegetical Commentary on Revelation*, 1:8. Furthermore, "The beatitude, of course, is true in itself independently of the time of consummation, but the closely impending recompense is repeatedly dwelt upon by our author to encourage his readers in the face of universal martyrdom." On this note Craig Keener remarks, "The 'blessing' form itself is general, but the context specifies the blessings of the end (Rev. 21–22) for which only the listener will be prepared ('the time is near,' 1:3)." Craig S. Keener, *Revelation* (Zondervan, 2000), 56.

18 Quarles, *Matthew*, 313.

	(2 Cor 1:20) ὅσαι γὰρ ἐπαγγελίαι θεοῦ, ἐν αὐτῷ τὸ ναί· διὸ καὶ δι' αὐτοῦ τὸ ἀμὴν τῷ θεῷ πρὸς δόξαν δι' ἡμῶν.

Revelation 1:7 consists of two Old Testament citations. The first is from Dan 7:13 and the second is from Zech 12:10.[19] Daniel 7:13 describes the enthronement of the "son of man" who will rule over all the nations after God judges the evil nations (Dan 7:9–12). Michael B. Shepherd argues that this early reference to Daniel indicates that "the [Revelation] depends upon a thorough knowledge of the book of Daniel for its comprehension."[20] Much like the reference to Daniel, Zech 12:10 is in the context of God defeating the wicked nations whenever "Israel will be redeemed after repenting of their sinful rejection of God and his messenger (i.e., 'the one they have pierced')."[21]

John uses the combination of Dan 7:13 and Zech 12:10 in Rev 1:7 to describe for his readers the reality of Christ's appearance. Revelation 1:7 is found within the broader section of John's greeting to the seven churches in Asia (cf. Rev 2–3), and this greeting (4–7) provides several Christological imageries by John and what the death of Jesus accomplished (5b). Once John has identified Jesus by various titles, he uses Dan 7:13 and Zech 12:10 in order to further buttress the divinity of Jesus. Thus, John identifies Jesus as the Son of Man from Dan 7:13 and as the messenger of God from Zech 12:10.

In Matt 24:30, Jesus is discussing the coming of the Son of Man to his disciples. The broader context of Matthew 24 is the prediction of Jesus for

---

19 For a helpful overview, see G. K. Beale and Sean M. McDonough, "Revelation," in *Commentary on the New Testament Use of the Old* (Baker, 2007), 1090–1091.

20 Michael B. Shepherd, *Daniel in the Context of the Hebrew Bible* (Peter Lang, 2009), 118.

21 Beale and McDonough, "Revelation," 1090. They further note, "The Zechariah text has been altered in two significant ways. The phrases 'every eye' and 'of the earth' (cf. Zech. 14:17) have been added to universalize its original meaning. This probably is a reference not to every person without exception, but rather to all among the nations who believe, as is indicated clearly by 5:9; 7:9 (cf. the plural 'tribes' as a universal reference to unbelievers in 11:9; 13:7; 14:6). The word *gē* ('earth, land') cannot be a limited reference to the land of Israel' rather, it is a universal denotation, since this is the only meaning that the phrase *pasai hai phylai tēs gēs* ('all the tribes of the earth') has in the OT (LXX: Gen. 12:3; 28:14; Ps. 71:17; Zech 14:17). The phrase 'all the tribes of Israel' occurs repeatedly in the OT (approximately twenty-five times), which highlights the different wording of Rev. 1:7b. This implies an extension of the OT concept of Israel, since what applied to that nation in Zech. 12 is now transferred to the peoples of the earth, who assume the role of repentant Israel. Some believe that the Zechariah quotation is utilized contrary to its original intentions to denote the grief of the nations over their impending judgment. However, John typically adheres to and consistently develops the contextual ideas of his OT references, and proposed exceptions to this rule must bear the burden of proof. The nations in 1:7b mourn not over themselves, but over Jesus, which fits better into an understanding of repentance than judgment." Ibid., 1090–1091.

the destruction of the temple (1–2), signs of the end of the age (3–14), and the abomination of desolation (15–28). Thus, it is fitting that, based upon the context, Jesus would discuss his identity as the Danielic Son of Man in Matt 24:30.

John uses these references similarly to Matthew, but he does so in reverse order. John first describes that Jesus ἔρχεται μετὰ τῶν νεφελῶν, whereas Matthew prioritizes the quotation from Zechariah (κόψονται πᾶσαι αἱ φυλαὶ τῆς γῆς). Second, John does not describe Jesus as the Son of Man and appears to believe his reader is familiar with both Dan 7:13 and perhaps Matt 24:30, for Matthew includes the Son of Man (υἱὸν τοῦ ἀνθρώπου) coming upon the clouds in his quotation.[22] Third, both writers include similar wording to depict a universal aspect of seeing the Son of Man coming upon the clouds. Both Matthew and John use αἱ φυλαὶ τῆς γῆς, but John structures his reference for emphasis.

It does not seem that John was dependent upon Matt 24:30 for his writing of Rev 1:7; rather, it does appear that a type of Christian tradition is in view.[23] However, Koester suggests that readers of John's work would have, like other early Christians, understood the passage as Christ's final return.[24] The wording and clause structure by John suggests a tradition rather than a dependence upon Matthew, but the correlation between the two make this verbal connection a clear reference. First, the context between the two references are similar. In both Rev 1:7 and Matt 24:30 the indication is that Jesus is the Son of Man who will come upon the clouds and he is the fulfillment of Zech 12:10. Second, although the wording and structuring is different, the main thought is present in both instances.

There is another reference in Rev 1:7 to 2 Cor 1:20, but this is an unlikely verbal connection. The reason for the use of ναί, ἀμήν in Rev 1:7 is for John to emphasize the coming of the Lord. However, in 2 Cor 1:20 the focus is upon prayers that find their fulfillment in Jesus (τὸ ναί) and "uttering our amen (τὸ ἀμήν) to God for his glory." The contexts are different as is the wording in both references.

---

22 Donald Hagner notes this connection and states, "The same combination of Zech 12:10–14 and the Dan 7:13 reference to the coming of the Son of Man is found in Rev 1:7, which suggests that the combination depends upon early Christian tradition rather than upon a common source." Donald A. Hagner, *Matthew 14–28*, WBC (Word, 1995), 714.

23 So also Aune, "The similarities between Matt 24:30 and Rev 1:7 make it highly probable that there is some kind of traditional link between the two, while the differences indicate that neither text is directly dependent upon the other." Aune, *Revelation 1–5*, 52.

24 Koester, *Revelation*, 229.

REVELATION 1:16; MATTHEW 17:2

(1:16) καὶ ἔχων ἐν τῇ δεξιᾷ χειρὶ αὐτοῦ ἀστέρας ἑπτὰ καὶ ἐκ τοῦ στόματος αὐτοῦ ῥομφαία δίστομος ὀξεῖα ἐκπορευομένη καὶ ἡ ὄψις αὐτοῦ ὡς ὁ ἥλιος φαίνει ἐν τῇ δυνάμει αὐτοῦ.	(Matt 17:2) καὶ μετεμορφώθη ἔμπροσθεν αὐτῶν, καὶ ἔλαμψεν τὸ πρόσωπον αὐτοῦ ὡς ὁ ἥλιος, τὰ δὲ ἱμάτια αὐτοῦ ἐγένετο λευκὰ ὡς τὸ φῶς.

In Rev 1:9–16 John informs the reader that he is exiled upon the island of Patmos on account of the word of God and the testimony of Jesus (διὰ τὸν λόγον τοῦ θεοῦ καὶ τὴν μαρτυρίαν Ἰησοῦ).[25] While he is in the Spirit on the Lord's Day, John hears a voice behind him which sounds like a loud trumpet.[26] After the voice gives John instructions to compose and to send it to the seven churches, John turns to see the voice that spoke to him and beholds the resurrected Christ in his glory (cf. 1:17). He provides a multitude of descriptions that correlate to various Old Testament themes and concludes that ἡ ὄψις αὐτοῦ ὡς ὁ ἥλιος φαίνει, his face was shining as the sun.[27]

This description of the face of Jesus bears much similarity to the transfiguration scene, where Jesus is transformed before Peter, James, and John, and ἔλαμψεν τὸ πρόσωπον αὐτοῦ ὡς ὁ ἥλιος. Here, Matthew seems to emphasize the parallels between this event and when Moses was on Mount Sinai (Exod 34:30–35).[28] But the differences are clear: Moses' face shone because it reflected God's glory, but Jesus was transformed (μετεμορφώθη) and the disciples were provided a glimpse into his "preincarnate glory ... and anticipate his coming exaltation."[29]

The backgrounds for both Matthew and Revelation are similar in that they are focused primarily upon the deification and glorification of Jesus. Rather than utilizing ἔλαμψεν to describe how the face of Jesus shone, John uses φαίνει, which appears to serve as further intertextual connections within Revelation (cf. 21:23).[30] Also, ὄψις is unique to John alone (cf. John 7:24; 11:44),

---

[25] For similarity between John and other Old Testament prophets, see Frederick David Mazzaferri, *The Genre of the Book of Revelation from a Source-Critical Perspective* (Walter de Gruyter, 1989), 259–378.

[26] John frequently states that he is ἐν πνεύματι when significant events occur. See 4:2; 17:3; 21:10.

[27] For these Old Testament themes, see Beale, *Revelation*, 205–212.

[28] So, Grant Osborne, *Matthew*, ZECNT (Zondervan, 2010), 646.

[29] Carson, "Matthew," 385.

[30] "The image is probably an important one. In Revelation 21:23, the New Jerusalem does not need the sun, because the glory of God and the Lamb provide light for the city. All of the Lamb's people will see his glory, just as he promised (John 17:24). In the New Jerusalem, the

but the word occurs with frequency in the LXX. In both the LXX and John's usage of ὄψις, the word carries the meaning of "appearance," or "face."[31] John certainly could have used τὸ πρόσωπον instead of ὄψις to describe Jesus, but he chose to use a word that is unique to him. This verbal connection, then, should be viewed as a clear connection.

Revelation 2:7; Matthew 11:15; Luke 8:8; 14:35; Mark 4:9

(2:7) Ὁ ἔχων οὖς ἀκουσάτω τί τὸ πνεῦμα λέγει ταῖς ἐκκλησίαις. Τῷ νικῶντι δώσω αὐτῷ φαγεῖν ἐκ τοῦ ξύλου τῆς ζωῆς, ὅ ἐστιν ἐν τῷ παραδείσῳ τοῦ θεοῦ. Phrase occurs throughout chs. 2–3	(Matt 11:15) ὁ ἔχων ὦτα ἀκουέτω. (cf. 13:9, 43)
	(Luke 8:8) καὶ ἕτερον ἔπεσεν εἰς τὴν γῆν τὴν ἀγαθὴν καὶ φυὲν ἐποίησεν καρπὸν ἑκατονταπλασίονα. ταῦτα λέγων ἐφώνει· ὁ ἔχων ὦτα ἀκούειν ἀκουέτω. (cf. Luke 14:35)
	(Luke 14:35) οὔτε εἰς γῆν οὔτε εἰς κοπρίαν εὔθετόν ἐστιν, ἔξω βάλλουσιν αὐτό. ὁ ἔχων ὦτα ἀκούειν ἀκουέτω.
	(Mark 4:9) καὶ ἔλεγεν· ὃς ἔχει ὦτα ἀκούειν ἀκουέτω. (cf. 4:23)

Chapters 2–3 of Revelation focus primarily upon the seven churches in Asia who are the initial recipient of Revelation (cf. 1:11). The phrase Ὁ ἔχων οὖς ἀκουσάτω τί τὸ πνεῦμα λέγει ταῖς ἐκκλησίαις occurs identically in all seven letters.[32] Also, the command to hear, which signifies a command to obey what is spoken, occurs throughout Revelation in an effort for believers to respond positively to what has been revealed to John (cf. 1:3; 13:9; 22:17–18). This command is no different in chapters 2–3 as each church is urged to hear what the Lord has just spoken to them.

Ὁ ἔχων οὖς ἀκουσάτω is identically cited in Matt 11:15; 13:9, 43. The occurrences in Luke 8:8 and 14:35 add the infinitive ἀκούειν, as does Mark 4:9.[33] In

---

people of God will see his face (22:4)." Paul M. Hoskins, *The Book of Revelation: A Theological and Exegetical Commentary* (ChristoDoulos Publications, 2017), 63.

31 See BDAG, s.v., "ὄψις."

32 See A. M. Enroth, "The Hearing Formula in the Book of Revelation," *NTS* 36 (1990): 596–608. Enroth believes that the hearing formula signifies that Jesus intended to address all congregations.

33 Some manuscripts include the infinitive ἀκούειν since it occurs in Mark and Luke. Although UBS5 gives this reading a "B" grade, it likely is original. Bruce Metzger remarks, "If the

every instance this formula occurs, the context is the same. Jesus is teaching to a group of people who have gathered around him. His topics range from John the Baptist as representing Elijah (Matt 11) to parables (Mark 4; Luke 8). The point, then, is that Jesus urges his hearers to listen to what he has to say. Robert H. Stein aptly notes, "This expression is always used to conclude a saying and therefore should be interpreted in light of what has preceded (4:1–8) rather than what follows."[34]

Stein's remark is helpful, for this is the manner one should interpret the phrase when it is used in Revelation. The contexts between how Revelation utilizes this phrase and how the Gospels use it readily parallel one another. The call to listen, believe, and obey is clearly seen in each example and, with the wording almost exactly identical between these examples, this verbal connection should be classified as clear.[35]

REVELATION 2:20, 24–25; ACTS 15:28–29

(2:20) ἀλλὰ ἔχω κατὰ σοῦ ὅτι ἀφεῖς τὴν γυναῖκα Ἰεζάβελ, ἡ λέγουσα ἑαυτὴν προφῆτιν καὶ διδάσκει καὶ πλανᾷ τοὺς ἐμοὺς δούλους πορνεῦσαι καὶ φαγεῖν εἰδωλόθυτα.	(Acts 15:28–29) 28 ἔδοξεν γὰρ τῷ πνεύματι τῷ ἁγίῳ καὶ ἡμῖν μηδὲν πλέον ἐπιτίθεσθαι ὑμῖν βάρος πλὴν τούτων τῶν ἐπάναγκες, 29 ἀπέχεσθαι εἰδωλοθύτων καὶ αἵματος καὶ πνικτῶν καὶ πορνείας, ἐξ ὧν διατηροῦντες ἑαυτοὺς εὖ πράξετε. Ἔρρωσθε.
(2:24–25) ὑμῖν δὲ λέγω τοῖς λοιποῖς τοῖς ἐν Θυατείροις, ὅσοι οὐκ ἔχουσιν τὴν διδαχὴν ταύτην, οἵτινες οὐκ ἔγνωσαν τὰ βαθέα τοῦ σατανᾶ ὡς λέγουσιν· οὐ βάλλω ἐφ' ὑμᾶς ἄλλο βάρος, 25 πλὴν ὃ ἔχετε κρατήσατε ἄχρι[ς] οὗ ἂν ἥξω.	

The church in Thyatira, although commended for their active service of love, faith, service, and patience endurance, are condemned by Jesus for its sexual

---

word had been present in the original text, there is no reason why it should have been deleted in such important witnesses as B D 700 al." Bruce M. Metzger, *A Textual Commentary on the Greek New Testament* (Deutsche Bibelgesellschaft, 1994), 24. David L. Turner notes, "The UBS4 reading ὦτα is found in B, D, and others, and the longer reading ὦτα ἀκούειν in ℵ, C, L, W *f* 1, *f* 13, *Byz*, *Lect*. The external evidence is stronger for the latter reading, but the former reading better explains the latter than vice versa. The same question arises in 13:9, 43. The longer reading is undisputed in Mark 4:9, 23; 7:16 (omitted in UBS4); Luke 8:8; 14:35 and may have been assimilated to Matt. 11:15 from those texts. David L. Turner, *Matthew*, BECNT (Baker, 2008), 297.

34 Robert H. Stein, *Mark*, BECNT (Baker, 2008), 201.

35 Koester remarks, "This saying can call for interpretation of something obscure (Mark 4:9 par.; *Gos. Thom.* 65, 96), but more often it summons listeners to accept or act on statements

immorality. This church receives neither a warning nor a reward in comparison to the other churches, because it appears that "the threat of punishment was already pronounced in the accusation due to the seriousness of their compromise."[36] The church has allowed Jezebel to teach and "seduce my servants to commit sexual immorality and eat food sacrificed to idols" (πλανᾷ τοὺς ἐμοὺς δούλους πορνεῦσαι καὶ φαγεῖν εἰδωλόθυτα).[37] Judgment will follow for those who do not repent of their sinful works, but for those who have not followed after the way of Satan, "I will not lay upon you another burden, yet hold strongly (πλὴν ὃ ἔχετε κρατήσατε) whatever you have until I come."

Similar language is found in Acts 15:28–29 where the apostles and the elders of the Jerusalem church composed and sent a letter to the Gentiles in Antioch, Syria, and Cilicia (15:23). This letter follows what was discussed in the Jerusalem council. There Barnabas and Paul argue vehemently with the believers who, like Paul, are members of the Pharisee party and demand that the Gentile believers conform to the law of circumcision.[38] Barnabas and Paul speak of the Holy Spirit's work and "what signs and wonders God had done through them among the Gentiles" (15:12), and recount that both Peter and James were able to convince the Jerusalem Council that all that is required for salvation was the inclusion of the Holy Spirit in the life of the believer. This salvific announcement provides the content for the letter that is sent to the Gentile believers by Barsabas and Silas.

Although the context of both sections of Scripture are different, the language is quite similar. In Acts 15:28–29, the Council informs the Gentile believers that they do not desire to lay any greater burden upon them (28b; μηδὲν πλέον ἐπιτίθεσθαι ὑμῖν βάρος πλὴν), but they must abstain from food

---

whose meaning is clear (Matt 11:15; 13:43; Mark 4:23), which is the case in Revelation." Koester, *Revelation*, 264.

36 Bandy, "The Prophetic Lawsuit," 210.

37 John does not provide a specific identity for Jezebel, but utilizes this imagery, like he did with Balaam (cf. 2:14), in order to show the severity of Thyatira's sin. The Old Testament Jezebel was married to King Ahab, and she was responsible for enticing her husband to follow after the Canaanite god Baal and commit spiritual immorality (1 Kgs 16). For various suggestions on the identity of Jezebel, see Robert H. Mounce, *Revelation*, NICNT (Eerdmans, 1997), 86–87; Koester, *Revelation*, 298. Richard Bauckham suggests that in Revelation the church fulfills a prophetic role, so that it "is connected with the idea of the church's newly revealed role of confronting the idolatry of Rome in a prophetic conflict, like that of Moses with Pharaoh and his magicians or of Elijah with Jezebel and her prophets of Baal, and in the power of the Spirit of prophecy winning the worship of the true God." Richard Bauckham, *The Theology of the Book of Revelation* (Cambridge University Press, 1993), 120. It may serve well to remember this point made by Bauckham and, rather than attempt to identify this Jezebel, understand that Jezebel here is presented as an enemy of the church.

38 John's recipients were most probably Gentile believers as well and resided in a pagan context.

that has been sacrificed to idols (ἀπέχεσθαι εἰδωλοθύτων). These commands, in essence, prohibited Gentiles from thinking they must first becomes Jews in order to become Christians.³⁹ These stipulations were addressed as a warning to the church in Thyratira, for they were committing the acts from which the Gentile Christians were prohibited from doing by the Jerusalem Council.⁴⁰ Furthermore, Rev 2:24 desires not to lay any other burden upon them, and βάρος also serves to connect these two passages. Thus, this verbal connection should be viewed as a clear since the words mirror the admonition of the Jerusalem Council closely. Furthermore, the themes of what is good for Christians as opposed to what Christians should abstain from is also readily apparent, thus strengthening this verbal connection.

REVELATION 3:3; 16:15; MATTHEW 24:42–43; 1 THESSALONIANS 5:2

(3:3) μνημόνευε οὖν πῶς εἴληφας καὶ ἤκουσας καὶ τήρει καὶ μετανόησον. ἐὰν οὖν μὴ γρηγορήσῃς, ἥξω ὡς κλέπτης, καὶ οὐ μὴ γνῷς ποίαν ὥραν ἥξω ἐπὶ σέ.	(Matt 24:42) Γρηγορεῖτε οὖν, ὅτι οὐκ οἴδατε ποίᾳ ἡμέρᾳ ὁ κύριος ὑμῶν ἔρχεται.
(16:15) Ἰδοὺ ἔρχομαι ὡς κλέπτης. μακάριος ὁ γρηγορῶν καὶ τηρῶν τὰ ἱμάτια αὐτοῦ, ἵνα μὴ γυμνὸς περιπατῇ καὶ βλέπωσιν τὴν ἀσχημοσύνην αὐτοῦ.	(Matt 24:43) Ἐκεῖνο δὲ γινώσκετε ὅτι εἰ ᾔδει ὁ οἰκοδεσπότης ποίᾳ φυλακῇ ὁ κλέπτης ἔρχεται, ἐγρηγόρησεν ἂν καὶ οὐκ ἂν εἴασεν διορυχθῆναι τὴν οἰκίαν αὐτοῦ.
	(1 Thess 5:2) αὐτοὶ γὰρ ἀκριβῶς οἴδατε ὅτι ἡμέρα κυρίου ὡς κλέπτης ἐν νυκτὶ οὕτως ἔρχεται.

Revelation 3:1–7 focuses upon the church of Sardis, a church that was thought to be alive but was near the point of death (3:1b). The risen Christ admonishes this church to remember what they received, keep it, and repent (3:2). This warning is precipitated by what Christ will do if the church fails to wake up (ἐὰν οὖν μὴ γρηγορήσῃς): "I will come as a thief, and you will not know the hour I will come against you" (καὶ οὐ μὴ γνῷς ποίαν ὥραν ἥξω ἐπὶ σέ). This warning also finds a parallel in Rev 16:15. There, the sixth bowl has been poured out upon the earth and demonic spirits assemble themselves for the great day of God the Almighty One. In the midst of this action, Christ announces "Behold, I am coming as a thief, blessed is the one who is staying awake" (Ἰδοὺ ἔρχομαι

---

39 Bock, *Theology of Luke-Acts*, 373.
40 See Eckhard J. Schnabel, *Acts*, ZECNT (Zondervan 2012), 650–651. Koester acknowledges the similarities between the two references and remarks, "It is more likely that Revelation and the decree reflect similar concerns but are not directly connected." Koester, *Revelation*, 301.

ὡς κλέπτης. μακάριος ὁ γρηγορῶν). In 3:3, Christ states that he will come (ἥξω), but in 16:15 ἔρχομαι is used to describe his future status. Also, κλέπτης and γρηγορήσῃς occur only in these verses in Revelation.[41] Whereas 3:3 is a warning for the church of Sardis, 16:15 also serves both as a warning and blessing since those who remain awake and keep on their garments are rewarded in the time to come.

This theme of Christ returning as a thief is also found in Matt 24:42–43 and 1 Thess 5:2. First, in Matt 24:42–43 the broader context of this section is concerned with the unknown hour of the return of the Son. It will be like the days of Noah and the return will not be expected.[42] Jesus commands that his followers stay awake (Γρηγορεῖτε), for they do not know (γινώσκετε) the day he will return. Furthermore, Jesus compares himself to the thief in v 43 (ὁ κλέπτης) and remarks that anyone who knows a thief intends to rob their house would stay awake (ἐγρηγόρησεν). A similar context is found in 1 Thess 5:2, where Paul reminds the Thessalonians that the day of the Lord will come as a thief in the night (ὡς κλέπτης ... ἔρχεται).[43] The usage of ἔρχεται here is meant to emphasize both the certainty of the return of Jesus but also the uncertainty of the day on which it will occur, for the Thessalonians already know that this day of the Lord will come as a thief.[44]

The theme of the Lord's return in Revelation appears to be a fulfillment of what was taught by Jesus and Paul.[45] Matthew 24:42–43 tells of the Lord's teaching of his return, and the apostle Paul's usage of this imagery in 1 Thess 5:2 indicates that this phrase is not unique to him, but likely handed down by another apostle. R.T. France claims that "Jesus' metaphor of the coming of a burglar as a model for the unexpected time of the *parousia* made a strong impression on the early church."[46] If this impression was indeed strong for the early church, then John is likely using this example in order to connect to the teaching of Jesus from Matt 24:42–43 and 1 Thess 5:2, which highlights the return of Christ is indeed imminent, and to stress the fulfillment of the

---

41 Charles, *Revelation*, 2:49. Some manuscripts attempt to change ἔρχομαι in order to parallel ἔρχεται in Matt 24:42 and 1 Thess 5:2.

42 Although Noah is called a "herald of righteousness," the focus of Jesus here is not necessarily upon Noah's message but upon the suddenness of God's judgment that came upon the earth. Thus, it will be with the return of Christ. Christians mirror Noah as a herald of righteousness and declare that the parousia will be imminent, but that specific day is unknown.

43 For the Old Testament theme of the day of the Lord, see Jeffrey A. D. Weima, *1–2 Thessalonians*, BECNT (Baker, 2014), 346.

44 Ibid., 346n4.

45 Cf. also 2 Pet 3:10. "Ἥξει δὲ ἡμέρα κυρίου ὡς κλέπτης, ἐν ᾗ οἱ οὐρανοὶ ῥοιζηδὸν παρελεύσονται, στοιχεῖα δὲ καυσούμενα λυθήσεται, καὶ γῆ καὶ τὰ ἐν αὐτῇ ἔργα οὐχ εὑρεθήσεται.

46 R. T. France, *The Gospel of Matthew*, NICNT (Eerdmans, 2007), 942. See also Koester, *Revelation*, 313.

return of Christ with that of the Day of the Lord. Therefore, this is a clear verbal connection.[47]

REVELATION 3:5, 8; MATTHEW 10:32; LUKE 12:8; 1 CORINTHIANS 16:9[48]

(3:5) Ὁ νικῶν οὕτως περιβαλεῖται ἐν ἱματίοις λευκοῖς καὶ οὐ μὴ ἐξαλείψω τὸ ὄνομα αὐτοῦ ἐκ τῆς βίβλου τῆς ζωῆς καὶ ὁμολογήσω τὸ ὄνομα αὐτοῦ ἐνώπιον τοῦ πατρός μου καὶ ἐνώπιον τῶν ἀγγέλων αὐτοῦ.	(1 Cor 16:9) θύρα γάρ μοι ἀνέῳγεν μεγάλη καὶ ἐνεργής, καὶ ἀντικείμενοι πολλοί. (Matt 10:32) Πᾶς οὖν ὅστις ὁμολογήσει ἐν ἐμοὶ ἔμπροσθεν τῶν ἀνθρώπων, ὁμολογήσω κἀγὼ ἐν αὐτῷ ἔμπροσθεν τοῦ πατρός μου τοῦ ἐν [τοῖς] οὐρανοῖς·
(3:8) οἶδά σου τὰ ἔργα, ἰδοὺ δέδωκα ἐνώπιόν σου θύραν ἠνεῳγμένην, ἣν οὐδεὶς δύναται κλεῖσαι αὐτήν, ὅτι μικρὰν ἔχεις δύναμιν καὶ ἐτήρησάς μου τὸν λόγον καὶ οὐκ ἠρνήσω τὸ ὄνομά μου.	(Luke 12:8) Λέγω δὲ ὑμῖν, πᾶς ὃς ἂν ὁμολογήσῃ ἐν ἐμοὶ ἔμπροσθεν τῶν ἀνθρώπων, καὶ ὁ υἱὸς τοῦ ἀνθρώπου ὁμολογήσει ἐν αὐτῷ ἔμπροσθεν τῶν ἀγγέλων τοῦ θεοῦ·

Revelation 3:5 concludes the letter to the church of Sardis by indicating that those who conquer will receive three rewards. First, the overcomers will be rewarded with white clothing. Second, Christ will never blot out their names from the book of life. Third, Christ "will confess his name before my Father and before his angels" (ὁμολογήσω τὸ ὄνομα αὐτοῦ ἐνώπιον τοῦ πατρός μου καὶ ἐνώπιον τῶν ἀγγέλων αὐτοῦ).[49]

Contextually, Matt 10:32 and Luke 12:8 are similar, but the one to whom Christ makes his confession is different.[50] For Matthew, it is "before my Father," (ἔμπροσθεν τοῦ πατρός μου), whereas in Luke it is before the angels

---

47 See also Beth M. Stovell, *Mapping Metaphorical Discourse in the Fourth Gospel: John's Eternal King* (Brill, 2012), 228–248.

48 Charles does not provide any reason for not following the sequential order of these verses, but instead groups these examples together. However, the examination will follow the sequential ordering of the verses in order to read the text of Scripture cohesively. This cohesive reading is why Matthew and Luke are treated before 1 Corinthians. The table reflects the order and grouping of Charles.

49 The future tense ὁμολογήσω is a predictive future stating that this specific event will happen. See Wallace, *Greek Grammar*, 568; A. T. Robertson, *A Grammar of the Greek New Testament in the Light of Historical Research* (Broadman Press, 1934), 872–873. BDF lists this option as a gnomic future "in order to express that which is to be expected under certain circumstances." F. Blass and A. Debrunner, *A Greek Grammar of the New Testament and Other Early Christian Literature* (The University of Chicago Press, 1961), 178.

50 "Though addressed to the Twelve (vv. 1–5), like much of vv. 17–42, this saying looks beyond the apostles to disciples at large. The point is made clear by 'Whoever.' (v. 21). A necessary criterion for being a disciple of Jesus is to acknowledge him publicly." Carson, "Matthew," 256.

of God (ἔμπροσθεν τῶν ἀγγέλων τοῦ θεοῦ).[51] However, it is important that both Matthew and Luke emphasize that Christ is confessed before men (ἔμπροσθεν τῶν ἀνθρώπων), and this parallel serves as a connection between the two texts.

In Rev 3:5 and both Matt 10:32 and Luke 12:8, the focus is upon confession that leads unto salvation.[52] This confession from Rev 3:5 is likely Jesus reading the names of the believers from the book of life, and this reading will take place before the Father (Matt 10:32) and his angels (Luke 12:8).[53] Furthermore, the example of confessing Christ before men and receiving the reward of Christ confessing their name before the Father is used only in these three locations. Therefore, this verbal connection should be viewed as a clear connection.

Revelation 3:8 begins the content of the letter to the church of Philadelphia. Here, Christ informs the church that he has set before them an open door (δέδωκα ἐνώπιόν σου θύραν ἠνεῳγμένην) before them. These two promises both offer the certainty of a future salvation and an escape from the impending judgment as described in the rest of Revelation. Charles believes a connection is made with 1 Cor 16:9, where Paul writes to the Corinthians because of a great door for effective work was opened there for him (θύρα γάρ μοι ἀνέῳγεν). The question, then, centers upon what does the "door" in Revelation mean, for it is clearly the missionary work of the Gospel in 1 Cor 16:9. Charles believes that the open door "means that a good opportunity is being given for missionary effort, and in our text and in the above Pauline passages the door stands for the privilege accorded to the Christian teachers."[54] However, the context in Revelation does not allow for this interpretation. Robert Mounce writes:

> The preceding verse spoke of a messianic kingdom whose access was under absolute control of Christ. He is the one who possesses the key and can open and shut at will. Now in v. 8 he reminds the Christians at Philadelphia who may have been excommunicated from the local synagogue

---

51 "The angels here constitute the heavenly royal court (as in 15:10) rather than a court specifically for judgment." John Nolland, *Luke 9:21–18:34*, WBC (Word, 1993), 679. Also, Bock, "Matthew 10:32 has a similar concept, except there Jesus says he will offer the confession before his Father in heaven. The Lucan reference to angels alludes to their role as witnesses of the confession at the heavenly court." Bock, *Luke 9:51–24:52*, 1139.

52 Koester also includes 2 Clement 3:2b. Koester, *Revelation*, 315–316.

53 Beale, *The Book of Revelation*, 280. Beale notes, "The second part of the saying, which John cites, is probably an abbreviation of the larger Synoptic statement and is meant to recall the first part."

54 Charles, *Revelation*, 1:87. See also Henry Barclay Swete, *The Apocalypse of St. John* (Macmillan and Co., 1907), 54.

(v. 9) that he has placed before them an open door into the eternal kingdom, and no one can shut it ... No matter if the door to the synagogue has been closed, the door into the messianic kingdom remains open.[55]

Therefore, there is no verbal connection between Rev 3:5 and 1 Cor 16:9.

REVELATION 5:5; LUKE 7:13; 8:52

(5:5) καὶ εἷς ἐκ τῶν πρεσβυτέρων λέγει μοι· μὴ κλαῖε, ἰδοὺ ἐνίκησεν ὁ λέων ὁ ἐκ τῆς φυλῆς Ἰούδα, ἡ ῥίζα Δαυίδ, ἀνοῖξαι τὸ βιβλίον καὶ τὰς ἑπτὰ σφραγῖδας αὐτοῦ.	(Luke 7:13) καὶ ἰδὼν αὐτὴν ὁ κύριος ἐσπλαγχνίσθη ἐπ᾽ αὐτῇ καὶ εἶπεν αὐτῇ· μὴ κλαῖε. (Luke 8:52) ἔκλαιον δὲ πάντες καὶ ἐκόπτοντο αὐτήν. ὁ δὲ εἶπεν· μὴ κλαίετε, οὐ γὰρ ἀπέθανεν ἀλλὰ καθεύδει.

In Rev 5, John states that he saw a sealed scroll in the hand of the one who sits upon the throne (καθημένου ἐπὶ τοῦ θρόνου). An angel loudly asks if anyone is able to open the scroll. After a thorough search in heaven, on earth, and under the earth, no one is found worthy to open or remove the scroll from the hand of God. As a result, John begins to weep loudly. He continues to weep only until an angel appears and commands him to stop weeping (μὴ κλαῖε), because the Lion from the tribe of Judah, the root of David, has conquered so that he is able to open the scroll and its seven seals.

The phrase μὴ κλαῖε occurs in both Luke 7:13 and 8:52, and in both references it is an imperative, as in Rev 5:5. In Luke 7:13 Jesus enters the town of Nain and a man, who had just died, was carried out to him. The man was the only son of a widow, and as he was carried out, she was crying; but Jesus tells her μὴ κλαῖε, do not weep. Upon this pronouncement, Jesus raises the man from the dead.[56] A similar event occurs in Luke 8:52 when Jesus visits the house of Jairus, whose daughter has just died. After Jesus walks through the house and arrives at the room where the daughter is laying, he tells all who were weeping and mourning μὴ κλαῖε, do not weep. Again, much like the event in Luke 7:13 the readers of Luke's gospel are able to predict the outcome, and Jesus raises the child from the dead (Luke 8:54–55).

Yet, the connection between Rev 5:5 and Luke 7:13; 8:52 appears to be weak at best. In the accounts of Luke's Gospel, the stories center upon people

---

55 Mounce, *Revelation*, 101.
56 For the parallel of this story with that of the Elijah/Elisha material, see Craig L. Blomberg, *Jesus and the Gospels: An Introduction and Survey* (B&H Academic, 2009), 317–318.

weeping over the death of some person, and Revelation depicts John weeping because none are found worthy to open the scroll. However, there is an apparent strength since all three instances use the imperative of κλαίω. The phrase μὴ κλαῖε also occurs in the plural imperative in Luke 23:38 and as a present participle in 1 Cor 7:30.[57] Considering the rarity of the command to stop weeping, it is best to consider this verbal connection as a possible connection since this example is difficult to prove given the context of each example, but the theme is similar.

Revelation 6:4; Matthew 10:34

(6:4) καὶ ἐξῆλθεν ἄλλος ἵππος πυρρός, καὶ τῷ καθημένῳ ἐπ' αὐτὸν ἐδόθη αὐτῷ λαβεῖν τὴν εἰρήνην ἐκ τῆς γῆς καὶ ἵνα ἀλλήλους σφάξουσιν καὶ ἐδόθη αὐτῷ μάχαιρα μεγάλη.	(Matt 10:34) Μὴ νομίσητε ὅτι ἦλθον βαλεῖν εἰρήνην ἐπὶ τὴν γῆν· οὐκ ἦλθον βαλεῖν εἰρήνην ἀλλὰ μάχαιραν

The Lamb, introduced in 5:6, was found worthy to take the scroll from the Father's hand and open the seals. Richard Bauckham notes that the scroll serves two purposes: (1), to reveal the way in which the Lamb's victory will occur, and (2) reveal how the followers of Christ are to participate in the coming of the kingdom of God.[58] The scope of their judgment is limited, and this limitation may be to encourage the earth-dwellers to repent (6:16; 9:20–21; 16:9).[59] As each seal is opened, judgment is brought forth upon the earth. In vv. 2–8 the initial four seals release four horses (cf. Zech 1:8–15; 6:1–8). The horses are given certain authority by the one sitting upon the throne in order to bring forth his judgment upon the earth.

The first seal reveals a white horse whose rider came out conquering (ἐξῆλθεν νικῶν) and was sent to conquer (νικήσῃ). The second seal is opened in 6:3, and a rider upon a bright red horse emerges. The color of this horse appears to mirror its judgment upon the earth, since the rider is given the authority to "take away peace form the earth" (λαβεῖν τὴν εἰρήνην ἐκ τῆς γῆς) so that those who dwell upon the earth will slay one another. This idea is further reinforced because of the great sword he also bears (ἀχαιρα μεγάλη). It

---

[57] The also occurs in the LXX in Mic 2:6; Jer 22:20, 18; Ezek 24:16, 23

[58] See the discussion of Richard Bauckham, *The Theology of the Book of Revelation* (Cambridge University Press, 1993), 80–84.

[59] So, I. Howard Marshall, *New Testament Theology* (InterVarsity Press, 2004), 554. This suggestion by Marshall seems unlikely considering the desire for the earth-dwellers to either hide from the wrath of God, refusal to repent, or to curse God for the judgments brought forth upon them.

appears that persecution of Christians is indicated here, for anytime σφάζω is used within Revelation it is in the context of death, whether it be the death of Christ (5:6, 9, 12), his followers (6:9; 13:8; 18:24), or even the first beast (13:8).[60]

In Matt 10:34 Jesus tells his disciples (10:1) that his coming was intended not to bring peace upon the earth, but rather a sword. He further expounds upon the wider context of universal hostility and persecution in vv. 34–37, which reinforces the prediction made in vv. 17–22.[61] His mission upon the earth would not bring peace, but strife and division among families (v. 35). The negated subjunctive, Μὴ νομίσητε, provides a warning for the followers of Christ, that the gospel message was not one simply of peace. Peace is unattainable until reconciliation to God precedes it.[62]

In both Rev 6:4 and Matt 10:34 the language is similar as there is considerable overlap with the usage of λαβεῖν τὴν εἰρήνην ἐκ τῆς γῆς. The red horse of Rev 6:4 takes peace away, and Christ brings a sword in Matt 10:34. Beale remarks:

> While the woe that this horseman inflicts may be international strife in general, persecution of Christians is also in mind. This is evident from the fact that Matt. 10:34 ... is alluded to in [Rev 6:4]. The point of the Matthew text is that Jesus' followers should not be discouraged from confessing his name to the world when persecution comes, since such persecution is part of God's sovereign will. Their faithfulness amid oppression may result in the loss of physical life, but it will also result in the salvation of spiritual life. Hence, their sufferings have a salutary effect. This idea is being developed in Rev. 6:4. Indeed, μάχαιρα is sometimes used outside this passage in contexts of persecution.[63]

However, it does not appear that an intentional connection should be made between Rev 6:4 and Matt 10:34. Despite the similar language, the contexts are different. Christ speaks of bringing a sword and not peace, which is in reference to the reception of his message to an unbelieving world. As mentioned previously, persecution will come (Matt 10:17–22). Yet, Rev 6:4 finds no parallel with the concept of Matt 10:34 other than the language of the sword and peace on the earth. Thus, this verbal connection is unlikely.

---

60 Beale also understands σφάζω to function in Revelation in this way. See Beale, *Revelation*, 379.

61 R. T. France, *The Gospel of Matthew*, NICNT (Eerdmans, 2007), 407. France also connects "do not suppose that I came to" with 5:17; 9:13; 20:28.

62 Turner, *Matthew*, 281.

63 Beale, *Revelation*, 379.

Revelation 6:10; Luke 18:7–8

(6:10) καὶ ἔκραξαν φωνῇ μεγάλῃ λέγοντες· ἕως πότε, ὁ δεσπότης ὁ ἅγιος καὶ ἀληθινός, οὐ κρίνεις καὶ ἐκδικεῖς τὸ αἷμα ἡμῶν ἐκ τῶν κατοικούντων ἐπὶ τῆς γῆς;	(Luke 18:7–8) 7 ὁ δὲ θεὸς οὐ μὴ ποιήσῃ τὴν ἐκδίκησιν τῶν ἐκλεκτῶν αὐτοῦ τῶν βοώντων αὐτῷ ἡμέρας καὶ νυκτός, καὶ μακροθυμεῖ ἐπ' αὐτοῖς; 8 λέγω ὑμῖν ὅτι ποιήσει τὴν ἐκδίκησιν αὐτῶν ἐν τάχει. πλὴν ὁ υἱὸς τοῦ ἀνθρώπου ἐλθὼν ἆρα εὑρήσει τὴν πίστιν ἐπὶ τῆς γῆς;

Revelation 6:9–11 comprises of the opening of the fifth seal. Unlike the previous four, and even the sixth and seventh seal, the fifth seal is a vision given to John of martyrs who were slain because of the word of God and the witness they bore (6:9; cf. Acts 7:60). These souls were under the altar (cf. Lev 4:7), which is most likely the altar of incense (cf. 8:3–5; 9:13).[64] They cry out for vengeance from God for their blood, and they ask how long (ἕως πότε) until "you avenge our blood?" (ἐκδικεῖς τὸ αἷμα ἡμῶν). Their cry is a plea for God to hold accountable the people who murdered them (cf. 6:4). In response to their plea, they are given a white robe and told to wait (6:11).

Luke 18:7–8 consists of the parable of the persistent widow who routinely went to a judge, who did not fear God nor respect man, and pleaded for justice against her adversary (18:2). Because of her relentless cry for justice to be served (18:3), the judge, tiring of her persistence, eventually grants her request (18:5). Jesus then applies the parable to the prayer life of the elect, so that they should always pray "and not lose heart" (18:1). Jesus then asks and answers the rhetorical question, when will God give justice for his elect (18:7), by stating that God will "do justice for them with haste" (18:8).

The parallels between Rev 6:10 and Luke 18:7–8 are strikingly similar, both contextually and verbally. Although the martyrs underneath the altar do not cry out repeatedly as the woman in Luke 18:2, they nonetheless cry out that their blood might be vindicated, and that God would judge (κρίνεις) those who murdered them. They are told to wait until those who must be slain are slain as they were (6:11), implying that God will hold their murders accountable. If one were to understand the martyrs as the elect, then the connection to Luke 8:7 is clearly seen, for "the promise imbedded in this

---

[64] Stephen Pattermore notes the similarities between Rev 6:10 and Lev 17:11 LXX. See Stephen Pattermore, *The People of God in the Apocalypse: Discourse, Structure, and Exegesis* (Cambridge University Press, 2004), 77.

question is that God will vindicate his elect."[65] Furthermore, the remark that implied vindication in 6:11 is a delay, which can also be presumed in the statement by Christ that God will do justice for them with haste, since "with haste" implies a delay as well. Yet, "Jesus assumes that the supplication is for God's final vindication of the elect," which is clearly seen at the end of Revelation.[66] Thus, this verbal connection should be understood as a clear verbal connection.

REVELATION 6:12–13; MATTHEW 24:29; MARK 13:24–25; LUKE 21:25

(6:12–13) Καὶ εἶδον ὅτε ἤνοιξεν τὴν σφραγῖδα τὴν ἕκτην, καὶ σεισμὸς μέγας ἐγένετο καὶ ὁ ἥλιος ἐγένετο μέλας ὡς σάκκος τρίχινος καὶ ἡ σελήνη ὅλη ἐγένετο ὡς αἷμα 13 καὶ οἱ ἀστέρες τοῦ οὐρανοῦ ἔπεσαν εἰς τὴν γῆν, ὡς συκῆ βάλλει τοὺς ὀλύνθους αὐτῆς ὑπὸ ἀνέμου μεγάλου σειομένη,	(Matt 24:29) Εὐθέως δὲ μετὰ τὴν θλῖψιν τῶν ἡμερῶν ἐκείνων ὁ ἥλιος σκοτισθήσεται, καὶ ἡ σελήνη οὐ δώσει τὸ φέγγος αὐτῆς, καὶ οἱ ἀστέρες πεσοῦνται ἀπὸ τοῦ οὐρανοῦ, καὶ αἱ δυνάμεις τῶν οὐρανῶν σαλευθήσονται.
	(Mark 13:24–25) 24 Ἀλλὰ ἐν ἐκείναις ταῖς ἡμέραις μετὰ τὴν θλῖψιν ἐκείνην ὁ ἥλιος σκοτισθήσεται, καὶ ἡ σελήνη οὐ δώσει τὸ φέγγος αὐτῆς, 25 καὶ οἱ ἀστέρες ἔσονται ἐκ τοῦ οὐρανοῦ πίπτοντες, καὶ αἱ δυνάμεις αἱ ἐν τοῖς οὐρανοῖς σαλευθήσονται.
	(Luke 21:25) Καὶ ἔσονται σημεῖα ἐν ἡλίῳ καὶ σελήνῃ καὶ ἄστροις, καὶ ἐπὶ τῆς γῆς συνοχὴ ἐθνῶν ἐν ἀπορίᾳ ἤχους θαλάσσης καὶ σάλου,

Revelation 6:12–17 concludes the seal narrative of chapter 6, only to be revisited once again in 8:1 after a brief interlude of a heavenly vision seen by John in 7:1–17. In Rev 6:12–13 the Lamb opens the sixth seal (12a) and, as reminiscent of the other seals, an event of judgment occurs subsequently thereafter (cf. Isa 3:10) with a great earthquake (cf. 16:18), and the sun became black as sackcloth, and the whole moon became as blood, and the stars of the heaven

---

65 Bock, *Luke 9:51–24:52*, 1451.
66 Garland, *Luke*, 712.

fall to the earth. Once this event occurs, the sky is rolled away (14) and the earth-dwellers hide themselves from the wrath of the Lamb.[67] It appears that John is reflecting upon Isa 3:10, which finds a close parallel verbally and contextually.

The Synoptic Gospels also use similar language to explain the day of the Lord, but the Gospels interpret this day as the coming of the Son of Man. Both Matt 24:29 and Mark 13:24–25 appear to quote Isa 3:10 and allude to Isa 34:4, as indicated by the indention in the UBS[5] and NA28.[68] Matthew does not provide a direct quotation from the LXX other than "the moon will not give its light," and Isa 3:10 omits stars falling from heaven, but 34:4 includes this phenomenon (cf. Ezek 32:7). Likewise, Joel 2:10, 31 and 3:15 refer to the sun turning black and the stars removing their light from shining upon the earth.[69] Thus, both Matthew and Mark, in almost an exact parallel, allude to key Old Testament texts in order to describe the coming of the Son of Man. Furthermore, Luke appears to draw from the "Markan text, where there is an evident connection with OT texts in which the heavenly bodies provide their own dramatic accompaniment to the execution of God's judgment upon the nations."[70]

The verbal parallels between Rev 6:12–13 and Matt 24:29, Mark 13:24–25, and Luke 21:25 are clear. In the case of the Synoptic Gospels, the writers allude to important Old Testament themes that discuss the coming of the day of the Lord. Clear signs are given as to when that day will appear with judgment contextually following, for "all the tribes of the earth will mourn" (Matt 24:30) at the arrival of the Son of Man. This thematic parallel is readily apparent in Rev 6:15–17 when the earth-dwellers hide from the wrath of the Lamb and essentially mourn his arrival. Also, both Matthew and Mark note that the return of the Son of Man will occur after the time of tribulation, and this tribulation could be understood as the first four seals, if not definitely the fifth seal. The verbal connections between these verses, therefore, should be understood as clear, as both thematically and verbally the parallels are strong.

---

67 The events described find a close parallel with the day of the Lord described in the Old Testament. For a study on the intertextual connection, thematic progression, and the day of the Lord texts, see Craig A. Blaising, "The Day of the Lord: Theme and Pattern in Biblical Theology," *BSac* 169 (2012): 8–19. See also John Christopher Thomas and Frank D. Macchia, *Revelation* (Eerdmans, 2016), 143–144.

68 οἱ γὰρ ἀστέρες τοῦ οὐρανοῦ καὶ ὁ Ὠρίων καὶ πᾶς ὁ κόσμος τοῦ οὐρανοῦ τὸ φῶς οὐ δώσουσιν, καὶ σκοτισθήσεται τοῦ ἡλίου ἀνατέλλοντος, καὶ ἡ σελήνη οὐ δώσει τὸ φῶς αὐτῆς. Isa 3:10, LXX.

69 It is based upon this examination that Blomberg does not agree with the NIV's usage of quotation marks in this verse. See Craig L. Blomberg, "Matthew," in *Commentary on the New Testament use of the Old Testament*, ed. G. K. Beale and D. A. Carson (Baker, 2007), 87. See also Donald A. Hagner, *Matthew 14–28*, 713.

70 John Nolland, *Luke 18:35–24:53*, WBC (Word, 1993), 1005.

REVELATION 6:15–16; LUKE 23:30[71]

(6:15–16) Καὶ οἱ βασιλεῖς τῆς γῆς καὶ οἱ μεγιστᾶνες καὶ οἱ χιλίαρχοι καὶ οἱ πλούσιοι καὶ οἱ ἰσχυροὶ καὶ πᾶς δοῦλος καὶ ἐλεύθερος ἔκρυψαν ἑαυτοὺς εἰς τὰ σπήλαια καὶ εἰς τὰς πέτρας τῶν ὀρέων 16 καὶ λέγουσιν τοῖς ὄρεσιν καὶ ταῖς πέτραις· πέσετε ἐφ᾽ ἡμᾶς καὶ κρύψατε ἡμᾶς ἀπὸ προσώπου τοῦ καθημένου ἐπὶ τοῦ θρόνου καὶ ἀπὸ τῆς ὀργῆς τοῦ ἀρνίου,	(Luke 23:30) τότε ἄρξονται λέγειν τοῖς ὄρεσιν· πέσετε ἐφ᾽ ἡμᾶς, καὶ τοῖς βουνοῖς· καλύψατε ἡμᾶς·

The group of people listed in 6:15 are pictured throughout Revelation as those who have sided with the unholy trinity. A strong connection is made with Isa 34:12 where Isaiah lists οἱ ἄρχοντες, οἱ βασιλεῖς, and οἱ μεγιστᾶνες as those who directly oppose God and must, like the context here, be destroyed.[72] Their idolatry (cf. Rev 13:1–18) is apparent when they cry out for the rocks to fall upon them and hide them from the wrath of the Lamb and the one who sits upon the throne, which draws a striking parallel with Hos 10:8 and is likely the source that John employs. The judgment from the sixth seal has come upon them, and the Lord has answered the prayers of those who were under his altar (6:10).

In a similar way, Jesus uses this quotation from Hos 10:8 at his crucifixion. Many were lamenting and weeping for him (Luke 23:27), but he encouraged them not to weep, for a day will come when some cry out for the mountains to fall upon and cover them. Mounce believes this statement by Jesus is meant for the destruction of Jerusalem.[73]

Contextually and verbally, the connections shared between Rev 6:15–16 and Luke 23:30 focus primarily upon their usage of Hos 10:8. In Hos 10:8, the people are judged for their idolatry, in Luke 23:30 the people are judged for their rejection and crucifixion of Jesus, and in Rev 6:15–16 they are judged for the persecution of God's people. In both Hos 10:8 and Rev 6:15–16 the response from the people is the same as they request the rock and hill to fall upon and cover them, respectively. Only in Luke 23:30 is no immediate response given from the people, but rather those words are prophesied by Jesus himself.

---

[71] For the context of Rev 6:15–16, see the previous section

[72] Beale, *Revelation*, 399–400.

[73] Mounce, *Revelation*, 152. Bock agrees and writes, "The suffering of Jerusalem's fall will be so great that it will be better to have no family ... In fact, the pain of Jerusalem's fall will be so great that people will desire their life to end." Bock, *Luke 9:51–24:53*, 1846.

Yet, verbally, thematically, and contextually Rev 6:15–16 and Luke 23:30 share a clear connection. First, both passages utilize Hos 10:8 appropriately and apply the passage within their own respective context to satisfy the connection. In both instances there is rejection and persecution of a certain person or group (Jesus/Christians), and in both references the persecutors will cry out to be hidden. Second, it is unclear whether Charles intends for οἱ μεγιστᾶνες καὶ οἱ χιλίαρχοι καὶ οἱ πλούσιοι καὶ οἱ ἰσχυροί to be included in his connection, but this group should not be omitted since the scope of God's judgment, and the prediction of Jesus, encompass all of humanity. Thus, the verbal connection between Rev 6:15–16 and Luke 23:30 is a clear connection.

REVELATION 6:17; LUKE 21:36

(6:17) ὅτι ἦλθεν ἡ ἡμέρα ἡ μεγάλη τῆς ὀργῆς αὐτῶν, καὶ τίς δύναται σταθῆναι;	(Luke 21:36) ἀγρυπνεῖτε δὲ ἐν παντὶ καιρῷ δεόμενοι ἵνα κατισχύσητε ἐκφυγεῖν ταῦτα πάντα τὰ μέλλοντα γίνεσθαι καὶ σταθῆναι ἔμπροσθεν τοῦ υἱοῦ τοῦ ἀνθρώπου.

After crying out for the rocks to fall upon them and hiding in the caves, the earth-dwellers recognize that the day of the Lord has arrived, and conclude their plea with a question: "Who is able to stand" (cf. Mal 3:2; Joel 2:11; Nah 1:6)?[74] The answer to their question is provided in Rev 7, as the Lord seals the 144,000 so that they are protected from the judgments that come forth. Furthermore, these sealed ones stand with the Lamb on Mount Zion (14:1), and follow him wherever he goes (14:4).

In Luke 21:34–38, Jesus warns his disciples to watch themselves, lest the day of the Lord come upon them quickly. He tells them to stay awake (ἀγρυπνεῖτε) and pray, so that they may have strength (κατισχύσητε) to escape what is about to arrive, in order to be able to stand before the Son of Man (σταθῆναι ἔμπροσθεν τοῦ υἱοῦ τοῦ ἀνθρώπου). The claim to be strong enough to flee that which is about to come should not be understood to mean literally to flee, but rather to "come through them victoriously."[75] Also, the phrase σταθῆναι ἔμπροσθεν τοῦ υἱοῦ τοῦ ἀνθρώπου is likely intended to recall Mal 3:2 which bears a similar question as that of Rev 6:17, who is able to stand? According to Jesus, it is those who watch and await the return of the Son of Man.[76]

---

74 Patterson understands this comment to be from John and not the earth-dwellers. See Paige Patterson, *Revelation*, NAC (Broadman and Holman, 2012), 188.

75 Ray Summers, *Commentary on Luke* (Word, 1972), 837.

76 Bock, *A Theology of Luke-Acts*, 197.

The contexts between Rev 6:17 and Luke 21:36 are very different from one another. Revelation 6:17 provides the context of judgment, whereas Luke 21:36 is a warning for the faithful to stay awake and pray so that they may stand before the Son of Man. In both references, it does appear that a clear allusion is meant to draw the reader back to Mal 3:2, Joel 2:11, and Nah 1:6 to seek an answer to the question of who can stand or be delivered from the day of the Lord. The answer to these questions is found in Luke 21:36, and the reader of Revelation will find the answer in Luke 21:36 as well as Rev 7. Thematically and verbally, the references share a clear connection.

REVELATION 9:20; LUKE 18:11

(9:20) Καὶ οἱ λοιποὶ τῶν ἀνθρώπων, οἳ οὐκ ἀπεκτάνθησαν ἐν ταῖς πληγαῖς ταύταις, οὐδὲ μετενόησαν ἐκ τῶν ἔργων τῶν χειρῶν αὐτῶν, ἵνα μὴ προσκυνήσουσιν τὰ δαιμόνια καὶ τὰ εἴδωλα τὰ χρυσᾶ καὶ τὰ ἀργυρᾶ καὶ τὰ χαλκᾶ καὶ τὰ λίθινα καὶ τὰ ξύλινα, ἃ οὔτε βλέπειν δύνανται οὔτε ἀκούειν οὔτε περιπατεῖν,	(Luke 18:11) ὁ Φαρισαῖος σταθεὶς πρὸς ἑαυτὸν ταῦτα προσηύχετο· ὁ θεός, εὐχαριστῶ σοι ὅτι οὐκ εἰμὶ ὥσπερ οἱ λοιποὶ τῶν ἀνθρώπων, ἅρπαγες, ἄδικοι, μοιχοί, ἢ καὶ ὡς οὗτος ὁ τελώνης·

Revelation 9:20–21 provides the conclusion to the sixth trumpet that was blown in 9:13. After the trumpet was blown, four angels are released to kill a third of mankind (15), and they rode upon horses, and they inflicted the earth-dwellers with three plagues (18). Those who survived the demonic slaughter (οἱ λοιποὶ τῶν ἀνθρώπων) failed to repent from the works of their hands. These remaining earth-dwellers are much like the Egyptians and Pharaoh (Exod 9:34–10:1) who continued to disobey God despite the plagues that were inflicted upon them.[77]

Luke 18:9–14 is the parable of the Pharisee and the Tax Collector. The parable was told to those who trusted in themselves that they were righteous (18:9). The Pharisee first prays and thanks God that he is not as the rest of men (οἱ λοιποὶ τῶν ἀνθρώπων), extortioners, unjust, adulterers or even like the tax collector. He then gives an account of his pharisaical duties that he accomplishes routinely (18:11). The main point of the parable is made evident with the tax collector whose prayer is recited in 18:13. Rather than attempting to justify himself with works, he pleads for mercy from God.

Neither Rev 9:20 nor Luke 18:11 share a contextual or thematic similarity. In fact, the verbal connection of οἱ λοιποὶ τῶν ἀνθρώπων is the only similarity

---

77 Hoskins, *The Book of Revelation*, 179.

the verses share with one another. Furthermore, one could argue that what the Pharisee does in Luke 18:12 are works of his hand and his failure to repent of them mirrors that of the οἱ λοιποὶ τῶν ἀνθρώπων in Revelation. Yet, this argument remains considerably weak considering the meaning of both references are contrasted. Therefore, there is no verbal connection between Rev 9:20 and Luke 18:11.

Revelation 11:3, 6; Luke 4:25; James 5:17

(11:3) Καὶ δώσω τοῖς δυσὶν μάρτυσίν μου καὶ προφητεύσουσιν ἡμέρας χιλίας διακοσίας ἑξήκοντα περιβεβλημένοι σάκκους.	(Luke 4:25) ἐπ᾽ ἀληθείας δὲ λέγω ὑμῖν, πολλαὶ χῆραι ἦσαν ἐν ταῖς ἡμέραις Ἠλίου ἐν τῷ Ἰσραήλ, ὅτε ἐκλείσθη ὁ οὐρανὸς ἐπὶ ἔτη τρία καὶ μῆνας ἕξ, ὡς ἐγένετο λιμὸς μέγας ἐπὶ πᾶσαν τὴν γῆν,
(11:6) οὗτοι ἔχουσιν τὴν ἐξουσίαν **κλεῖσαι τὸν οὐρανόν, ἵνα μὴ ὑετὸς βρέχῃ τὰς ἡμέρας τῆς προφητείας αὐτῶν**, καὶ ἐξουσίαν ἔχουσιν ἐπὶ τῶν ὑδάτων στρέφειν αὐτὰ εἰς αἷμα καὶ πατάξαι τὴν γῆν ἐν πάσῃ πληγῇ ὁσάκις ἐὰν θελήσωσιν.	(Jas 5:17) Ἠλίας ἄνθρωπος ἦν ὁμοιοπαθὴς ἡμῖν, καὶ προσευχῇ προσηύξατο τοῦ μὴ βρέξαι, καὶ οὐκ ἔβρεξεν ἐπὶ τῆς γῆς ἐνιαυτοὺς τρεῖς καὶ μῆνας ἕξ·

In Rev 11:1–14 John is given a reed to measure the temple of God but is told not to measure the outside of the temple, for that is given to the nations (11:2) to trample over the holy city for forty-two months. Outside the temple, God will allow his two witnesses to prophesy for 1,260 days (προφητεύσουσιν ἡμέρας χιλίας διακοσίας ἑξήκοντα; cf. Dan 7:25; 12:7) clothed in sackcloth. These witnesses are presumably given authority over natural occurrences, as they are allowed to close the heavens so that it does not rain upon their days of prophesying (κλεῖσαι τὸν οὐρανόν, ἵνα μὴ ὑετὸς βρέχῃ τὰς ἡμέρας τῆς προφητείας αὐτῶν). These witnesses, after their time of prophesy, are killed and lay in the street for three days (11:11) until God calls them into heaven (11:12).

The actions these witnesses perform find two parallels within the New Testament. First, in Luke 4:25, after Jesus has read and applied Isa 61:1 to himself in the temple, he is rejected within Nazareth. Jesus takes a story of Elijah (1 Kgs 17:8–24), where Elijah is rejected by a Jewish king but accepted by a Gentile. Here, Jesus is rejected by Jews but will eventually be welcomed by the Gentiles and sinners throughout the Gospel.[78] Jesus recounts what Elijah did in his explanation: namely, that he closed the sky for three years and six months (ἐκλείσθη ὁ οὐρανὸς ἐπὶ ἔτη τρία καὶ μῆνας ἕξ). James, in like manner,

---

78 David W. Pao and Eckhard J. Schnabel, "Luke," in *Commentary on the New Testament use*

utilizes this brief story from Elijah in his epistle. In the context of James, it is the prayer of faith, and the Elijah story is recounted to suggest that since Elijah was a man like themselves, they should pray fervently. Elijah's prayer was answered, and it did not rain upon the earth for three years and six months.[79]

However, the connection Rev 11:3, 6 appear to share with Luke 4:25 and Jas 5:17 is not from what Elijah did, but rather in the identity of one of the two witnesses. Revelation 11 does not identify these witnesses, but rather provides possible connections with Old Testament figures, of whom Moses and Elijah are the most notable examples.[80] However, within the broader narrative of Rev 11:1–13 there are descriptions provided about these witnesses. They are labeled as the two olive trees and the two lampstands that stand before the Lord of the earth (Zech 4:3, 11, 14), and lampstands appear in 1:12–13 and throughout chapters 2–3. Also, what these two witnesses do mimic the actions of both Moses and Elijah, and it is likely significant that these two prophets appeared with Jesus on the Mount of Transfiguration (Matt 17:1–9; Mark 9:2–8; Luke 9:28–36). First, 11:5 states that fire comes from their mouth if any should harm them, which occurs in 2 Kgs 1:10 with Elijah and King Ahaziah. Second, they are able to shut the sky, which occurs in 1 Kgs 17:1 with Elijah and the prophets of Baal. Third, they have the ability to change the waters into blood, and that is what Moses did in Exod 7:17–19 to the Nile River.

Some choose to identify the identity of the two witnesses as that of the church. Beale notes that the two witnesses "represent the whole community of faith, whose primary function is to be a prophetic witness."[81] Bandy, likewise, argues that the description provided by John in 11:4 and its connection to Zech 4 identifies the two witnesses as the church.[82] Considering the evidence within Rev 11:1–13, it appears that the church is in view. Yet, the verbal connection that Rev 11:3, 6 shares with Luke 4:25 and Jas 5:17 suggest that John envisioned the witnesses to function in the same manner as that of the Old Testament prophets. Thus, these two verbal connections should be understood as clear.

---

of the Old Testament, ed. G. K. Beale and D. A. Carson (Baker, 2007), 290.

79 Peter Davids believes that Elijah was chosen because he "was simply another human being like all those in the congregation reading the epistle, not a heavenly being or a specially perfect person, despite the many legends circulating about him and the story of his ascension into heaven. The example was probably selected because Elijah in legend (not in the OT) was a well-known person with a reputation for prayer." Peter H. Davids, *The Epistle of James*, NIGTC (Eerdmans, 1982), 197.

80 See Osborne, *Revelation*, 417–418; Beale, *Revelation*, 572–573; Aune, *Revelation 6–16*, 610–611; Seth Turner, "Revelation 11:1–13: History of Interpretation" (PhD diss., University of Oxford, 2004); Koester, *Revelation*, 496–498.

81 Beale, *Revelation*, 573.

82 Bandy, "The Prophetic Lawsuit," 299–300.

Revelation 11:15; Matthew 4:8

(11:15) Καὶ ὁ ἕβδομος ἄγγελος ἐσάλπισεν· καὶ ἐγένοντο φωναὶ μεγάλαι ἐν τῷ οὐρανῷ λέγοντες· ἐγένετο ἡ βασιλεία τοῦ κόσμου τοῦ κυρίου ἡμῶν καὶ τοῦ χριστοῦ αὐτοῦ, καὶ βασιλεύσει εἰς τοὺς αἰῶνας τῶν αἰώνων.	(Matt 4:8) Πάλιν παραλαμβάνει αὐτὸν ὁ διάβολος εἰς ὄρος ὑψηλὸν λίαν καὶ δείκνυσιν αὐτῷ πάσας τὰς βασιλείας τοῦ κόσμου καὶ τὴν δόξαν αὐτῶν.

Revelation 11:15 brings the seven-trumpet narrative (8:2–9:21) to a conclusion, as the seventh angel blows his trumpet. Rather than a judgment scene of cosmic proportions, a declaration from voices in heaven declare that the kingdom of the world (ἡ βασιλεία τοῦ κόσμου) has now become the kingdom of the Lord and of his Christ. These heavenly voices are able to make this declaration because the enemies of the kingdom of God have been defeated and judged, as described in 11:18. This announcement does not usher in the final judgment reserved for the earth-dwellers (20:11–15), but rather provides a brief vision of the final worship scene in heaven. The seventh trumpet is the third woe (11:14), and 11:15–19 functions much like 7:9–17, as well as mirrors the narrative and interlude of the seven seals in 6:1–7:17.[83] Nevertheless, this proclamation embodies a full orbed notion of the kingdom of God ruling, and the "not yet" of the eschatological reign of Christ has finally been realized.[84] After the second woe has been announced, the narrative returns to the blowing of the trumpets with the final trumpet blown in 11:15. Once the trumpet is blown, a loud voice from heaven announces, "The kingdom of this world has become the kingdom of our Lord and his Christ, and he will reign forever and ever." Charles notes ἡ βασιλεία τοῦ κόσμου may be compared to τὰς βασιλείας τοῦ κόσμου from Matt 4:8.[85]

Matthew 4:1–11 is the familiar text depicting the temptation of Jesus by

---

83 Osborne, *Revelation*, 340.
84 George Eldon Ladd, *A Theology of the New Testament* (Eerdmans, 1993), 54–67; Leonard Goppelt, *Theology of the New Testament: Volume 1*, trans. John E. Alsup (Eerdmans, 1981), 43–76.
85 Charles firmly believes that the author had access to Matthew. "That our author has used Matthew is deducible from the following facts. In 17 he has had Matt 2430 before him, where our author's combination of Dan 713 and Zech 1210.12 occurs already. Our author derives from Matthew the words πᾶσαι αἱ φυλαὶ τ. γῆς, which are not in the O.T. or Versions. Next, a reference to 27 shows that it is the Matthaean (or Lucan: cf. 88) form of the command, ὁ ἔχων οὖς κτλ., Matt 1115 139 etc., that our author was familiar with. The dependence of 33, 1615 on Matt 2442. 43. 46 is obvious at the first glance. 35 presupposes both Matt 1032 and the parallel passage in Luke 128. Other passages showing dependence on Matthew, though not so conclusively, will be found under 13d 116 64 1115 below." Charles, *Revelation*, lxvi.

the devil in the wilderness.⁸⁶ The first two temptations offer Jesus a way to "satisfy a legitimate bodily appetite in an illegitimate way and then ... use his supernatural power to rebel against God, even while demonstrating great faith."⁸⁷ It is the final temptation, to worship the devil and then receive the kingdoms of the world, that Jesus rebukes the devil and declares that worship is reserved for God alone.

Again, in exchange for worshipping the devil Jesus would receive the kingdoms of the world (τὰς βασιλείας τοῦ κόσμου). Worshipping the devil would provide a way around the cross whereby Jesus could receive the kingdoms that he was to receive later, as the Son of Man (Dan 7:13–14). The kingdoms that Jesus would have compete rule over would be given to him at that moment.

Charles makes the verbal connection from Rev 11:15 to Matt 4:8 based on the τὰς βασιλείας τοῦ κόσμου and the surrounding theme between the two contexts.⁸⁸ It may be a stretch to base a verbal connection on τὰς βασιλείας τοῦ κόσμου, yet the phrase does not occur again within the New Testament. In fact, other than Rev 11:15 and Matt 4:8, ὁ βασιλεία and ὁ κόσμος do not appear in any other text together in sequence. The editors of both NA27 and NA28, and Charles as well, allude to a connection with Rev 21:10 rather than 11:15, and there the connection appears with the high mountain and the holy city Jerusalem coming down out of heaven. Yet, the contextual and verbal connections appear stronger between Rev 11:15 and Matt 4:8. What the devil offers Jesus in Matt 4:8 is fully realized in Rev 11:15 and strengthened with the verbal connection of τὰς βασιλείας τοῦ κόσμου. The connection between these two verses should be considered clear.⁸⁹

REVELATION 12:9; LUKE 10:18

(12:9) καὶ ἐβλήθη ὁ δράκων ὁ μέγας, ὁ ὄφις ὁ ἀρχαῖος, ὁ καλούμενος Διάβολος καὶ ὁ Σατανᾶς, ὁ πλανῶν τὴν οἰκουμένην ὅλην, ἐβλήθη εἰς τὴν γῆν, καὶ οἱ ἄγγελοι αὐτοῦ μετ' αὐτοῦ ἐβλήθησαν.	(Luke 10:18) εἶπεν δὲ αὐτοῖς· ἐθεώρουν τὸν σατανᾶν ὡς ἀστραπὴν ἐκ τοῦ οὐρανοῦ πεσόντα.

---

86 Nicholas P. Lunn, "The Temple in the Wilderness: Allusions to the Hebrew Sanctuary in the Baptism and Temptations of Christ," *JETS* 59 (2016): 701–716.

87 Craig L. Blomberg, *Matthew*, NAC (Broadman and Holman: Nashville, 1992), 85.

88 See also Osborne, *Matthew*, 135.

89 David Aune likewise makes the connection between Rev 11:15 and Matt 4:8. "There is a verbal parallel elsewhere in the NT only in Matt 4:8 (in the context of the temptation of Jesus), where the plural phrase αἱ [sic] βασιλείας τοῦ κόσμου, "the kingdoms of the world," occurs and refers to the many individual kingdoms, each with its particular ruler, which make up the

The preceding context of Rev 12:9 tells the story of a woman who is to give birth (12:2) to the male child who will rule the nations (12:5), and the dragon who sought to devour the child at birth (12:4). The child is caught up to God and his throne (12:5), the woman flees into the wilderness (12:6) and the dragon, with his angels, fight against Michael in heaven (12:7). After their defeat, the dragon, identified as the great serpent (cf. Gen 3:1, 14) and Satan (ὁ Σατανᾶς), is thrown down to the earth (ἐβλήθη εἰς τὴν γῆν).[90] This removal not only explains the phrase why there was no room left for them (12:8), but it also describes the role Satan has in deceiving the world; namely, the earth-dwellers.[91]

The unit of Luke 10:1–24 can aptly be summarized as the sending of the seventy-two disciples (10:1–12), a pronouncement of woe by Jesus to unrepentant cities (10:13–16), the report of the seventy-two (10:17–20), and a thanksgiving by Jesus for them (10:21–24). Returning from their mission (10:1–12), the seventy-two report that the demons are subject to "us in your name" (10:17), thus implying a defeat of the kingdom of Satan upon the earth. Jesus responds and says, 'I saw Satan fall as a star from heaven (ἐθεώρουν τὸν σατανᾶν ὡς ἀστραπὴν ἐκ τοῦ οὐρανοῦ πεσόντα)." The imperfect ἐθεώρουν lends itself to two possible interpretations: either an event that occurred in the past or one that will occur in the future. The context of the passage makes this verse difficult, for some understand the event which Jesus describes as having already occurred, while others view it as a future event.[92]

Despite how one may interpret Luke 10:18, the connection Charles make between this verse and Rev 12:9 is not based upon *when* Satan fell but rather the event itself. Of course, the context of Rev 12 does indicate a fall prior to

---

world. Yet the implication is that all these kingdoms belong to Satan and that he is able to deliver them to whomever he pleases." David Aune, *Revelation 6–16*, WBC (Thomas Nelson, 1998), 638. UBS5 and NA28 do not list the plural form which Aune references.

90 The term ὁ Σατανᾶς derives from the Hebrew שטן, and this term carries the notion of a legal adversary (cf. Num 22:22, 31; 1 Sam 29:4; 2 Sam 19:23). He is also identified in 12:10 as ὁ κατήγωρ, which likely carries across a literal translation of שטן. See Aune, *Revelation 6–16*, 700. See also the discussion of Satan as an accuser in Bandy, "The Prophetic Lawsuit," 303–304. A persuasive argument is made by Ryan Stokes, that שטן does not necessarily mean "accuser" in the Hebrew Bible, but here the reference appears as such. He suggests that the thought developed among the Greek-speaking theologians and the semantic range of διάβλος and its usage in Num 22:22, 32 "opened the door for later interpreters to view the śāṭān (LXX ὁ διάβλος) as 'the Accuser.'" Ryan E. Stokes, "Satan, YHWH's Executioner" *JBL* 133, 2 (2014): 269n42.

91 "Thus the story of the original expulsion of Satan and his angels from heaven is complete. The reader now understands not only how the evil angels fell but why they fell and what kind of beings Satan and his messengers are." Osborne, *Revelation*, 473.

92 See Simon J. Gathercole, "Jesus' Eschatological Vision of the Fall of Satan: Luke 10.18 Reconsidered," *ZNW* 94 (2003): 143–163; Mounce, *Revelation*, 237. For the past, see Beale, *Revelation*, 655–666; Bock, *Luke 9:51–24:53*, 1006–1007; Nolland, *Luke 9:21–18:34*, 563–564.

the birth of Jesus since he is the baby from 12:5; yet, the focus of the verbal connection is upon the fall of Satan. Notably, in Rev 12:9 Satan is cast (ἐβλήθη) to the earth, whereas in Luke 10:18 he is falling (πεσόντα). Both ἐβλήθη and πεσόντα are passive, which leads to the understanding that Satan did not leave willingly (Rev 12:7–8). Furthermore, a description of Satan falling out of heaven is only found in the New Testament in Luke 10:18 and Rev 12:9. However, the verbal connection appears only to be linked together thematically rather than verbally. Thus, it is perhaps wise to label this verbal connection as probable.

REVELATION 13:11; MATTHEW 7:15

(13:11) Καὶ εἶδον ἄλλο θηρίον ἀναβαῖνον ἐκ τῆς γῆς, καὶ εἶχεν κέρατα δύο ὅμοια ἀρνίῳ καὶ ἐλάλει ὡς δράκων.	(Matt 7:15) Προσέχετε ἀπὸ τῶν ψευδοπροφητῶν, οἵτινες ἔρχονται πρὸς ὑμᾶς ἐν ἐνδύμασιν προβάτων, ἔσωθεν δέ εἰσιν λύκοι ἅρπαγες.

The context of Rev 13:1–18 introduces the second and third members of the unholy trinity, which mirror the Holy Trinity closely. This section focuses on the second beast who rose from the earth (13:11). He exercises authority that was given to him from the first beast (13:12), performs miraculous signs (13:13), and compels the earth-dwellers to make an image to the first beast (13:14b) that he breathed upon and caused to speak (13:15). The description of this beast is significant, for he mirrors the dragon by his speech (καὶ ἐλάλει ὡς δράκων) but he also has two horns like a lamb (εἶχεν κέρατα δύο ὅμοια ἀρνίῳ).

Charles finds a parallel, based upon the two horns, with the false prophets from Matt 7:15. In Matt 7:15, Jesus is concluding the Sermon on the Mount and warns the hearers to beware of false prophets, for they "come among you with the clothing of sheep, but inwardly they are ravenous wolves." Matthew 7:15 may be an allusion to Ezek 22:27, where the "simile of the roaring lion tearing its prey to depict the false prophets of Jerusalem and the image of 'wolves tearing their prey, shedding blood, and destroying lives' to portray corrupt officials who use their positions of authority and influence to pursue 'unjust gain'" is employed.[93]

There are close parallels thematically between these two passages. First, the second beast disguises itself as a lamb, but is inwardly a false prophet as

---

[93] Charles L. Quarles, *The Sermon on the Mount: Restoring Christ's Message to the Modern Church* (B&H Academic, 2011), 322. Koester makes a similar connection. Koester, *Revelation*, 590.

he is called in Revelation (ὁ ψευδοπροφήτης; 16:13; 19:20; 20:10). This label of false prophet only strengthens the parallel with Matt 7:15. Second, "sheep" are identified in Matthew (cf. 10:16; 25:32–33; 26:31) as those who are Jesus' disciples and those who received "Jesus' representatives and their message."[94] Thus, it would be relevant for the false prophets to disguise themselves as one of Christ's own and dwell undetected with those within the church. Also, considering that the first beast (13:1–10) mirrors the Son, it is the job of the second beast to cause the earth-dwellers to worship the first beast. Thus, this verbal connection should be understood as clear, since what Jesus warned his hearers in Matt 7:15 finds a strong connection with Rev 13:11.

Revelation 14:4; Luke 9:57

(14:4) ὗτοί εἰσιν οἳ μετὰ γυναικῶν οὐκ ἐμολύνθησαν, παρθένοι γάρ εἰσιν, οὗτοι οἱ ἀκολουθοῦντες τῷ ἀρνίῳ ὅπου ἂν ὑπάγῃ.[95] οὗτοι ἠγοράσθησαν ἀπὸ τῶν ἀνθρώπων ἀπαρχὴ τῷ θεῷ καὶ τῷ ἀρνίῳ,	(Luke 9:57) Καὶ πορευομένων αὐτῶν ἐν τῇ ὁδῷ εἶπέν τις πρὸς αὐτόν· ἀκολουθήσω σοι ὅπου ἐὰν ἀπέρχῃ. (cf. Mark 2:14; 10:21)

After the first and second beast are introduced in Rev 13:1–18, John is given a vision of the 144,000 (cf. 7:1–8) who stand upon Mount Zion with the Lamb (14:1) who are given a new song to sing (14:3) and none could learn it except them. John, then, describes the 144,000 in three ways: (1) they have not defiled themselves with women for they are virgins, (2) they follow the Lamb wherever he goes, and (3) they have been redeemed from man as firstfruits for God and the Lamb.[96] Thus, the 144,000 have followed the Lamb through hardships and persecution and finally arrive at Mount Zion and stand with him (cf. 6:17).

Charles suggests a possible verbal connection with Luke 9:57. There, the context describes the cost of following Jesus in various ways, most notably Jesus's command to let the dead bury the dead, for "anyone who puts their hand to the plow and looks back is fit for the kingdom of God" (9:62). Yet, the apparent verbal connection with Rev 14:4 and Luke 9:57 is sufficiently weak. First, the contexts find no connection with one another. In Rev 14:4 the

---
94 Ibid.
95 Charles lists ὑπάγει.
96 The comment about defilement with women is connected to the Old Testament and Israel's description as a virgin (2 Kgs 19:21; Lam 2:13; Jer 18:13; Amos 5:2). Also, Paul exhorts the Corinthians that he is to present them to Christ as a pure virgin (2 Cor 11:2). These 144,000 are the promised bride of Christ who have kept themselves pure until his return (cf. 19:6–10). See also Keener, *Revelation*, 371.

144,000 are following Jesus wherever he goes; however, the one from Luke 9:57 does not follow him despite requesting to do so. Second, it is difficult to build a verbal connection primarily upon ἀκολουθέω (οἱ ἀκολουθοῦντες/ἀκολουθήσω) since the word frequently occurs in the New Testament. Disciples follow Jesus (Matt 4:20), crowds follow Jesus (Matt 8:1), tax collectors and sinners follow Jesus (Mark 2:15), and Jesus's sheep follow him (John 10:27). The harmony between the two references is minute and verbally weak and should be understood as having no verbal connection.

REVELATION 14:7; ACTS 4:24; 14:15

(14:7) λέγων ἐν φωνῇ μεγάλῃ· φοβήθητε τὸν θεὸν καὶ δότε αὐτῷ δόξαν, ὅτι ἦλθεν ἡ ὥρα τῆς κρίσεως αὐτοῦ, καὶ προσκυνήσατε τῷ ποιήσαντι τὸν οὐρανὸν καὶ τὴν γῆν καὶ θάλασσαν καὶ πηγὰς ὑδάτων.	(Acts 4:24) οἱ δὲ ἀκούσαντες ὁμοθυμαδὸν ἦραν φωνὴν πρὸς τὸν θεὸν καὶ εἶπαν· δέσποτα, σὺ ὁ ποιήσας τὸν οὐρανὸν καὶ τὴν γῆν καὶ τὴν θάλασσαν καὶ πάντα τὰ ἐν αὐτοῖς,
	(Acts 14:15) καὶ λέγοντες· ἄνδρες, τί ταῦτα ποιεῖτε; καὶ ἡμεῖς ὁμοιοπαθεῖς ἐσμεν ὑμῖν ἄνθρωποι εὐαγγελιζόμενοι ὑμᾶς ἀπὸ τούτων τῶν ματαίων ἐπιστρέφειν ἐπὶ θεὸν ζῶντα, ὃς ἐποίησεν τὸν οὐρανὸν καὶ τὴν γῆν καὶ τὴν θάλασσαν καὶ πάντα τὰ ἐν αὐτοῖς·

After the 144,000 are introduced to the reader, John turns his attention to an angel who flies directly overhead, proclaiming an eternal gospel to the earth-dwellers (14:6).[97] He proclaims loudly for the earth-dwellers to fear God and give him glory, and that the hour of his judgment has finally arrived. He also identifies God as the one who made heaven and earth and the sea (τῷ ποιήσαντι τὸν οὐρανὸν καὶ τὴν γῆν καὶ θάλασσαν), which shows the extent of his power upon the created order.[98]

There are two instances where this divine title is employed in the New Testament, and both appear to draw from Old Testament imagery. In Acts

---

97 The language John uses (those who dwell on earth) suggests this announcement is dedicated primarily to the earth-dwellers and not the Christians. A parallel can be found in 5:9 where the Lamb is said to have ransomed people from every "nation and tribe and language and people" like here, but it appears that this language is intended for the reader to see the scope of the dragon's influence upon the earth.

98 See Beale, *Revelation*, 754, who provides a comparison between Dan 4:34 LXX and Rev 14:6–7.

4:24, after Peter and John are released from prison (4:23), the two apostles report to their friends all that the chief priests and elders had said to them. The phrase ποιήσας τὸν οὐρανὸν καὶ τὴν γῆν καὶ τὴν θάλασσαν corresponds exactly to Ps 145:6 LXX, where the psalm "contrasts the inability of human rulers with the power of God as creator of the universe; he is the God of Jacob, who reigns forever and cares for the needy."[99] Darrell Bock remarks, "The mention of creation underscores the initial address, as this sovereign God is the one who made the heaven, earth, seas, and all that is in them. It is God's creation, and so God's lordship is the highest court of appeal."[100] Although the context of Acts 14:15 is different, the phrase is used in the same manner.

Between these two references the phrase is quoted almost verbatim, only differing with the tense of ποιέω. Beale provides a strong parallel with Dan 4:34, 37 LXX with this phrase, but this overlap does not diminish its verbal connection with Acts 4:24 and 14:15.[101] Furthermore, Aune notes that "the divine title 'the one who made the heaven and earth' occurs only here in Revelation, but it is a frequent designation for God in the OT ... and is used occasionally in early Christianity."[102] This verbal connection, then, should be viewed as clear.

REVELATION 17:14; MATTHEW 22:14

(17:14) οὗτοι μετὰ τοῦ ἀρνίου πολεμήσουσιν καὶ τὸ ἀρνίον νικήσει αὐτούς, ὅτι κύριος κυρίων ἐστὶν καὶ βασιλεὺς βασιλέων καὶ οἱ μετ' αὐτοῦ κλητοὶ καὶ ἐκλεκτοὶ καὶ πιστοί.	(Matt 22:14) πολλοὶ γάρ εἰσιν κλητοί, ὀλίγοι δὲ ἐκλεκτοί.

In Rev 17:1–18, John is shown a vision of the great prostitute who sits upon a scarlet beast, drunk with the blood of the martyrs of Jesus (17:7). This woman represents Babylon the Great, the "Mother of Prostitutes" (17:5), and she is a physical representation of Rome.[103] She leads the nations astray with her

---

99 I. Howard Marshall, "Acts" in *Commentary on the New Testament Use of the Old Testament*, ed. G. K. Beale and D. A. Carson (Baker, 2007), 552.
100 Darrell L. Bock, *Acts*, BECNT (Baker, 2007), 205.
101 Beale, *Revelation*, 751.
102 Aune, *Revelation 6–16*, 828.
103 The majority of commentaries cite Rome as Babylon. Mounce, *Revelation*, 308. Charles argues that "throughout the chapter [the judgment of the Great Harlot] is not referred to save once (in xvii. 16) and alike the vision in xvii. 3b–6 and its interpretation by the angel are concerned with the Beast, which according to the present form of the text symbolizes the demonic Nero, or Nero returning from the abyss to lead the Parthian powers against Rome." Charles, *Revelation*, 2:54. She also may symbolize the goddess Roma. See Richard Bauckham,

wickedness (17:2), but the nations take advantage of her for financial gain (18:3, 9). The harlot has accumulated great wealth and her opulence is seen by her attire: purple, scarlet, gold, jewels, pearls, and a golden cup full of her sexual immoralities (17:4). The angel explains to John that the woman is seated on seven heads that represent seven mountains (17:9), and these mountains are seven kings. The ten horns (cf. 13:1) are ten kings who will receive authority as kings with the beast for one hour, and their goal is to make war on the Lamb (17:14a; cf. Dan 7:21 LXX). However, the Lamb will conquer them, and those with him are called chosen and faithful (κλητοὶ καὶ ἐκλεκτοὶ καὶ πιστοί). These chosen and faithful ones, then, provide the answer to the earth-dwellers question in 13:4.

Matthew 22:1–14 contains the parable of the wedding feast which focuses upon the divine justice (22:11–14) and divine mercy (22:1–10) of God.[104] This parable "condemns the contempt with which Israel as a whole treats God's grace."[105] Thus, the parable is focused upon two groups of people, those that are called and not chosen and those that are both called and chosen (πολλοὶ γάρ εἰσιν κλητοί, ὀλίγοι δὲ ἐκλεκτοί).[106]

The comparison between Rev 17:14 and Matt 22:14 is focused primarily upon the theme of those who are called. In the parable of the wedding feast, the many represent those found in 22:3–6 who refused to attend the wedding feast, but the chosen ones are those found in the roads (22:9). However, the key verbal connection is ἐκλεκτοί, as κλητοί in both references are used differently. In Rev 17:14 it is used to represent the redeemed, those who follow the Lamb, and in Matt 22:14 it is used to identify those who attended the wedding feast. Both groups, then, have been chosen.

However, much like Rev 14:4 it is perhaps difficult to suggest that this verbal connection is clear. Ἐκλεκτός occurs frequently in the New Testament, as well as the LXX, suggesting a wide realm of meaning and usage.[107] Also, the contexts of both passages are different, with one that depicts the chosen following the Lamb (Rev 17:14) and the other as an explanatory statement of

---

The Climax of Prophecy: Studies on the Book of Revelation (T&T Clark, 1993), 343–350; David E. Aune, Revelation 17–22 (Thomas Nelson, 1998), 920–922; Beale, Revelation, 854; Bandy, "The Prophetic Lawsuit," 315.

104 "God is just in his wrath and judgment on those who flaunt his invitation and gracious in inviting both 'the bad and the good' (v. 10) to the messianic banquet." Osborne, Matthew, 796.

105 Carson, "Matthew," 456.

106 B. F. Meyer, "Many (= All) Are Called, but Few (= Not All) Are Chosen," NTS 36 (1990): 89–97. Quarles understands that γάρ functions as the reason for the exclusion of the man with no wedding garment. See Quarles, Matthew, 259.

107 Matt 22:14; 24:22, 24, 31; Mark 13:20, 22; 13:27; Luke 18:7; 23:35; Rom 8:33; 16:13; Col 3:12; 1 Tim 5:21; 2 Tim 2:10; Titus 1:1; 1 Pet 1:1; 2:4, 6, 9; 2 John 1, 13.

the parable (Matt 22:14). Thus, this verbal connection should be labeled as a probable connection.

Revelation 18:24; Luke 11:50

(18:24) καὶ ἐν αὐτῇ αἷμα προφητῶν καὶ ἁγίων εὑρέθη καὶ πάντων τῶν ἐσφαγμένων ἐπὶ τῆς γῆς.	(Luke 11:50) ἵνα ἐκζητηθῇ τὸ αἷμα πάντων τῶν προφητῶν τὸ ἐκκεχυμένον ἀπὸ καταβολῆς κόσμου ἀπὸ τῆς γενεᾶς ταύτης,

After the events of Rev 17, John hears an angel cry out "Fallen, fallen is Babylon the great" (18:1). This chapter focuses primarily upon the fall of Babylon with various descriptions of how she fell and who has betrayed her, and it is divided into three main movements. First, in 1–8 there is the proclamation of Babylon's fall. Second, in 9–20 the world mourns of her demise. Third, the finality of Babylon's judgment and fall is fully realized in 21–24. Another movement could possibly be found in 19:1–6 as a great multitude in heaven glorifies God over the judgments that were brought forth against Babylon. The earth-dwellers will mourn, weep, and wail at the judgment that is brought unto Babylon, their beloved city and provider of all things they need. There are primarily three sins that Babylon has committed, but the one emphasized is the murder of God's saints.[108] "Thus, this becomes not only the third reason but a separate indictment on its own, summarizing the emphasis on Babylon's martyrdom of the saints (6:9–11; 7:14; 11:7; 13:7, 15; 14:13; 16:6; 17:6; 19:2)."[109]

Luke 11:37–54 contains the woes to the Pharisees and Lawyers from Jesus, with the main focus that those who misinterpret God's word "leads to an empty religiosity that spills over into violence against those messengers from God who challenge it."[110] God, in his wisdom (11:49), declared he would send prophets and apostles, some of whom were killed, so that their blood, shed from before the foundation of the world, might judge this generation.

The martyrs are in view in Rev 18:24, and they are specifically identified as prophets and saints (προφητῶν καὶ ἁγίων εὑρέθη). The parallel in Luke 11:50 omits saints, but that is not in the immediate context of the final woe pronounced by Christ. In both instances there are prophets who have died, and Rev 18:24 provides a holistic view whereas Luke 11:50 is limited to the prophets

---

[108] As with the previous two sins that were introduced with the causal ὅτι, v 24 omits it and the tone shifts from second (18:22–23) back to third person (18:1–20). Osborne agrees. See Osborne, *Revelation*, 658–659.

[109] Ibid., 659.

[110] Garland, *Luke*, 489.

of the Old Testament. Other than prophets that provide a verbal connection between the two passages, there is little else to suggest a plausible verbal connection. Therefore, this verbal connection should be understood as probable since it appears to echo this source in concept.

REVELATION 19:7; MATTHEW 5:12

(19:7) χαίρωμεν καὶ ἀγαλλιῶμεν καὶ δώσωμεν τὴν δόξαν αὐτῷ, ὅτι ἦλθεν ὁ γάμος τοῦ ἀρνίου καὶ ἡ γυνὴ αὐτοῦ ἡτοίμασεν ἑαυτήν	(Matt 5:12) χαίρετε καὶ ἀγαλλιᾶσθε, ὅτι ὁ μισθὸς ὑμῶν πολὺς ἐν τοῖς οὐρανοῖς· οὕτως γὰρ ἐδίωξαν τοὺς προφήτας τοὺς πρὸ ὑμῶν.

Babylon has been destroyed in Rev 18, and now there is great rejoicing in Rev 19:1–5. Revelation 19:6–10 presents the climax of Christ and his church, the marriage supper of the Lamb.[111] The praise of "Hallelujah" rings forth (19:6) from a great multitude as they announce the omnipotent reign of God. They further declare that those who were invited to this marriage supper should rejoice and be glad (χαίρωμεν καὶ ἀγαλλιῶμεν) as the Bride has made herself ready by clothing herself with fine linen, bright and pure.[112]

In Matt 5:2–12, Jesus has just concluded his first main portion of the Sermon on the Mount. After he notes several ways in which God's people are blessed (Μακάριοι), he concludes this account by exhorting his hearers to rejoice and be glad (χαίρετε καὶ ἀγαλλιᾶσθε) even in the midst of intense persecution. The force of this statement by Jesus is felt in the imperatives as they are "in the present tense and thus command continual joy and gladness."[113]

In these two instances, the evidence suggests an intentional verbal connection. First, both χαίρω and ἀγαλλιάω never appear together in the New Testament nor the LXX outside of these two examples. Second, Christ commanded his hearers in Matt 5:12 to rejoice in the midst of persecution because their reward is great in heaven. The reward is then realized in Rev 19:7 at this marriage supper with the Lamb. Furthermore, the remnant upon the earth have experienced great persecution by the unholy trinity throughout Revelation, so the encouragement by Christ to χαίρετε καὶ ἀγαλλιᾶσθε and the reward to come would also apply to them. Therefore, this verbal connect should be understood as a clear connection.

---

111 For a description of the wedding garment and Old Testament background, see Beale, *Revelation*, 934–944.

112 It is not until Rev 21 that the reader understands the Bride is the New Jerusalem. See Hoskins, *The Book of Revelation*, 366–367.

113 Quarles, *The Sermon on the Mount*, 74.

REVELATION 19:9;[114] LUKE 14:16–17

| (19:9) Καὶ λέγει μοι· γράψον· **μακάριοι οἱ εἰς τὸ δεῖπνον τοῦ γάμου τοῦ ἀρνίου κεκλημένοι.** καὶ λέγει μοι· οὗτοι οἱ λόγοι ἀληθινοὶ τοῦ θεοῦ εἰσιν. | (Luke 14:16–17) 16 Ὁ δὲ εἶπεν αὐτῷ· ἄνθρωπός τις ἐποίει **δεῖπνον** μέγα, καὶ ἐκάλεσεν πολλοὺς 17 καὶ ἀπέστειλεν τὸν δοῦλον αὐτοῦ τῇ ὥρᾳ τοῦ δείπνου εἰπεῖν τοῖς **κεκλημένοις**· ἔρχεσθε, ὅτι ἤδη ἕτοιμά ἐστιν. |

After John hears of the declaration for the marriage supper of the Lamb and his bride, he is told by an angel to write, "Blessed are those who are called (οἱ κεκλημένοι) to the marriage supper (εἰς τὸ δεῖπνον) of the Lamb." Those who are called are those identified in 17:14, as evidenced by the usage of ἐκλεκτοὶ in 17:14. These called ones are blessed, as indicated by 19:7. In Luke 14:16–17 Jesus tells the parable of the great banquet where a man gave a great banquet (δεῖπνον) and invited many.[115] Evidently these people accepted, for he sent his servants to get those whom were called (τοῖς κεκλημένοις).

The parallels between Rev 19:9 and Luke 14:16–17 are evident when one considers the context and verbal connections. Both texts focus specifically upon the feast (δεῖπνον). The term δεῖπνον carries with it the understanding of a formal meal in which it is a dinner of celebration.[116] Both texts suggest this type of elaborate meal prepared for all who would attend (Luke 14:16–17); however, it is only those who were called (Rev 19:9; cf. 17:14) that will attend. Yet, this verbal connection is best viewed as a probable connection, since Rev 19:9 includes the idea and wording of Luke 14:16–17.

REVELATION 21:10; MATTHEW 4:8

| (21:10) καὶ ἀπήνεγκέν με ἐν πνεύματι ἐπὶ **ὄρος μέγα καὶ ὑψηλόν**, καὶ ἔδειξέν μοι τὴν πόλιν τὴν ἁγίαν Ἰερουσαλὴμ καταβαίνουσαν ἐκ τοῦ οὐρανοῦ ἀπὸ τοῦ θεοῦ. | (Matt 4:8) Πάλιν παραλαμβάνει αὐτὸν ὁ διάβολος εἰς **ὄρος ὑψηλὸν λίαν** καὶ δείκνυσιν αὐτῷ πάσας τὰς βασιλείας τοῦ κόσμου καὶ τὴν δόξαν αὐτῶν. |

Revelation 21:9–27 introduces the reader to the New Jerusalem, who is the Bride and wife of the Lamb (cf. 19:7).[117] After John listens to the voice of one

---

114 For the context of Rev 19:9, see the section of Rev 19:7 and Matt 5:12.

115 Luke's account differs from Matthew's (Matt 22:1–14) in several ways. For a comparison, see Carson, "Matthew," 455–456; Hagner, *Matthew 14–28*, 626–629; Bock, *Luke 9:51–24:53*, 1268–1271.

116 So BDAG, δεῖπνον. BDAG also shows an apparent connection between Rev 19:9 and Luke 14:16.

117 See also the verbal parallel between Rev 21:9–10 and Rev 17:1, 3.

of the seven angels who had one of the seven bowls, he is carried away in the Spirit to a great and high mountain (ἐπὶ ὄρος μέγα καὶ ὑψηλόν) and the angel showed him (ἔδειξέν μοι) the holy city coming down out of heaven from God.

Matthew 4:1–11 depicts the temptation of Jesus by Satan in the wilderness.[118] After Jesus successfully thwarts the devil's temptation to utilize his Messiahship in an inappropriate way (3–7), the devil takes Jesus to a very high mountain (εἰς ὄρος ὑψηλὸν λίαν) in order to tempt Jesus to worship him.[119] Donald Hagner also notes that the mountain(s) function in Matthew's Gospel primarily as a revelatory location, notably either with a teaching or healing ministry of Jesus.[120]

The parallels between Rev 21:10 and Matt 4:8 focus primarily upon the mountain. Jesus is lead up to a high mountain and shown the kingdoms of the world, while John is lead to a high mountain and watches the New Jerusalem descend from God. Yet, the language and context are too different for there to be a plausible connection between Rev 21:10 and Matt 4:8; thus, there is no verbal connection between these texts.

Concluding Observations

The analysis of Revelation's possible usage of the Synoptic Gospels and Acts has revealed several observations. First, of the twenty-seven examples listed by Charles, the results varied as to whether the examples were clear, probable, possible, or no verbal connection. Of the twenty-nine examples provided, sixteen were determined to be clear, five probable, one possible, and seven that were unlikely or provided no verbal connection.[121]

Clear	Probable	Possible	Unlikely/No
1:1, 1:7, 16; 2:7, 20; 3:3, 5 (Matt 10:32; Luke 12:8); 6:10, 12–13, 15–16, 17; 11:3, 6, 15; 13:11; 14:7; 19:7	1:3 (Luke 11:28); 12:9; 17:14; 18:24; 19:9	5:5	1:3 (Matt 26:18), 1:7 (2 Cor 1:20); 3:5 (1 Cor 16:9); 6:4; 9:20; 14:4; 21:10

Figure 4.1: Categorization of Revelation's Possible Use of the Synoptic Gospels and Acts

---

118 It is worth noting that in Rev 21:9 and Matt 4:1 both John and Jesus are carried away by the Spirit.

119 For parallels between Jesus and Old Testament figures, see Donald Hagner, *Matthew 1–13*, WBC (Thomas Nelson, 1993), 68.

120 Ibid., 86.

121 Technically, there are twenty-seven possible occurrences. However, there were two instances, Rev 1:7 with 2 Cor 1:20 and Rev 3:5 with 1 Cor 6:9, that provided no verbal connection with a Pauline letter but did with a synoptic Gospel.

The above table shows the high probability that John may have been familiar with certain texts of the Synoptic Gospels and Acts, as well as some Pauline Epistles.[122] Thus, one can conclude that John expected that his readers are familiar with the Synoptic Gospels and Acts. By making these apparent verbal connections to key passages from the Synoptics and Acts, John seems to intend for his readers to remember New Testament themes and see their fulfillment within Revelation.

Second, as John does not explain the Old Testament imagery and allusions found within Revelation, the suggested verbal connections from the Synoptics and Acts appear to function in the same way. In other words, John simply believed that the reader of Revelation would be familiar with various New Testament texts. As such, he appears to leave various keys of interpretation for Revelation through the verbal connections.

Beale's model for determining the allusions of the New Testament in Revelation has provided a helpful model for determining the possible verbal connections between Revelation and the Synoptic Gospels and Acts. These verbal connections, then, suggests a particular reading strategy for Revelation. Once the connections are examined for the Pauline and Catholic Epistles, then one is able to conclude that there is a reading strategy for Revelation given its location within the canon.

---

[122] These examples are dealt with in the next chapter.

CHAPTER 5

REVELATION'S USAGE OF THE PAULINE AND CATHOLIC EPISTLES

INTRODUCTION

In chapter four, the argument was presented that the author of Revelation utilized various passages from the Synoptic Gospels and Acts in his work. These examples were analyzed using Beale's model for determining the strength of various Old Testament images within Revelation. The three categories are clear, probable, and possible. Adding to Beale's categories a fourth category, that of unlikely or no connection present, was necessary considering the aspects of this work. The strategy employed in the fourth chapter will continue within this chapter. Each example, as provided by Charles, are examined verbally and contextually in order to determine a possible connection. Furthermore, this chapter is divided into two main sections, that of the Pauline Epistles and those of the Catholic Epistles. Dividing the chapter in this manner affords the opportunity to examine the possible influence of the canon upon Revelation's usage of the respective epistolary section.

THE PAULINE EPISTLES

The Pauline Epistles constitute the second largest collection of possible verbal connection by John in Revelation. Of the fifteen connections by R. H. Charles, Colossians is referenced six times, 2 Corinthians five times, Ephesians four times, 1 Corinthians and 1 Thessalonians twice, and Galatians and 1 Timothy once.[1] There is one instance in which a Pauline Epistle overlaps with material from a Catholic Epistle (Rev 2:9; 2 Cor 6:10; Jas 2:5). This material, in similar vein with chapter four, has been kept together per the outline of Charles.

---

1 In this section, 2 Corinthians appears four times and 1 Thessalonians once. This total is calculated by the combination of these references with Chapter Four.

Revelation 1:4; Colossians 1:2

(1:4) Ἰωάννης ταῖς ἑπτὰ ἐκκλησίαις ταῖς ἐν τῇ Ἀσίᾳ· χάρις ὑμῖν καὶ εἰρήνη ἀπὸ ὁ ὢν καὶ ὁ ἦν καὶ ὁ ἐρχόμενος καὶ ἀπὸ τῶν ἑπτὰ πνευμάτων ἃ ἐνώπιον τοῦ θρόνου αὐτοῦ	(Col 1:2) τοῖς ἐν Κολοσσαῖς ἁγίοις καὶ πιστοῖς ἀδελφοῖς ἐν Χριστῷ, χάρις ὑμῖν καὶ εἰρήνη ἀπὸ θεοῦ πατρὸς ἡμῶν. (cf. Rom 1:7; 1 Cor 1:3; 2 Cor 1:2; Gal 1:3; Eph 1:2; Phil 1:2; 1 Thess 1:1; 2 Thess 1:2; Phlm 3)

John begins the epistolary section of his work by addressing the seven churches in Asia (chps. 2–3) as the recipients of his letter. He begins with the customary greeting of grace to you and peace (χάρις ὑμῖν καὶ εἰρήνη) followed by the identity of the one who wishes grace and peace, God (ἀπὸ ὁ ὢν καὶ ὁ ἦν καὶ ὁ ἐρχόμενος) and the seven spirits before his throne (cf. Rev 3:1; 4:5). Thus, at the outset of his work the apostle brings forth a Trinitarian theology.[2]

The greeting χάρις ὑμῖν καὶ εἰρήνη is found throughout the New Testament epistles and is not simply limited to Col 1:2.[3] Elsewhere, the phrase is found in Rom 1:7; 1 Cor 1:3; 2 Cor 1:2; Gal 1:3; Eph 1:2; Phil 1:2; 1 Thess 1:1; 2 Thess 1:2; and Phlm 3.[4] Furthermore, Titus 1:4 does not contain ὑμῖν, but is otherwise identical to Rev 1:4, and the phrase likewise occurs 1 Pet 1:2; 2 Pet 1:2. Jude 2 substitutes χάρις for ἔλεος, but the phrase is still closely paralleled. In every instance, the phrase introduces the epistle in much the same way that Rev 1:4 introduces the work as a whole.

The significant correlation between Rev 1:4 and several other epistles suggests intentionality of the part of John. Although it can be argued that the phrase is the typical greeting for the historical epistolary genre, and Revelation does share some aspects of an epistolary genre, this argument should not exclude the possible intentionality on the part of John. Excluding an intentionality on the part of John, Matthew Emerson argues such an exclusion disregards "the fact that the Holy Spirit has inspired the writers in such a way as to use similar, if not identical, structure and language."[5] Emerson believes

---

2 See Richard Bauckham, *The Theology of the Book of Revelation* (Cambridge University Press, 1993), 23–25. Grant Osborne, *Revelation*, BECNT (Baker, 2006), 59. See also Brandon D. Smith, "Vision of the Triune God: Reading Revelation through the Father, Son, and Spirit," PhD diss., (Ridley College Melbourne, 2020).

3 See the helpful study by T. Y. Mullins, "Greeting as a New Testament Form," *JBL* 87 (1968): 418–426.

4 "This distinctively Christian formula is related to the traditional Gk. greeting (χαῖρε or χαίρειν, 'greetings!') and the customary Jewish greeting (šālôm, 'peace!')." Murray J. Harris, *Colossians and Philemon*, EGGNT (Broadman and Holman, 2010), 9. F. F. Bruce believes that the change from the normal "grace and peace" is "amplified to χάρις ἔλεος εἰρήνη" in the 1 and 2 Timothy. See F. F. Bruce, *The Epistles to the Colossians, to Philemon, and to the Ephesians*, NICNT (Eerdmans, 1984), 39n4.

5 Matthew Y. Emerson, *Christ and the New Creation: A Canonical Approach to the Theolo-*

that this intentionality on the part of John indicates that Revelation is read as the climax of the New Testament.⁶ Thus, this verbal connection is clear.

Revelation 1:5; Colossians 1:18

(1:5) καὶ ἀπὸ Ἰησοῦ Χριστοῦ, ὁ μάρτυς, ὁ πιστός, ὁ **πρωτότοκος τῶν νεκρῶν** καὶ ὁ ἄρχων τῶν βασιλέων τῆς γῆς. Τῷ ἀγαπῶντι ἡμᾶς καὶ λύσαντι ἡμᾶς ἐκ τῶν ἁμαρτιῶν ἡμῶν ἐν τῷ αἵματι αὐτοῦ.	(Col 1:18) καὶ αὐτός ἐστιν ἡ κεφαλὴ τοῦ σώματος τῆς ἐκκλησίας· ὅς ἐστιν ἀρχή, **πρωτότοκος ἐκ τῶν νεκρῶν**, ἵνα γένηται ἐν πᾶσιν αὐτὸς πρωτεύων.

The greeting from Rev 1:4 continues into v 5 and brings forth the fullness of the Trinitarian greeting. This traditional greeting "precedes the normal beginning, and the greeting itself goes beyond the norm: in 1:4–5a there is a Trinitarian formula, and in the doxology of 1:5b–6 John goes beyond custom to build a case for the soteriological (v. 5b) and ecclesiological (v. 6) core of the book."⁷ Thus, the letter is from the Father and the Holy Spirit, identified as the seven spirits (1:4), and from the Son himself. John identifies Jesus in three distinct manners: (1) the faithful witness, (2) the firstborn from the dead (ὁ πρωτότοκος τῶν νεκρῶν), and (3) the ruler of the kings of the earth. This three-part introduction to Jesus interprets three events from the life of Jesus: (1) his death upon the cross, (2) his resurrection, and (3) his exaltation.⁸

The Christological hymn of Col 1:15–20 is perhaps the most famous portion of this letter.⁹ This hymn, widely debated as to its purpose, focuses on several Christological themes in its three-fold division.¹⁰ Within these themes, Paul remarks that Christ is the firstborn from the dead (πρωτότοκος ἐκ τῶν νεκρῶν), which parallels an earlier expression of Paul in Rom 8:29 (πρωτότοκον ἐν πολλοῖς ἀδελφοῖς). The point made by Paul in Col 1:18 signifies that Christ, who previously died, will never die again (cf. Rom 6:9).

---

gy of the New Testament (Wipf and Stock, 2013), 144. See also David Aune, *Revelation 1–5*, WBC (Thomas Nelson, 1997), 26–28; Craig R. Koester, *Revelation* (Yale, 2014), 215.

6 Emerson, *Christ and the New Creation*, 143–144.

7 Osborne, *Revelation*, 59.

8 Paul Hoskins, *The Book of Revelation: A Theological and Exegetical Commentary* (ChristoDoulos Publications, 2017), 52.

9 Per Douglas J. Moo, *The Letter to the Colossians and to Philemon* (Eerdmans, 2008), 107. For the argument that this section is a hymn, see J. M. Robinson, "A Formal Analysis of Colossians 1:15–20," *JBL* 76 (1957): 270–287. See also Bruce Francis Vawter, "The Colossians Hymn and the Principle of Redaction," *CBQ* 33 (1971): 62–81.

10 Bruce believes this hymn "occupies this position because an intelligent appreciation of the doctrine of Christ is the best safeguard against most forms of heretical teaching, and certainly against that which was currently threatening the peace of the Colossian Christians." Bruce, *The Epistles to the Colossians, to Philemon, and to the Ephesians*, 55.

For both John and Paul, the emphasis centers upon the claim that Jesus is the firstborn from the dead.[11] In both instances πρωτότοκος is employed, and the only distinction made appears to be temporal. In Col 1:18, Christ is the firstborn from the dead (ἐκ τῶν νεκρῶν), whereas Rev 1:14 he is simply the firstborn *of* the dead (τῶν νεκρῶν). Murray J. Harris notes this distinction well when he writes that "πρωτότοκος may refer to both time and status, here only temporal priority is signified, since the word is followed by ἐκ τῶν νεκρῶν, and not simply τῶν νεκρῶν (as in Rev 1:5, where both time and status may be denoted."[12] Charles agrees, noting that in the Pauline passages "the sense of being first in point of time appears in certain passages to be displaced wholly by the secondary idea of Sovereignty," and that Rev 1:5 requires the meaning of πρωτότοκος to reflect the idea of his sovereignty.[13] The point of Rev 1:14, then, is to recognize both the Pauline truth that Christ was raised from the dead and that he now exercises his sovereign authority over the kings of the earth, which is a theme that appears frequently in Revelation. Thus, this verbal connection is clear both thematically and verbally.

REVELATION 1:5; GALATIANS 2:20

(1:5) καὶ ἀπὸ Ἰησοῦ Χριστοῦ, ὁ μάρτυς, ὁ πιστός, ὁ πρωτότοκος τῶν νεκρῶν καὶ ὁ ἄρχων τῶν βασιλέων τῆς γῆς. Τῷ ἀγαπῶντι ἡμᾶς καὶ λύσαντι ἡμᾶς ἐκ τῶν ἁμαρτιῶν ἡμῶν ἐν τῷ αἵματι αὐτοῦ,	(Gal 2:20) ζῶ δὲ οὐκέτι ἐγώ, ζῇ δὲ ἐν ἐμοὶ Χριστός· ὃ δὲ νῦν ζῶ ἐν σαρκί, ἐν πίστει ζῶ τῇ τοῦ υἱοῦ τοῦ θεοῦ τοῦ ἀγαπήσαντός με καὶ παραδόντος ἑαυτὸν ὑπὲρ ἐμοῦ.

The second possible verbal connection that Charles sees in Rev 1:5 is centered upon the phrase "to him who loves us" (Τῷ ἀγαπῶντι ἡμᾶς).[14] G. K. Beale sees a connection between Ps 88 (89 LXX) in that John meditates upon the connection between the kingship of Christ and his royal lineage which causes "the writer to break into a doxology beginning with the phrase τῷ ἀγαπῶντι ἡμᾶς ... and continuing through v 6."[15] This type of doxology, beginning with the dative τῷ (*dativus commodi*), only appears in three other place in the New Testament: Rom 16:25–27, Eph 3:20–21, and Jude 24–25.[16]

---

11 "Royal connotations are evident in Colossians, where Christ is 'the firstborn of the dead' and has the 'first place in everything' (Col 1:18; cf. Heb 1:6)." Koester, *Revelation*, 217.
12 Harris, *Colossians and Philemon*, 44.
13 R. H. Charles, *A Critical and Exegetical Commentary on Revelation of St. John*, ICC (T&T Clark, 1985), 1:14.
14 For the context of Rev 1:5, see the previous section.
15 G. K. Beale, *Revelation*, NIGTC (Eerdmans, 1999), 191.
16 Aune, *Revelation 1–5*, 45–46.

In Gal 2:15–21 Paul transitions from a series of rebukes (2:1–14) to an exposition on the nature of the Gospel itself. Paul continues his address to Peter in Gal 2:15–21 by noting, among other things, that doing the works of the law never justifies (2:16) and the restoring of the law as the basis for one's standing before God would condemn the people as sinners (2:18).[17] The new life is not obtained by works of the law but by faith (2:19), and now the believer lives both in the flesh and by faith in "the Son of God who loved me (τῇ τοῦ υἱοῦ τοῦ θεοῦ τοῦ ἀγαπήσαντός με) and gave his life for me." The participial phrase τοῦ ἀγαπήσαντός is one of two parallel phrases that describe "the Son of God," and the apostle "rarely refers to Christ's love for us (Rom. 8:37)."[18]

For his doxology, John appears to draw from Gal 2:20 and includes the theme of Christ loving the church. A similar participial construction is found in Gal 2:20, albeit in a different case and with a different object of Christ's love. Koester remarks, "Revelation sees Christ's love being expressed in his death but here uses the present tense to convey the ongoing love that the risen Christ shows."[19] Regardless, the emphasis in Gal 2:20 is upon the two participles that describe the Son of God loving (ἀγαπήσαντός) and giving himself (παραδόντος ἑαυτὸν) specifically for Paul (ὑπὲρ ἐμοῦ).

However, it may be more appropriate to include the other instances in which τῷ ἀγαπῶντι ἡμᾶς is used in order to strengthen the verbal connection. The phrase also occurs in John 14:21; Rom 8:37; 2 Thess 3:16 and, with the exception of John 14:21, all explicitly focus on Christ's love for the believer. However, Gal 2:20 and 2 Thess 3:16 also find the parallel with Christ giving himself for believers which, though the words are different, also find a connection with the second portion of Rev 1:5. Therefore, the verbal connection between Rev 1:5 and Gal 2:20 is a clear connection.

REVELATION 1:18; 2 CORINTHIANS 6:9

(1:18) καὶ ὁ ζῶν, καὶ ἐγενόμην νεκρὸς καὶ ἰδοὺ ζῶν εἰμι εἰς τοὺς αἰῶνας τῶν αἰώνων καὶ ἔχω τὰς κλεῖς τοῦ θανάτου καὶ τοῦ ᾅδου.	(2 Cor 6:9) ὡς ἀγνοούμενοι καὶ ἐπιγινωσκόμενοι, ὡς ἀποθνήσκοντες καὶ ἰδοὺ ζῶμεν, ὡς παιδευόμενοι καὶ μὴ θανατούμενοι,

Revelation 1:17–20 is part of the larger section of 1:9–20 in which John has the heavenly vision of the Son of Man.[20] After John turns to see the Son of Man

---

17 Thomas R. Schreiner, *Galatians*, ZECNT (Zondervan, 2010), 153.
18 Douglas J. Moo, *Galatians*, BECNT (Baker, 2013), 172. Although, see Eph 5:2, 25; 2 Thess 3:16.
19 Koester, *Revelation*, 217.
20 For the context of 1:9–16, see the discussion of Rev 1:16 and Matt 17:2 in Chapter Four.

(cf. Dan 7:13–14), he falls at his feet as if he were a dead man (1:17), only to have Christ tell him not to fear for he is the living one who was dead but is now alive (νεκρὸς καὶ ἰδοὺ ζῶν).

2 Corinthians 6:3–10 provides an abrupt change of tone from 2 Cor 5:14–6:2 in that "Paul shifts from a call for the Corinthians to be reconciled to God, to a catalog of his credentials as an apostle."[21] He highlights several facets of his journey as an apostle in order to contrast the opponents (cf. 3:1–3; 6:14–7:1) and show the sacrifices that he endured in light of his divine call.[22] Among those sacrifices is "as dying, and behold, we live" (ἀποθνῄσκοντες καὶ ἰδοὺ ζῶμεν). Ralph P. Martin helpfully navigates through Paul's "paradoxical rhetoric" and notes the various times Paul was exposed to the "perils of death (Acts 14:19; 1 Cor 15:30; 2 Cor 1:8, 9; 11:23–26)," as well as under a death penalty (1 Cor 4:9).[23] Yet, there appears more to what Paul means here rather than simply experiencing the perils of death or escaping a death penalty. Frequently in the Pauline Epistles Paul cites various theological implications, such as Gal 2:20 ("I no longer live, but Christ lives in me"). Martin concludes that "Paul was constantly aware of death (noted by [the] present participle) but God's power for triumph over death was also known to the apostle.[24]

This same argument could be suggested as a parallel with Rev 1:18, that Christ died but is living, as indicated by ζῶν. One could say that just as Christ has died and is alive forevermore, the believer will also be one day. However, this argument is weak and establishes the believer in the place of Paul in 2 Cor 6:9. Furthermore, contextually 2 Cor 6:9 shares more parallel with Ps 118:17–18 (117:17–18 LXX) as attested below.[25]

2 Cor 6:9	Ps 117:17–18
ἀποθνῄσκοντες καὶ ἰδοὺ ζῶμεν	οὐκ ἀποθανοῦμαι, ἀλλὰ ζήσομαι
As *dying* and behold, we live	I will not *die*, but I shall *live*

Thus, this verbal connection between Rev 1:18 and 2 Cor 6:9 is probable as it merely echoes the possible source of 2 Cor 6:9 only thematically.

---

21 George H. Guthrie, *2 Corinthians*, BECNT (Baker, 2015), 321.
22 Andreas J. Köstenberger, L. Scott Kellum, Charles L. Quarles, *The Cradle, the Cross, and the Crown: An Introduction to the New Testament*, 2nd ed. (B&H Academic, 2016), 574.
23 Ralph P. Martin, *2 Corinthians*, WBC (Thomas Nelson, 1986), 181.
24 Ibid., 182.
25 Guthrie, *2 Corinthians*, 336.

Revelation 2:9; 2 Corinthians 6:10; James 2:5

(2:9) οἶδά σου τὴν θλῖψιν καὶ τὴν πτωχείαν, ἀλλὰ πλούσιος εἶ, καὶ τὴν βλασφημίαν ἐκ τῶν λεγόντων Ἰουδαίους εἶναι ἑαυτοὺς καὶ οὐκ εἰσὶν ἀλλὰ συναγωγὴ τοῦ σατανᾶ.	(2 Cor 6:10) ὡς λυπούμενοι ἀεὶ δὲ χαίροντες, ὡς πτωχοὶ πολλοὺς δὲ πλουτίζοντες, ὡς μηδὲν ἔχοντες καὶ πάντα κατέχοντες. (Jas 2:5) Ἀκούσατε, ἀδελφοί μου ἀγαπητοί· οὐχ ὁ θεὸς ἐξελέξατο τοὺς πτωχοὺς τῷ κόσμῳ πλουσίους ἐν πίστει καὶ κληρονόμους τῆς βασιλείας ἧς ἐπηγγείλατο τοῖς ἀγαπῶσιν αὐτόν;

In Rev 2:8–11, Jesus addresses the church of Smyrna, and this church is one of two churches that does not receive a rebuke from the Lord. Rather, they receive only encouragement together with an exhortation not to fear the persecution that will arrive soon (2:10). As is customary of every letter to the seven churches in Asia, Jesus states that he knows (οἶδά σου) their persecution and their supposed poverty (τὴν πτωχείαν), for he contrasts their poverty by claiming that they are rich (ἀλλὰ πλούσιος εἶ). Mounce believes their poverty was materialistic, as it was difficult "for a Christian to make a living, and thus many were economically destitute ... spiritually they were rich."[26]

Charles believes there are two possible verbal connections with Rev 2:9. The first is 2 Cor 6:10, where the apostle Paul remarks that "as poor, but making many rich."[27] Clearly, since the apostle Paul did not maintain possession of many worldly goods, then the poverty and riches he mentions must be a spiritual richness (cf. Phil 3:8; 4:19; Eph 1:7; 2:7, 8; 3:8).[28] Paul "possessed and shared the riches of the Gospel" with the Corinthians, and any who would listen to his message.[29]

The second possible verbal connection is to Jas 2:5 where, in 2:1–13, James discusses the sin of favoritism amongst the people of God. After providing an illustration of what the recipients of his letter may be doing in their gatherings (2:1–4), he reminds the readers that God has chosen the poor in the world to be rich in faith (τοὺς πτωχοὺς τῷ κόσμῳ πλουσίους ἐν πίστει).[30] Chris A. Vlachos rightfully suggests that τῷ κόσμῳ is a dative of respect and that

---

26 Robert H. Mounce, *Revelation*, NICNT (Eerdmans, 1997), 74.

27 For the context of 2 Cor 6, see the previous section.

28 In 2 Cor 8–9 the apostle Paul discusses, at length, the literal giving from the church in Macedonia (8:1) and collections taken for Christians in Jerusalem (9:1–5). It appears that 2 Cor 6:10, and the surrounding context of 2 Cor 6, lays the groundwork for Paul's argument in 2 Cor 8–9; however, it does not negate the spiritual wealth of this present situation.

29 Martin, *2 Corinthians*, 184. Also, Philip E. Hughes, "Having learnt that it is not according to human resources but 'according to His riches in glory in Christ Jesus' that God supplies our every need (Phil. 4:19), he considered no man richer than himself." Philip E. Hughes, *The Second Epistle to the Corinthians* (Eerdmans, 1962), 236.

30 "Present faith and future hope reinforce each other." Koester, *Revelation*, 274.

πλουσίους serves as an appositive to τοὺς πτωχοὺς and describes "what God intends for the poor."[31] The poor here are contrasted to the rich from 2:2–3, and the purpose of this comparison is to show that the materially poor are rich in faith.[32]

In both 2 Cor 6:10 and Jas 2:5, there appears to be a clear verbal connection to Rev 2:9. Paul, in 2 Cor 6:10, declares that he makes many rich and, as this brief survey showed, this statement should be taken to reference a spiritual wealth. The same occurs in Jas 2:5, where James declares that it is the poor who are to be rich in faith, and the comparison is between the rich materially in 2:1–3. As was shown in Rev 2:9, the church of Smyrna claimed to be poor, but Christ declared they were rich, implying that their faith is what made them wealthy.[33] These verbal connections, then, are clear.

Revelation 2:24; 1 Corinthians 2:10

(2:24) ὑμῖν δὲ λέγω τοῖς λοιποῖς τοῖς ἐν Θυατείροις, ὅσοι οὐκ ἔχουσιν τὴν διδαχὴν ταύτην, οἵτινες οὐκ ἔγνωσαν τὰ βαθέα τοῦ σατανᾶ ὡς λέγουσιν· οὐ βάλλω ἐφ' ὑμᾶς ἄλλο βάρος,	(1 Cor 2:10) ἡμῖν δὲ ἀπεκάλυψεν ὁ θεὸς διὰ τοῦ πνεύματος· τὸ γὰρ πνεῦμα πάντα ἐραυνᾷ, καὶ τὰ βάθη τοῦ θεοῦ.

Jesus concludes his rebuke to the church in Thyatira in 2:23, and 2:24 begins his brief exhortation to those who do not hold to the teaching of Jezebel (2:20).[34] To these people, Jesus declares that he will not lay any other burden upon them for they have rejected the "depths of Satan" (τὰ βαθέα τοῦ σατανᾶ). The term βάθος is used in the Gospels as a reference to both the depth of soil (Matt 13:5; Mark 4:5), and of water (Luke 5:4). Paul uses the term in reference to all creation (Rom 8:39), the knowledge of God (Rom 11:33), poverty (2 Cor 8:2), and the riches of God's glory (Eph 3:18).

In 1 Cor 2:10 Paul appears to use βάθος in a similar way as he did in Rom 11:33 and Eph 3:18. Here, Paul discusses the "secret and hidden wisdom of God" (1 Cor 2:7) as what is imparted unto the Corinthians, and he compares this secret wisdom with what the "rulers of this age understood" (1 Cor 2:8). 1 Corinthians 2:10–13 reveals the essential point that the hidden wisdom of

---

[31] Chris A. Vlachos, *James*, EGGNT (B&H Academic, 2013), 72–73.
[32] Douglas J. Moo, *The Letter of James*, PNTC (Eerdmans, 2000), 105.
[33] Aune understands this wealth to be eschatological. See Aune, *Revelation 1–5*, 161.
[34] For the context of Rev 2:18–29 see "Revelation 2:20, 24–25; Acts 15:28–29" in Chapter Four.

God is revealed by the Spirit of God.³⁵ It is the Spirit, then, that reveals the depths of God (τὰ βάθη τοῦ θεοῦ).³⁶

The contexts of Rev 2:24 and 1 Cor 2:10 are reversed, and the central word τὰ βαθέα is used in strikingly different ways. In Rev 2:24 it is utilized in the realm of Satanic teaching, which connects τὰ βαθέα τοῦ σατανᾶ to the teaching of Jezebel in 2:20. Yet, in 1 Cor 2:8 τὰ βάθη focuses upon the depths of God; that is, the hidden message of the gospel as it is revealed through the work of the Holy Spirit. Contextually the word is used differently, and even throughout the New Testament it varies in range of meaning.³⁷

But there appears to be a probable connection between the two references. First, the discussion is focused on the "depth" of things, and in both instances it is either to the teachings of Satan (Rev 2:24) or to the teaching of the Gospel (1 Cor 2:10).³⁸ Second, the church of Thyatira has apparently two communities within it: those who follow Jezebel and those who follow God. The followers of Jezebel have not received τὰ βάθη τοῦ θεοῦ, but rather τὰ βαθέα τοῦ σατανᾶ. The contrast between the verses is a probable connection, since it includes the wording, since it is linguistically constructed as a genitive phrase, even though the object of the genitive is different in the two examples.

REVELATION 3:14; COLOSSIANS 1:18, 15

| (3:14) Καὶ τῷ ἀγγέλῳ τῆς ἐν Λαοδικείᾳ ἐκκλησίας γράψον· Τάδε λέγει ὁ ἀμήν, ὁ μάρτυς ὁ πιστὸς καὶ ἀληθινός, ἡ ἀρχὴ τῆς κτίσεως τοῦ θεοῦ· | (Col 1:18) καὶ αὐτός ἐστιν ἡ κεφαλὴ τοῦ σώματος τῆς ἐκκλησίας· ὅς ἐστιν ἀρχή, πρωτότοκος ἐκ τῶν νεκρῶν, ἵνα γένηται ἐν πᾶσιν αὐτὸς πρωτεύων, (Col 1:15) ὅς ἐστιν εἰκὼν τοῦ θεοῦ τοῦ ἀοράτου, πρωτότοκος πάσης κτίσεως, |

Revelation 3:14 identifies Laodicea as the final church to be addressed before John begins the narrative of his Apocalypse. As customary in the previous six churches, Jesus identifies his recipient (to the angel of the church in "X") and then describes part of his Christological nature that normally is found in the Old Testament or, as in 2:1 and even here, may be found in the opening chapter of Revelation.³⁹ In 3:14 Jesus identifies himself Τάδε λέγει ὁ ἀμήν, ὁ μάρτυς

---

35 Richard B. Hays, *1 Corinthians* (Westminster John Knox, 2011), 45.
36 "The spirit is the key, the crucial reality, for life in the new age." Gordon D. Fee, *The First Epistle to the Corinthians*, NICNT (Eerdmans, 1987), 147.
37 In the LXX, τὰ βάθη occurs frequently with the overwhelming sense of physical depths, much like its usage in Matt 13:5 and Mark 4:5. See also Anthony C. Thiselton, *The First Epistle to the Corinthians*, NIGTC (Eerdmans, 2000), 257; Koester, *Revelation*, 300–301.
38 David E. Garland makes this connection as well. See David E. Garland, *1 Corinthians*, BECNT (Baker, 2003), 98.
39 Harris, *Colossians and Philemon*, 40.

ὁ πιστὸς καὶ ἀληθινός, ἡ ἀρχὴ τῆς κτίσεως τοῦ θεοῦ· In 1:5 John identifies Jesus in similar language (ὁ πρωτότοκος τῶν νεκρῶν), and Charles lists 1:5 as another possible allusion to Col 1:18; yet it is the language of ἡ ἀρχὴ τῆς κτίσεως τοῦ θεοῦ that draws a strong parallel to both Col 1:18 and 1:15.

Colossians 1:15–20 provides the Christological hymn concerning the deity of Jesus, and various themes are present throughout the hymn. The focus that John appears to draw from is present within v 18 and v 15, respectively. In Col 1:18 Paul says that ὅς ἐστιν ἀρχή, "he is the beginning," and in 1:15 πρωτότοκος πάσης κτίσεως, "the firstborn of all creation."[40] The designations of Jesus as the "beginning" and "firstborn of all creation" does not affirm a creation of Jesus by the Father but rather they are "in respect of the old and the new creation alike [and] he enjoys the status of the 'firstborn.'"[41]

John appears to draw on this designation from the apostle Paul in both 3:14 and 1:5. Mounce is bold enough to say that John undoubtedly links to Col 1:18 and 15 but also believes that the "close geographical proximity of the two cities and Paul's instructions to Colossae that they exchange letters make it all but certain that the writer of Revelation knew the Colossian epistle."[42] As in Col 1:18 and 15, Christ, as the beginning of God's creation, makes him "the divine creator along with God (4:11) [since] God is Jesus' title for the Father" in Revelation.[43] Thus, the reference in Rev 3:14 is a clear verbal connection to both Col 1:18 and 15.

REVELATION 3:17; COLOSSIANS 1:27

(3:17) ὅτι λέγεις ὅτι πλούσιός εἰμι καὶ πεπλούτηκα καὶ οὐδὲν χρείαν ἔχω, καὶ οὐκ οἶδας ὅτι σὺ εἶ ὁ ταλαίπωρος καὶ ἐλεεινὸς καὶ πτωχὸς καὶ τυφλὸς καὶ γυμνός,	(Col 1:27) οἷς ἠθέλησεν ὁ θεὸς γνωρίσαι τί τὸ πλοῦτος τῆς δόξης τοῦ μυστηρίου τούτου ἐν τοῖς ἔθνεσιν, ὅ ἐστιν Χριστὸς ἐν ὑμῖν, ἡ ἐλπὶς τῆς δόξης·

Another possible verbal connection in the section addressed to the church at Laodicea is Rev 3:17.[44] After Jesus announces that he will spit the Laocideans out of his mouth for their lukewarmness (3:16), Jesus takes issue with their statements of wealth. The Laodiceans have declared themselves to be wealthy and in need of nothing (πλούσιός εἰμι), when in reality they do not know their

---

40 Daniel B. Wallace, *Greek Grammar Beyond the Basics: An Exegetical Syntax of the New Testament* (Zondervan, 1996), 103.
41 Bruce, *The Epistles to the Colossians, to Philemon, and to the Ephesians*, 56.
42 Mounce, *Revelation*, 108. Koester argues against the comparison with Rev 3:14 and Col 1:15 (Koester, *Revelation*, 336), but when combined one can see the emphasis John makes.
43 Hoskins, *The Book of Revelation*, 113.
44 For the context of Rev 3:14–22, see the previous section.

current state of poverty. Christ declares that they are poor (πτωχός; cf. 2:9). Osborne captures the sentiments of Christ well, "The Laodiceans were immensely wealthy, and this led to self-sufficiency and complacency, a deadly combination for the Christian ... Because they were materially 'rich,' they assumed that they were also spiritually 'rich.'"[45]

In Col 1:24-29 Paul relays to the Colossians that he both suffered (1:24) and served as a steward (1:25) of the mystery that was hidden (1:26) but is now revealed to the saints (1:27). It is to the Gentiles that God chose to make known the glorious riches of this mystery (τὸ πλοῦτος τῆς δόξης τοῦ μυστηρίου), "which is Christ in you" (ὅ ἐστιν Χριστὸς ἐν ὑμῖν).[46] The "riches" (τὸ πλοῦτος) do not have a specific content, but Paul frequently used similar expressions elsewhere (cf. Rom 2:4; 9:23; 2 Cor 8:2; Eph 1:7, 18; 2:7; 3:8, 16; Col 2:2), and the addition of the interrogative τί that precedes is intended to "heighten the value of these riches."[47]

There appears to be no verbal connection between Rev 3:17 and Col 1:27, and the only possible link between the two references is πλούσιός. Charles provides no argument for why he includes several of the bolded words from Rev 3:17 and Col 1:27. A possible case for a verbal connection could be made by highlighting that what made the Laodiceans poor was their lack of spiritual riches, which would be Christ in them. Yet, that argument is unlikely. Thus, there is no verbal connection.

REVELATION 3:21; COLOSSIANS 3:1; EPHESIANS 2:6

(3:21) Ὁ νικῶν δώσω αὐτῷ καθίσαι μετ' ἐμοῦ ἐν τῷ θρόνῳ μου, ὡς κἀγὼ ἐνίκησα καὶ ἐκάθισα μετὰ τοῦ πατρός μου ἐν τῷ θρόνῳ αὐτοῦ.	(Col 3:1) Εἰ οὖν συνηγέρθητε τῷ Χριστῷ, τὰ ἄνω ζητεῖτε, οὗ ὁ Χριστός ἐστιν ἐν δεξιᾷ τοῦ θεοῦ καθήμενος· (Eph 2:6) καὶ συνήγειρεν καὶ συνεκάθισεν ἐν τοῖς ἐπουρανίοις ἐν Χριστῷ Ἰησοῦ,

The final possible verbal connection in the section written to the Laodiceans is found in Rev 3:21. At the end of Christ's admonition and exhortation to Laodicea, he states that the conqueror, a refrain repeated throughout the seven letters, will be granted the authority to sit with Christ on his throne (δώσω

---

45 Osborne, *Revelation*, 206.
46 Moo believes this translation of τὸ πλοῦτος τῆς δόξης τοῦ μυστηρίου is the most appropriate translation. See Moo, *The Letters to the Colossians and to Philemon*, 156.
47 Ibid., 157. See also Christopher R. Seitz, *Colossians* (Brazos Press, 2014), 109–110. James D. G. Dunn believes τὸ πλοῦτος τῆς δόξης has a liturgical "ring and again heightens the sense both of divine condescension and that what has been revealed is itself a manifestation of the heavenly majesty of God." James D. G. Dunn, *The Epistles to the Colossians and to Philemon*, NIGTC (Eerdmans, 1996), 121.

αὐτῷ καθίσαι μετ' ἐμοῦ ἐν τῷ θρόνῳ μου), in the same manner as Christ conquered and sat down with his Father upon his throne (ἐκάθισα μετὰ τοῦ πατρός μου ἐν τῷ θρόνῳ αὐτοῦ). As Aune notes, the concept of believers reigning with Christ occurs in the New Testament, but it occurs with greater frequency in Revelation (1:6; 5:10; 20:4, 6; 22:5).[48]

Charles notes two possible verbal connection with Rev 3:21. The first is Col 3:1, where Paul commands that the Colossians "seek the things that are above, where Christ is seated at the right hand of God" (τὰ ἄνω ζητεῖτε, οὗ ὁ Χριστός ἐστιν ἐν δεξιᾷ τοῦ θεοῦ καθήμενος).[49] Similar language is found in Eph 2:6, where Paul claims that believers have been raised and seated in the heavenly places in Christ Jesus (συνεκάθισεν ἐν τοῖς ἐπουρανίοις ἐν Χριστῷ Ἰησοῦ). The overlap between Col 3:1, as well as Col 2:12–13, is seen in the believer seated with Christ, but the concept of reigning is unique only to Ephesians.[50] Clinton Arnold remarks, "This is not a resurrection of our bodies; that is still future. This is a participation with Christ in his resurrection."[51]

The conqueror, who overcomes the pressures to compromise and mirrors the faithful and true witness (3:14b), will sit with Christ upon his throne. This inauguration, however, is ambiguous. Does this event occur at the death of the believer, the final coming of Christ, or both?[52] It is difficult to be certain, and it appears that this decision would be significant in how one determines the validity of a possible connection with Eph 2:6. Although Paul employs the aorist συνεκάθισεν, this seating is undefined. However, in the instance of Col 3:1 Paul discusses the present reign of Christ and its concept is different than Rev 3:21. Thus, it is perhaps wise to conclude that Col 3:1 is a possible verbal connection and Eph 2:6 is a clear verbal connection.

Revelation 7:3; Ephesians 4:30

(7:3) λέγων· μὴ ἀδικήσητε τὴν γῆν μήτε τὴν θάλασσαν μήτε τὰ δένδρα, ἄχρι σφραγίσωμεν τοὺς δούλους τοῦ θεοῦ ἡμῶν ἐπὶ τῶν μετώπων αὐτῶν.	(Eph 4:30) καὶ μὴ λυπεῖτε τὸ πνεῦμα τὸ ἅγιον τοῦ θεοῦ, ἐν ᾧ ἐσφραγίσθητε εἰς ἡμέραν ἀπολυτρώσεως.

---

48 Aune, *Revelation 1–5*, 261. He also remarks that this reigning with Christ is a concept carried over from Dan 7:18, 27.
49 This reference appears to be an explicit contrast with the religion discussed in 2:12–23. See N. T. Wright, *The Epistles of Paul to the Colossians and to Philemon* (Eerdmans, 1986), 131–132; Moo, *The Letters to the Colossians and Philemon*, 144.
50 So Frank Thielman, *Ephesians*, BECNT (Baker, 2010), 134n8.
51 Clinton E. Arnold, *Ephesians*, ZECNT (Zondervan, 2010), 137.
52 Richard Bauckham believes Luke 22:29–30 is the source of this text. See Richard Bauckham, "Synoptic Parousia Parables and the Apocalypse," *NTS* 23 (1977): 173

After the sixth seal is opened (6:12–17), John sees a vision of four angels who stand and hold back the four winds of the earth (7:1), and another angel, who ascends from the sun and has the seal of God (7:2), calls in a loud voice to the four. He entreats the four angels not to harm the earth, sea, or the trees until the servants of God are sealed (ἄχρι σφραγίσωμεν τοὺς δούλους τοῦ θεοῦ) upon their foreheads. Although the seal is not identified here, later in Rev 14:1 it is described as the name of the Lamb and "his Father's name." This seal is intended to contrast against the mark of the beast's name (cf. 13:17; 14:11; 16:2; 19:20) and mirrors the sealing from Ezek 9.[53]

Ephesians 4:17–32 is Paul's exhortation to the believers in Ephesus to walk not as the Gentiles (4:17–19), but to walk in Christ (4:20–24). In 4:25–31 he provides numerous practical applications, but above all the climax of these applications is found in 4:30. There, Paul tells the believers not to grieve the Holy Spirit, for it is by him that they were sealed for the day of redemption (ἐσφραγίσθητε εἰς ἡμέραν ἀπολυτρώσεως). There are also two other Pauline usages of σφραγίζω that depict God "sealing" believers (2 Cor 1:22; Eph 1:3), and in both occurrences the contexts are the same: God has placed his seal on believers (2 Cor 1:22), and believers are sealed with the promise of the Holy Spirit (Eph 1:3).[54]

There appears to be a clear verbal connection between Rev 7:3 and Eph 4:30. First, the concept of sealing God's believers occurs not just in Eph 4:30 but also in 2 Cor 1:22 and Eph 1:3. Coupled together, the comparison with Rev 7:3 is strong. Second, the contexts also appear similar as well. In Rev 7:3 the believers will be sealed, which happens in 7:5–8, and they are spared the painful tribulations that the earth-dwellers must endure.[55] Likewise, Paul highlights the sealing of the Holy Spirit in Eph 4:13 for the day of redemption (εἰς ἡμέραν ἀπολυτρώσεως), which is the future day of judgment (cf. Rev 20:11–15). On that day, God will redeem his people, those who have been sealed.[56] Therefore, this verbal connection is clear.

---

[53] G. K. Beale and Sean M. McDonough, "Revelation," in *Commentary on the New Testament Use of the Old* (Baker, 2007), 1106–1107. See the helpful discussion by Koester, *Revelation*, 416.

[54] There is a difference, however, in the sealing of the believer for salvation and the sealing in Rev 14:1; the former being sealed for salvation, and the latter for preservation.

[55] I understand the 144,000 in 7:5–8 to refer to the church. See Chapter Three.

[56] See Bruce, *The Epistles to the Colossians, to Philemon, and to the Ephesians*, 364.

Revelation 14:13; 1 Thessalonians 4:16

(14:13) Καὶ ἤκουσα φωνῆς ἐκ τοῦ οὐρανοῦ λεγούσης· γράψον· μακάριοι οἱ νεκροὶ οἱ ἐν κυρίῳ ἀποθνήσκοντες ἀπ' ἄρτι. ναί, λέγει τὸ πνεῦμα, ἵνα ἀναπαήσονται ἐκ τῶν κόπων αὐτῶν, τὰ γὰρ ἔργα αὐτῶν ἀκολουθεῖ μετ' αὐτῶν.	(1 Thess 4:16) ὅτι αὐτὸς ὁ κύριος ἐν κελεύσματι, ἐν φωνῇ ἀρχαγγέλου καὶ ἐν σάλπιγγι θεοῦ, καταβήσεται ἀπ' οὐρανοῦ καὶ οἱ νεκροὶ ἐν Χριστῷ ἀναστήσονται πρῶτον,

At the conclusion of the message of the three angels, a voice from heaven declares the second beatitude (μακάριοι); namely, that the dead who die in the Lord (οἱ ἐν κυρίῳ ἀποθνήσκοντες) are blessed.[57] The location of this beatitude is significant, for it follows after the declaration that those who worship the beast and receive his mark will drink the wine of God's wrath (14:9–10) and will be judged with no rest (14:11). Thus, in light of this forthcoming judgment, John calls for an endurance of the saints (14:12) to keep the commandments of God and their faith in Jesus.[58]

The apostle Paul addresses the topic of the return of the Lord in 1 Thess 4:13–18. Among other things, he primarily focuses his writing upon encouraging the Thessalonians to grieve with hope (4:13), and states that those who are alive when the Lord returns will not precede those who have fallen asleep (4:15).[59] The dead in Christ (οἱ νεκροὶ ἐν Χριστῷ) will rise first when the Lord gives the cry of command and the sound of a trumpet. Those who have remained in Christ during their life on the earth will remain in Christ after death.[60]

Thus, the focus of this possible verbal connection centers upon the dead in Christ. Rev 14:12 is connected with 14:13 in that faithful obedience in the Lord may result in death, and these who have died are blessed. In 1 Thess 4:16,

---

57 For the context of Rev 14:6–13, see "Revelation 14:4; Luke 9:57" and "Revelation 14:7; Acts 4:24; 14:15" in Chapter Four.

58 Although no one is explicitly identified as speaking, John appears to meditate on what he has just heard from the third angel in 14:9–11. He calls for an endurance that believers will remain steadfast, and the beatitude that is mentioned in 14:13 may strengthen this Johannine comment. David deSilva connects the beatitude in Rev 14:13 with another in 20:6 and notes that "In both, people who die (οἱ νεκροὶ οἱ ἐν κυρίῳ ἀποθνήσκοντες, 14:13; τὰς ψυχὰς τῶν πεπελεκισμένων διὰ τὴν μαρτυρίαν Ἰησοῦ καὶ διὰ τὸν λόγον τοῦ θεοῦ καὶ οἵτινες οὐ προσεκύνησαν τὸ θηρίον οὐδὲ τὴν εἰκόνα αὐτοῦ , 20:4) are pronounced 'honorable' or 'favored' (Μακάριοι, 14:13; μακριος). people. These become the positive models for John's audience—those whom they will emulate if they submit to John's vision and the ideology it inscribes." David A. deSilva, "A Sociorhetorical Interpretation of Revelation 14:6–13: A Call to Act Justly toward the Just and Judging God," *BBR* 9 (1999): 81.

59 This euphemistic language is used until 4:16 when Paul finally labels them as the dead in Christ.

60 F. F. Bruce, *1 & 2 Thessalonians*, WBC (Thomas Nelson, 1982), 101.

however, the context is clearly upon what will happen within the resurrection from the dead. They are believers *in Christ* who will be called up to heaven by the voice of Christ. It is difficult to see a verbal connection between these two passages. F. F. Bruce sees a parallel between the two, but unfortunately provides no argument or reasoning for this belief other than the theme as suggested above.[61] However, thematically a connection is visible in the fact that believers have died, and they die in Christ. This verbal connection, then, should be seen as possible since it simply echoes the theme of death in Christ.

REVELATION 17:14; 1 TIMOTHY 6:15

(17:14) οὗτοι μετὰ τοῦ ἀρνίου πολεμήσουσιν καὶ τὸ ἀρνίον νικήσει αὐτούς, ὅτι **κύριος κυρίων ἐστὶν καὶ βασιλεὺς βασιλέων** καὶ οἱ μετ' αὐτοῦ κλητοὶ καὶ ἐκλεκτοὶ καὶ πιστοί.	(1 Tim 6:15) ἣν καιροῖς ἰδίοις δείξει ὁ μακάριος καὶ μόνος δυνάστης, ὁ **βασιλεὺς τῶν βασιλευόντων καὶ κύριος τῶν κυριευόντων**,

After a thorough description of the woman and the beast, John is shown what must happen to the ten kings in 17:12.[62] These kings, who sided with the prostitute, will make war with the Lamb (cf. 5:6), but the Lamb will conquer them because "he is Lord of lords and King of kings" (κύριος κυρίων ἐστὶν καὶ βασιλεὺς βασιλέων; cf. 19:16; Deut 10:17; Dan 2:47).[63] The Lamb, by his defeat of these ten kings, "has authority and power that exceeds that of all other claimants to the title of lord and king, including the beast."[64]

In his conclusion of his first epistle to Timothy, Paul gives Timothy an outline of godliness that should characterize his ministry. Within this section there are a series of commands (11–12), a charge to keep God's commandments (13–14), and a doxology (15–16).[65] In the first portion of his doxology, Paul declares that Jesus is "King of kings and Lord of lords (ὁ βασιλεὺς τῶν βασιλευόντων καὶ κύριος τῶν κυριευόντων)."[66]

The connection between Rev 17:14 and 1 Tim 6:15 is a clear verbal connection. First, contextually in both references the emphasis is upon the sovereign rule of Christ. When Rev 17:14 is coupled with Rev 19:16, the emphasis

---

61 Ibid.
62 For the context of Rev 17:1–18, see the section Revelation 17:14; Matthew 22:14 in Chapter Four.
63 See the thorough analysis of this phrase by David Aune, *Revelation 17–22*, WBC (Thomas Nelson, 1998), 953–955.
64 Hoskins, *The Book of Revelation*, 333.
65 Thomas D. Lea and Hayne P. Griffin, Jr. *1,2 Timothy, Titus*, NAC (Broadman Press, 1992), 171.
66 It is worth noting that both τῶν βασιλευόντων and τῶν κυριευόντων are present participles and could be translated "reigning," and "ruling" respectively.

is even clearer. Furthermore, the emphasis is the same in 1 Tim 6:15, and the "implication of the fact that God is the 'only sovereign' is now made explicit: He is the sovereign over every other kind of rulership."[67] Second, not only are there contextual and thematic similarities, but there are clear verbal parallels as well. What was emphasized by Paul in 1 Tim 6:15, as well as the parallels in Deut 10:17 and Dan 2:47, is brought forth once more in Rev 17:14 to emphasize the sovereign rule of Christ over the kings and lords of the earth.

REVELATION 18:4; 2 CORINTHIANS 6:17; EPHESIANS 5:11

(18:4) Καὶ ἤκουσα ἄλλην φωνὴν ἐκ τοῦ οὐρανοῦ λέγουσαν· ἐξέλθατε ὁ λαός μου ἐξ αὐτῆς ἵνα μὴ συγκοινωνήσητε ταῖς ἁμαρτίαις αὐτῆς, καὶ ἐκ τῶν πληγῶν αὐτῆς ἵνα μὴ λάβητε,	(2 Cor 6:17) διὸ ἐξέλθατε ἐκ μέσου αὐτῶν καὶ ἀφορίσθητε, λέγει κύριος, καὶ ἀκαθάρτου μὴ ἅπτεσθε· κἀγὼ εἰσδέξομαι ὑμᾶς (Eph 5:11) καὶ μὴ συγκοινωνεῖτε τοῖς ἔργοις τοῖς ἀκάρποις τοῦ σκότους, μᾶλλον δὲ καὶ ἐλέγχετε.

In Rev 18:1–24, John sees another angel (18:1) who declares with a mighty voice that Babylon the great has fallen (18:2). There appear to be three movements in Rev 18:1–24. First, in chs. 1–8 the angel pronounces the destruction of Babylon. Second, chs. 9–20 describes the world mourning her fall. Third, in chs. 21–24 the description of Babylon's final judgment and fall is provided, and she is now viewed as "Babylon the Less." Before her ultimate destruction, however, another voice from heaven, presumably an angel, cries out for God's people to come out from her (ἐξέλθατε ... ἐξ αὐτῆς) so that they may not partake in her sins (ἵνα μὴ συγκοινωνήσητε ταῖς ἁμαρτίαις).

Charles understands two possible verbal connections between 2 Cor 6:17 and Eph 5:11. First, in 2 Cor 6:17 Paul, as he exhorts the Corinthians not to be unequally yoked with unbelievers (2 Cor 6:14–16) draws upon Lev 26:11 and Isa 52:11 in order to demonstrate the ethical consequences of the relationship between God and his people in the Old Testament. "Paul applies the quotations to the Christian community as the people of God; this new community has to be different from the pagan environment as well."[68] Thus, Paul encourages the Corinthians by quoting from Isa 52:11, to go out from their midst (ἐξέλθατε ἐκ μέσου αὐτῶν). Second, Paul also makes a similar argument in Eph 5:11 where he tells the Ephesians not to take part in unfruitful works of

---

67 George W. Knight, *The Pastoral Epistles*, NIGTC (Eerdmans, 1992), 269. William D. Mounce, *Pastoral Epistles*, WBC (Thomas Nelson, 2000), 361.
68 Peter Balla, "2 Corinthians" in *Commentary on the New Testament Use of the Old*, ed. G. K. Beale and D. A. Carson (Baker, 2007), 773.

darkness (μὴ συγκοινωνεῖτε τοῖς ἔργοις ... τοῦ σκότους,). Unlike 2 Cor 6:17, Paul is not quoting an Old Testament text but he is relaying an admonition he previously mentioned in 5:7. Furthermore, those sons of disobedience (Eph 5:7) had a behavior that was "marked by greed and sexual immorality (5:3–6)."[69]

Contextually and verbally, the connection between Rev 18:4 with 2 Cor 6:17 and Eph 5:11 are clear. The similarity in words that Rev 18:4, 2 Cor 6:17, and Eph 5:11 employ suggest an intentionality on the part of John. In other words, John was, at least, familiar with Isa 52:11 and Paul's adaptation of it to his specific context.[70] Paul only changes the possessive pronoun from "her" (αὐτῆς) to "their" (αὐτῶν). It could be argued, however, that John is alluding to Isa 52:11, but the call to both the Ephesians and those in Babylon are similar. Furthermore, the command is quite similar in Rev 18:4 as in Eph 5:11. Revelation 18:4 uses ταῖς ἁμαρτίαις whereas Eph 5:11 τοῖς ἔργοις τοῦ σκότους, which is euphemistic for sin. Thus, this verbal connection is clear.

REVELATION 21:4D–5B; 2 CORINTHIANS 5:17

(21:4d–5b) ⁴ καὶ ἐξαλείψει πᾶν δάκρυον ἐκ τῶν ὀφθαλμῶν αὐτῶν, καὶ ὁ θάνατος οὐκ ἔσται ἔτι οὔτε πένθος οὔτε κραυγὴ οὔτε πόνος οὐκ ἔσται ἔτι, [ὅτι] τὰ πρῶτα ἀπῆλθαν. ⁵ Καὶ εἶπεν ὁ καθήμενος ἐπὶ τῷ θρόνῳ· ἰδοὺ καινὰ ποιῶ πάντα καὶ λέγει· γράψον, ὅτι οὗτοι οἱ λόγοι πιστοὶ καὶ ἀληθινοί εἰσιν.	(2 Cor 5:17) ὥστε εἴ τις ἐν Χριστῷ, καινὴ κτίσις· τὰ ἀρχαῖα παρῆλθεν, ἰδοὺ γέγονεν καινά·

After the judgment before the great white throne (Rev 20:11–15), John sees the new heaven and new earth (21:1) that God has created, as well as the new Jerusalem (21:2) which comes down from heaven. After this event, a voice declares that the dwelling place of God is now with man (21:3a) and God is their God (21:3b). Furthermore, God provides his people with hope, in that pain, suffering, and even death has now passed away (τὰ πρῶτα ἀπῆλθαν). Subsequently, in 21:5 God speaks and declares, "Behold, I am making all things new" (ἰδοὺ καινὰ ποιῶ πάντα).

In 2 Cor 5:16–21, Paul discusses what it means to live in the new age of the Christian life. A transition in the believer has occurred; they have been

---

69 Thielman, *Ephesians*, 342. He also notes that he preposition σύν that begins συγκοινωνεῖτε "suggests the incompatibility of participating both in the community of God's people, which Paul has also described with σύν compounds (2:5, 6, 19, 21–22; 3:6; 4:3, 16), and participating in the activities of those who practice the 'works of darkness.'"

70 See the discussion in Martin, *2 Corinthians*, 205–206; Victor Paul Furnish, *II Corinthians* (Doubleday, 1984), 364; Guthrie, *2 Corinthians*, 355–356.

transferred from one kingdom to another (cf. Col 1:13). This is because the believer is now in Christ, and he is a new creation, for "the old has passed away, behold the new has come" (τὰ ἀρχαῖα παρῆλθεν, ἰδοὺ γέγονεν καινά).[71]

The themes of God creating and recreating are evident in both Rev 21:4d–5b and 2 Cor 5:17, however, the contexts of both passages differ. Revelation 21:4d–5b focuses primarily upon the former things passing away; that is, the list provided in 21:4a–c. Next, the passage establishes that God is making all things new, which is an eschatological reference since the former things have just passed away. Beale notes that 21:5 is the third reference back to the Isaiah prophecies of a new creation and the insertion of this reference "suggests not thoroughgoing universal salvation but the culmination of the new creation previously begun only in part."[72] Furthermore, the language in 2 Cor 5:17 is quite similar in that καινὴ κτίσις, which precedes the apparent verbal connection, is an eschatological term "for God's age of salvation" which suggests that Paul is speaking of a new act of creation within the Christian.[73] As David Garland notes, "Paul also never uses the noun 'creation' (*ktisis*) to refer to an individual person (see Rom 1:2, 25; 8:19–22, 39), and the concept of a new creation appears prominently in Jewish apocalyptic texts that picture the new age as inaugurating something far more sweeping than individual transformation—a new heaven and a new earth."[74] Thus, this is a clear verbal connection between Rev 21:4–5b and 2 Cor 5:17.

REVELATION 22:21; EPHESIANS 6:24; COLOSSIANS 4:18

(22:21) Η χάρις τοῦ κυρίου Ἰησοῦ μετὰ πάντων.	(Eph 6:24) ἡ χάρις μετὰ πάντων τῶν ἀγαπώντων τὸν κύριον ἡμῶν Ἰησοῦν Χριστὸν ἐν ἀφθαρσίᾳ. (Col 4:18) Ο ἀσπασμὸς τῇ ἐμῇ χειρὶ Παύλου. μνημονεύετέ μου τῶν δεσμῶν. ἡ χάρις μεθ᾽ ὑμῶν.

Revelation concludes with a farewell address that is often repeated throughout the New Testament: Η χάρις τοῦ κυρίου Ἰησοῦ μετὰ πάντων. Charles notes

---

71 "εν Χριστῷ governs the expression καινὴ κτίσις, 'new creation,' not τις, 'anyone.'" Martin, *2 Corinthians*, 152.

72 Beale, *Revelation*, 1052.

73 Martin, *2 Corinthians*, 152. See also Christopher P. Azure, "A New Humanity in the Risen Christ: Paul's Use of ΚΑΙΝΗ ΚΤΙΣΙΣ in 2 Corinthians 5:17 as a Metaphor from New Foundations" (PhD diss., Midwestern Baptist Theological Seminary, 2017).

74 David Garland, *2 Corinthians*, NAC (Broadman and Holman, 1999), 286. "For Paul, the old has already passed away in Christ (2 Cor 5:17), though the defeat of death remains in the future (1 Cor 15:27); Revelation also emphasizes the future dimension." Koester, *Revelation*, 798.

that "some form of this grace is found at the close of the Pauline Epp. and in them only in the N.T."[75] The list can be expanded to include Rom 16:20; 1 Cor 16:23; 2 Cor 13:14; Gal 6:18; Phil 4:23; 1 Thess 5:28; 2 Thess 3:18; 1 Tim 6:21; 2 Tim 4:22; Titus 3:15; Plhm 25; Heb 13:25. This verbal connection functions much in the same way as with Rev 1:4 and the common greeting that is associated with Paul; yet, this verbal connection appears weak. Osborne notes that when John asks Christ to impart "his grace to πάντων, [it is] similar to some epistles (2 Corinthians, 2 Thessalonians, Titus, Hebrews) but different in that they have 'you all.'"[76] Thus, it is unlikely that John intended for his readers to make a connection between his benediction and that of the epistles listed above.

The Catholic Epistles

The Catholic Epistles fall last in the possible verbal connections that are used in Revelation. There are potentially seven instances that John may be employing languages from these texts. Of the seven books that are labeled as the Catholic Epistles, only two according to Charles, are used by Revelation: (1) 1 Peter, and (2) James. First Peter potentially occurs four times, and James twice.[77]

Revelation 1:6; 1 Peter 2:9

(1:6) καὶ ἐποίησεν ἡμᾶς βασιλείαν, ἱερεῖς τῷ θεῷ καὶ πατρὶ αὐτοῦ, αὐτῷ ἡ δόξα καὶ τὸ κράτος εἰς τοὺς αἰῶνας [τῶν αἰώνων]· ἀμήν.	(1 Pet 2:9) ὑμεῖς δὲ γένος ἐκλεκτόν, βασίλειον ἱεράτευμα, ἔθνος ἅγιον, λαὸς εἰς περιποίησιν, ὅπως τὰς ἀρετὰς ἐξαγγείλητε τοῦ ἐκ σκότους ὑμᾶς καλέσαντος εἰς τὸ θαυμαστὸν αὐτοῦ φῶς·

Near the end of his epistolary greeting, and after he has introduced the author of Revelation with various theological themes, John moves into a doxology in 1:5–6.[78] Christ has freed his people from their sins (1:5) and he has made them a "kingdom, priests to God" (βασιλείαν, ἱερεῖς τῷ θεῷ; cf. Exod 19:6; 23:22 LXX; Isa 61:6). The term ἱερεύς occurs just three times in Revelation (1:6; 5:10; 20:6), and in both 1:6 and 5:10 it alludes to Exod 19:6 (מַמְלֶכֶת כֹּהֲנִים).[79]

---

75 Charles, *Revelation*, 1:lxxxvi.
76 Osborne, *Revelation*, 798.
77 In this section on the Catholic Epistles, James occurs once, but the other possible occurrence was discussed in the Pauline Epistles.
78 For the context of this greeting, see the appropriate discussion in "The Pauline Epistles."
79 Aune, *Revelation 1–5*, 47. Furthermore, "Yet it is clear that, when Rev 1:6 is compared with 5:10 (where the phrase βασιλείαν καὶ ἱερεῖς, 'kingdom and priests,' is found, also alluding to

In 1 Pet 2:1–10, Peter encourages the exiles in the Dispersion (1 Pet 1:1–2) to put away the old and put on the new if they have tasted that the Lord is good (2:1–3). In 2:4–8 the Old Testament image of the stone to describe Jesus is used to indicate a new pattern of living, for he is the "living stone" (2:4) who was rejected by men. Like Jesus, the exiles are also rejected by men and, with a string of Old Testament citations (2:6, Isa 28:16; 2:7, Ps 118:22; 2:8, Isa 8:14), Peter enables "a people shamefully and dishonored by their culture to seek a different kind of honor through their association with Jesus."[80] He appropriately concludes this section by alluding to Exod 19:6 and tells the exiles that they are a royal priesthood (βασίλειον ἱεράτευμα).[81]

There are several things to observe in these two texts. First, both Rev 1:6 and 1 Pet 2:9 utilize Exod 19:6, but both John and Peter do so in a different way. The phrase from Exod 19:6 that both texts employ is βασίλειον ἱεράτευμα. 1 Pet 2:9 quotes this reference verbatim, whereas Rev 1:6 simply alludes to its theme.[82] Second, John uses ἱερεύς whereas Peter uses ἱεράτευμα, which is the term used for the priesthood itself. This distinction may be significant, because it seems to make a distinction between priests and priesthood. Yet, Beale argues that there is little difference. "In view of the redemptive-historical and prophetic-eschatological fulfillment context of Revelation, use of the Exod. 19:6 description of God's people does not merely compare the church to the nation Israel but also conveys the tacit notion that the church now functions as true Israel, while unbelieving ethnic Israelites, who claims to be true [Jews] ... are 'liars' (3:9)."[83]

Yet, it is difficult to classify this verbal connection as clear. The evidence has shown that 1 Pet 2:9 uses the exact phrase from Exod 19:6 within its context, and the argument can be made that John is not drawing from 1 Pet 2:9 but rather from Exod 19:6. Thus, it is perhaps wise to conclude that this verbal connection is possible. If 1 Pet 2:9 did not quote Exod 19:6, then the likelihood of 1 Pet 2:9 and Rev 1:6 would be a clear verbal connection.

Exod 19:6), John is thinking in terms of two privileges of the people of God rather than just one (as in the MT, LXX, and Aquila)."

80 David R. Nienhuis and Robert W. Wall, *Reading the Epistles of James, Peter, John and Jude as Scripture: The Shaping and Shape of a Canonical Collection* (Eerdmans, 2013), 119.

81 For the usage of this theme within 1 Peter and how Peter employs this Old Testament allusion, see D. A. Carson, "1 Peter," in *Commentary on the New Testament Use of the Old*, ed. G. K. Beale and D. A. Carson (Baker, 2007), 1030–1031.

82 Karen Jobes mentions that 1 Peter is the only epistle to call God's people a "royal priesthood." See Karen H. Jobes, *1 Peter*, BECNT (Baker, 2005), 160.

83 Beale, *Revelation*, 193–194.

REVELATION 2:10; JAMES 1:12

(2:10) μηδὲν φοβοῦ ἃ μέλλεις πάσχειν. ἰδοὺ μέλλει βάλλειν ὁ διάβολος ἐξ ὑμῶν εἰς φυλακὴν ἵνα πειρασθῆτε καὶ ἕξετε θλῖψιν ἡμερῶν δέκα. γίνου πιστὸς ἄχρι θανάτου, καὶ δώσω σοι τὸν στέφανον τῆς ζωῆς.	(Jas 1:12) Μακάριος ἀνὴρ ὃς ὑπομένει πειρασμόν, ὅτι δόκιμος γενόμενος λήμψεται τὸν στέφανον τῆς ζωῆς ὃν ἐπηγγείλατο τοῖς ἀγαπῶσιν αὐτόν.

Revelation 2:8–11 addresses the church in Smyrna. At the end of the address Jesus tells those who are about to suffer that if they remain faithful he will give them the crown of life (τὸν στέφανον τῆς ζωῆς).[84] The "crown of life" is a metaphor for eternal life, as indicated in v 11, and is the reward for the one who conquers since this one will not be hurt by the second death.[85] James 1:12 appears to employ the imagery of the crown of life in much the same way. After discussing the various trials and temptations that the believer must endure (Jas 1:2–11), James tells his readers that the one who remains steadfast under trial is blessed, because after this period of his tribulation he will receive the crown of life (τὸν στέφανον τῆς ζωῆς).

Contextually and verbally, Rev 2:10 and Jas 1:12 are quite similar. First, the verbal parallels are used in the exact same manner, even to the point of case, number, and gender of both words. Furthermore, the "crown of life" is only found in Rev 2:10 and Jas 1:12 within the New Testament. Second, both contexts present the issue of trials and tribulations. Jesus warns those in the church of Smyrna that they will soon suffer, be cast into prison, and suffer tribulation. If they are faithful unto death, their reward is the crown of life, which is eternal life. James also exhorts his readers in this same manner. They will meet trials of various kinds (1:2), and they are encouraged to ask God for wisdom in order to be faithful (1:5–8) so that they may remain steadfast under the trial and receive the crown of life.[86] Thus, the verbal connection between Rev 2:10 and Jas 1:12 is clear.[87]

---

84 For the context of Rev 2:8–11 see Revelation 2:9; 2 Corinthians 6:10; James 2:5 in "The Pauline Epistles," in Chapter Four.

85 For a concise discussion on the crown of life, see Osborne, *Revelation*, 135–136.

86 "The actual reward is salvation itself, for (eternal) life is certainly the content of the crown. It is useless to speculate whether this is a victor's crown ... or a royal crown ... although the former would fit best in this context if 2 Tim. 4:8 is any parallel, for the image is a stock one in apocalyptic writings for the eternal reward." Peter H. Davids, *James*, NIGTC (Eerdmans, 1982), 80.

87 Dan G. McCartney makes an interesting comment. "Although a few scholars who date James late think that he borrowed the expression from Revelation, it is more likely that both John the seer and the author of James found the phrase in early Christian or Jewish vocabulary. Both life and a crown are gifts of wisdom in Proverbs (3:18; 4:9)." Dan G. McCartney, *James*, BECNT (Baker, 2009), 101n17. See also Vlachos, *James*, 40.

Revelation 7:17; 1 Peter 2:25

| (7:17) ὅτι τὸ ἀρνίον τὸ ἀνὰ μέσον τοῦ θρόνου **ποιμανεῖ** αὐτοὺς καὶ ὁδηγήσει αὐτοὺς ἐπὶ ζωῆς πηγὰς ὑδάτων, καὶ ἐξαλείψει ὁ θεὸς πᾶν δάκρυον ἐκ τῶν ὀφθαλμῶν αὐτῶν. | (1 Pet 2:25) ἦτε γὰρ ὡς πρόβατα πλανώμενοι, ἀλλὰ ἐπεστράφητε νῦν ἐπὶ τὸν **ποιμένα** καὶ ἐπίσκοπον τῶν ψυχῶν ὑμῶν. |

Revelation 7:1–17 contains two sets of visions for John. The first is the vision of the 144,000 (7:1–8) and the second is the vision of the great multitude from every nation (7:9–17). This nation is so numerous that John cannot number them all (7:9), and they cry out in a loud voice to God in worship (7:10). An angel explains the vision to John (7:14–17) and tells him that these are the ones who have come out of the great tribulation (7:14). They will never hunger nor thirst anymore (7:16; cf. 21:22) because the Lamb (τὸ ἀρνίον), who is in the midst of the throne, will be their shepherd (ποιμανεῖ αὐτούς).

1 Peter 2:11–4:11 constitutes the third major section of 1 Peter, and in 2:11–3:12 the focus is primarily upon how the people of God should conduct their lives. The exiles are to conduct their lives honorably among the Gentiles (2:11–12), submit to every human institution (2:13–17), and look to the example of Christ in suffering and guidance, for they have returned to the Shepherd (τὸν ποιμένα) and the chief overseer of their souls (τῶν ψυχῶν ὑμῶν).[88]

The verbal connections are primarily focused upon Jesus as the Shepherd of the people. In Rev 7:17 he is identified as τὸ ἀρνίον (cf. Rev 5:6) and ποιμανεῖ, and in 1 Pet 2:25 he is likewise identified as τὸν ποιμένα. The strength between the two verses is evident when one considers that Christ is identified as a shepherd in the New Testament (Matt 26:31; Mark 14:27; John 10:2, 11–12, 14, 16; Heb 13:20.[89] Furthermore, in Rev 7:17 he is labeled as "their" shepherd, and this is a reference to the great multitude from 7:9–17. Thus, one can conclude that just as Christ is the chief Shepherd of the exiles in 1 Peter, he is also the Shepherd of the souls from the great multitude. Yet, because of the lack of a specific exactness, this verbal connection is best viewed as a probable connection since it mirrors the imagery of 1 Pet 2:25.

---

[88] "I would render the clause thus, 'But you have been now restored,' that is, from your wandering 'to the shepherd and the bishop (or, overseer) of your souls.'" John Calvin, *Calvin's Commentaries* (Baker, 2009), 22:94.

[89] Thomas R. Schreiner, *1, 2 Peter, Jude*, NAC (Broadman Press, 2003), 147.

Revelation 13:8; 1 Peter 1:19–20

(13:8) καὶ προσκυνήσουσιν αὐτὸν πάντες οἱ κατοικοῦντες ἐπὶ τῆς γῆς, οὗ οὐ γέγραπται τὸ ὄνομα αὐτοῦ ἐν τῷ βιβλίῳ τῆς ζωῆς τοῦ ἀρνίου τοῦ ἐσφαγμένου ἀπὸ καταβολῆς κόσμου.	(1 Pet 1:19–20) ¹⁹ ἀλλὰ τιμίῳ αἵματι ὡς ἀμνοῦ ἀμώμου καὶ ἀσπίλου Χριστοῦ, ²⁰ προεγνωσμένου μὲν πρὸ καταβολῆς κόσμου φανερωθέντος δὲ ἐπ' ἐσχάτου τῶν χρόνων δι' ὑμᾶς

Revelation 13 introduces the second person of the unholy trinity as the beast who rises out of the sea. This second person of the unholy trinity mirrors the second person of the Holy Trinity.[90] After John describes the appearance of the first beast, he informs the reader that the earth-dwellers will worship the beast. These people are identified as those who do not have their name written in the book of life of the Lamb who was slain before the foundation of the world (τοῦ ἀρνίου τοῦ ἐσφαγμένου ἀπὸ καταβολῆς κόσμου).[91]

This description of the slain Lamb is the connection for Charles to 1 Pet 1:19–20. Although Peter uses ἀμνοῦ in v 19 rather than ἀρνίου, as does John in 13:8, the comparisons are nonetheless similar. Believers in Christ are ransomed by the blood of the Lamb (1:18–19). Furthermore, where John describes the Lamb as slain from before the foundation of the world, Peter describes the Lamb as *foreknown* (προεγνωσμένου) before the foundation of the world. Different words, but same eternality for the Son (cf. Acts 2:23).

Charles believes that John has a possible acquaintance with 1 Pet 1:19–20 and the language is strikingly similar. David Aune notes, "There is a striking parallel to Rev 13:8 in 1 Pet 1:18–20 in which several of the same motifs occur: 'You were ransomed ... with the precious blood of Christ, like that of a *lamb* [ἀμνοῦ] without defect or blemish. He was destined before the foundation of the world [πρὸ καταβολῆς κόσμου].'"[92] It is perhaps wise to conclude that Rev 13:8 is a probable connection to 1 Pet 1:19–20 considering the words are different but the overall theme is present.

---

90 Osborne notes, "the beast is the 'son' of the dragon, a further parody on Christ, and this imitation motif continues in the 'mortal wound' that 'is healed' (13:3–4), a parody on the death and resurrection of Christ. It seems obvious that the beast builds on the Antichrist theme of the NT. As such, he conducts the final war against God and his people (13:5–8) as well as demanding universal worship (13:4, 8), probably alluding to the imperial cult demanding worship of the emperor." Osborne, *Revelation*, 488.

91 How this verse should be translated is debated. See the helpful discussion in Ibid., 503–504.

92 Aune, *Revelation 6–16*, 747. J. Ramsey Michaels disagrees: "Rev 13:8, despite its reference to Jesus as the Lamb, is a doubtful parallel: the phrase ἀπὸ καταβολῆς κόσμου ('ever since [not 'before'] the beginning of the world') refers not to the death of the Lamb (or to God's knowledge of it), but simply strengthens 'not' to 'never' ... in asserting the nonelection of those not inscribed in the Lamb's book of life (cf. Rev 17:8)." J. Ramsey Michaels, *1 Peter*, WBC (Thomas Nelson, 1988), 67.

Revelation 16:19; 1 Peter 5:13

(16:19) καὶ ἐγένετο ἡ πόλις ἡ μεγάλη εἰς τρία μέρη καὶ αἱ πόλεις τῶν ἐθνῶν ἔπεσαν. καὶ Βαβυλὼν ἡ μεγάλη ἐμνήσθη ἐνώπιον τοῦ θεοῦ δοῦναι αὐτῇ τὸ ποτήριον τοῦ οἴνου τοῦ θυμοῦ τῆς ὀργῆς αὐτοῦ. (cf. 14:8; 17:5)	(1 Pet 5:13) Ἀσπάζεται ὑμᾶς ἡ ἐν Βαβυλῶνι συνεκλεκτὴ καὶ Μᾶρκος ὁ υἱός μου.

Revelation 16:1–21 details the final judgment of God upon the earth-dwellers, as the angels begin to pour out the seven bowls of God's wrath. These bowls affect humanity with painful sores (16:2) and kill the creatures in the waters and turns the water to blood (16:3–7). The sun inflicts pain upon the earth-dwellers (16:8–9) and the throne of the beat is plunged into darkness (16:10–11), and the battle of Armageddon is prepared (16:12). Finally, in the seventh bowl an angel pronounces that the judgment is complete, the great city is split into three parts, and God makes Babylon the great (Βαβυλὼν ἡ μεγάλη) drain the cup of his fury (16:19).

Peter concludes his first epistle by sending greetings to the exiles in the Dispersion (cf. 1 Pet 1:1–2) from various people: Silvanus, Mark, and she who is in Babylon (5:12–14). Peter did not mean the historical Babylon from the Old Testament, for that city had been destroyed. Thus, it is likely that Peter drew upon the Old Testament tradition that presents Babylon as this enemy of God (Gen 11; Isa 3–14; 46–47; Jer 50–51), and at this time it appears to be Rome.[93]

The verbal connection between Rev 16:19 and 1 Pet 5:13 can be deemed probable if the argument is set forth that Babylon, in both instances, reference the great enemy of God as it does through the Old Testament. Thus, in Rev 16:19 Babylon is understood to mean the great city that opposes God and oppresses his people. However, in 1 Pet 5:13 the reference is clearly to Rome, although it is identified as Babylon as well. Yet, unless one believes that Rome will one day return to its former position of power and wealth, it is unlikely that Rev 16:19 is meant to be taken as a literal Rome. Therefore, it is best to conclude that this final verbal connection is probable.

Concluding Observations

The examination of the possible verbal connections Revelation may share with the Pauline and Catholic Epistles has provided several observations from which to conclude. First, the fifteen examples provided by Charles produced

---

93 So, most scholars. For helpful overviews see Schreiner, *1, 2 Peter, Jude*, 37–38; Jobes, *1 Peter*, 13–14.

a variety of results that, along with the examples from the Synoptic Gospels and Acts, suggests a possible reading strategy for the book. Of the twenty examples provided, ten were determined to be clear, four probable, one possible, and five as having an unlikely or no verbal connection.

Clear	Probable	Possible	Unlikely/No
1:4, 6; 2:9, 10; 3:14, 21; 7:3; 17:14; 18:4; 21:4d–5b	2:24; 7:17; 13:8; 16:19	14:13	1:5 (twice), 18; 13:17; 22:21

Figure 5.1: Categorization of Revelation's Possible Use of the Pauline and Catholic Epistles

This table suggests that John may have known, or at least have been familiar with, certain texts that are found within the Pauline and Catholic Epistles. Coupled with the examples from the Synoptic Gospels and Acts and the location of Revelation within the New Testament canon, the probability that John intended for a particular reading strategy for this book greatly increases.

Second, as with the Old Testament and the Synoptic Gospels and Acts, it appears that John believed his readers would be familiar with portions of the New Testament or, at least, familiar with the books of the Pauline and Catholic Epistles that he references. The themes that are present within the sections of the Pauline and Catholic Epistles likewise appear here and, at times, are strengthened by the word choices of the apostles.

Thus, given the strong likelihood of these verbal connections, one is now able to conclude that John may have intended for his work to be read in a certain fashion. In other words, given the evidence that has been provided it appears that John did not solely rely upon the Old Testament for his work. He seems to have drawn upon other New Testament texts and themes in order for his reader to fully understand the book. Furthermore, considering the location of Revelation within the New Testament canon, one can argue that it is intentionally placed at the conclusion of the canon in order for the reader to draw specific conclusions about the work. Thus, it is now appropriate to ask, considering all of the evidence that has been shown, who is the ideal-reader of Revelation?

CHAPTER 6

AT THE END OF ALL THINGS: THE IDEAL-READER OF REVELATION

INTRODUCTION

At the end of J. R. R. Tolkien's magisterial work, *The Return of the King*, the destruction of the One Ring causes the tide to turn in favor of the army of Middle Earth and against the soldiers of Mordor. The sky begins to clear, the Eagles arrive to assist the race of men, and Gandalf urges the Men of the West to stand and fight. It is at the moment when all hope appears lost that Tolkien notes the ground began to groan, the Towers of the Teeth began to fall, the Black Gate is hurled into ruin, and a "long echoing roll of a ruinous noise" fills the land.[1] This final scene concludes with Frodo and Sam escaping from Mount Doom after the One Ring was taken, and destroyed, by Gollum. As everything collapses around them, the hobbits reflect upon their newfound freedom from the heavy burden of the ring. Tolkien describes the event for Sam as, "In all that ruin of the world for the moment [Sam] felt only joy, great joy. His master has been saved; he was himself again, he was free."[2] Yet, what is perhaps the most pointed illustration that Tolkien provides for the reader is found in the final words spoken by Frodo. Even though Gollum had previously bitten off his finger, Frodo shows little concern for it now. "For the Quest is achieved, and now all is over. I am glad you are here with me. Here at the end of all things, Sam."[3]

In many ways, Revelation is considered the book that brings about "the end of all things." The metanarrative of the Bible has been leading up to the point of a new creation, the new heaven and the new earth. Much like the

---

[1] J. R. R. Tolkien, *The Return of the King*, 2nd ed. (Houghton Mifflin, 1988), 227.
[2] Ibid., 225.
[3] Ibid.

hobbits, who throughout *The Lord of the Rings*, longed to return to the Shire, this narrative of Scripture portrays a longing to return to Eden when all things were perfect and God walked with man. In fact, Tolkien scatters the Edenic like nature of the Shire throughout the three books so that when the reader has journeyed there and back again he is shocked to find that the Shire has been overtaken by Saurman and Wormtongue. It is only after a scouring in the Shire occurs that a new Shire begins to emerge, filled with peace, hope, and prosperity.

The thesis of this volume is that a canonical approach to Revelation should inform our understanding of its ideal-reader. Most scholars will agree that a working knowledge of the Old Testament is important for interpreting Revelation because the author employs several Old Testament allusions and themes. The present volume, however, seeks to advance that discussion by arguing that Revelation also incorporates several New Testament texts and themes.

Summary of the Study

The preceding chapters focused on interpreting Revelation from a canonical vantage-point. Chapter One examined the recent scholarship concerning the canonical approach within the field of New Testament studies. The canonical approach, introduced by Brevard Childs, was contrasted with the traditional historical-critical approach that has dominated the field of both Old and New Testament studies. In this context, we saw that John Sailhamer contributed another voice to the canonical approach by suggesting that "shape" affects the emphasis of a particular text, narrative, or book within the biblical canon. The methods proposed by Childs and Sailhamer were primarily limited to the Old Testament, but recently New Testament scholars have begun to explore this area of study within the New Testament. An overview of various approaches reflected differing contributions to the field, but none of these studies focused extensively upon Revelation. Thus, it can be suggested that Revelation is the final frontier, of sorts, within the canonical study of the New Testament.

Chapter Two explored the question of interpretation versus methodology. In the study of Revelation, four views are prominent: preterist, historical (historicist), futurist, and idealist. Yet, this chapter demonstrated that these four views of interpretation are simply conclusions of their own respective hermeneutic. Chapter Two primarily focused upon three hermeneutic examples that command the study of Revelation. First, the "History of Religions" section analyzed the contributions of David Aune and Adele Yarbro Collins. These scholars rely upon the historical background of the Greco-Roman world to understand Revelation. Second, the "Hebrew Bible and Jewish Theology" method, utilized by scholars Elisabeth Schüssler Fiorenza and G. K. Beale, argues that the Hebrew Bible, as well as the historical context of Revelation, influences how one reads and interprets Revelation. Third, a "Theological" approach suggested by Richard Bauckham proposes a theological reading of Revelation that focuses upon various themes John references in the historical context and his application of these themes to his readers. Yet, bound within the three categories is the discussion of how the historical background of Revelation influences its interpretation. For a canonical approach, the interpreter focuses primarily upon the written biblical text and argues that the text is God's locus of revelation. The recent commentary by Christopher R. Seitz provides a helpful case-study as to the manner in which a canonical approach might illuminate a New Testament book, and his work laid the groundwork for interpreting Revelation within the canon.

Chapter Three analyzed the concept of canon and noted the importance that this term has in the canonical hermeneutic. "Canon" is defined as "a collection of books that are regarded as authoritative for Christians," since the term itself, historically, was used to mean the criteria or standard by which something else was measured. Thus, "canon" is an appropriate term to use when describing the collection of books within the New Testament, as these books are the ruling "norm." Also examined was the development of a canonical list in order to determine the regular location of Revelation within the biblical canon. Of the various studies provided, Revelation is consistently placed at the end of the canon, most likely because of its apocalyptic and eschatological overtones. After Revelation's position in the canon was analyzed, several proposed structures were suggested that ranged from a simple structure that focused upon the narrative to the more complex chiastic structures proposed by various authors. In a canonical hermeneutic, however, both the structure and the bridge between the preceding collections of books are seen as essential to understanding the book's message.

Chapters Four and Five constituted an exegetical analysis of the possible verbal connections that Revelation may share with other New Testament texts. Chapter Four focused upon the Gospels and Acts, while Chapter Five searched for these connections in the Pauline and Catholic Epistles. An examination of these verbal connections was accomplished through the model proposed by Beale in which he classifies John's usage of the Old Testament in Revelation to three categories: clear, probable, and possible. Also, this study added a fourth category, that of unlikely or no verbal connection, because there appears to be no verbal connection between some of the examples provided by Charles. Twenty-six were determined to be clear, nine were probable, two are possible, and twelve were judged as unlikely or provided no verbal connection.

The Ideal-Reader of Revelation

Our task is to understand Revelation from the perspective intended by John, which is labeled as the "ideal-reader" perspective in this study. We argued throughout this work that the ideal-reader of Revelation must take into account the wider biblical canon. This conclusion follows from the fact that Revelation is consistently found near the end in the various canonical lists of books from the early church. Given its consistent location, it also follows that the reader needs more than the Old Testament in order to understand the message of Revelation. One must know much of what the New Testament includes as well. The importance of the New Testament in Revelation is indicated from the fact that Revelation contains exact verbal parallels to certain passages of the New Testament. Based on the extensive emphasis that Revelation places upon the Old Testament and New Testament, it is wise to conclude that the ideal-reader of Revelation is one who, by various means, has developed an extensive knowledge of the Old and New Testaments. In other words, the ideal-reader of Revelation is one who is familiar with the entirety of the Christian Scriptures.

The fact that Revelation concludes the canon must also be taken into consideration when interpreting Revelation from the ideal-reader perspective. Indeed, there are many parallels between the beginning and ending of the Christian Bible, as evidenced by the creation of the heavens and the earth (Gen 1) and the *new* heaven and *new* earth.[4] There is also the introduction of the rightful heir of David's throne in Matt 1:1–17, with the final plea from John that Jesus would come and, by implication, establish his realized kingdom upon the earth (Rev 22:20). Thus, the ideal-reader of Revelation is one who reads the words of this prophecy (cf. Ps 1:2) and keeps it (Rev 1:3), for the time is near. Therefore, in this sense, the ideal-reader of Revelation knows the Old and New Testaments thoroughly. As stated previously, this demand arises from the fact that John sees no need to clarify his allusions to the Old Testament and to various parts of the New Testament tradition. He assumes

---

4 For a helpful study, see Ched Spellman, *Toward a Canon-Conscious Reading of the Bible: Exploring the History and Hermeneutics of the Canon* (Sheffield Phoenix Press, 2014), 225–234.

that such explanations are not essential for making his words understandable. The verbal connections that John uses throughout the book also function in the same way as the Old Testament in that John offers no explanation or interpretation to the reader; rather, he expects the reader to be familiar with and know both testaments. John's implicit use of the Old Testament and New Testament causes his book to place a heavy demand for biblical literacy upon his readers.

Contribution to the Field of Study

This volume has contributed to the study of Revelation in two ways. First, all would agree that Revelation uses themes and allusions from the Old Testament. The continual usage of the Old Testament by the author of Revelation indicates that his readers understood the Old Testament and were, perhaps, steeped within the literature of the Old Testament itself. However, this study also argued that the author of Revelation incorporates themes, allusions, and actual texts from the New Testament. Chapters four and five demonstrated that there is enough evidence to conclude that the New Testament was used in Revelation and, as a result, that Revelation must be read in light of the New Testament as well as the Old Testament.

Second, this volume examined Revelation in the context of its location within the canon. A main thesis of the canonical approach, as proposed by John Sailhamer, is that the location of a book within the canon of Scripture places a certain degree of emphasis upon its content. For example, the book of Proverbs concludes by seeking for the "excellent wife." In the Hebrew Bible, Proverbs is read before Ruth who, after reading the book, adequately fulfills the "excellent wife" of Prov 31.

Revelation concludes not just the New Testament canon but the canon of the Christian Bible as a whole. As chapter three indicated, the traditional place of Revelation within the major codices is near the end of every canon. It can be inferred, then, that the early compilers of these codices all understood that Revelation belongs at the end due to its content, themes, and fulfillments that are prophesied throughout the canon.

Suggestions for Further Research

More research is still needed to be done in the field of canonical hermeneutics in the New Testament. Although this volume sought to be as comprehensive as possible, there are other aspects of interpreting Revelation in a canonical approach that will contribute to this field of biblical studies. First, this volume focused on identifying the ideal-reader of Revelation by analyzing the various verbal connections Revelation shares with the New Testament. Yet, this study did not provide a full orbed canonical approach to Revelation as it is found within the context of the canon.[5] A study that is more in-depth on how the interpretation of Revelation is influenced by its relative placement within the canon is a needed area of focus.

Second, this volume focused upon the list of possible verbal connections that were provided by R. H. Charles. He noted several parallels between Revelation and the Synoptic Gospels, but Charles does not provide any examples of John using texts from his own Gospel. This exclusion of any reference to the Gospel of John is consistent with his self-effacing references to himself as simply "beloved disciple" in the Gospel, but there should be thematic parallels between these two works. For example, the introduction of John 1:6–7 and Rev 1:1–2 include Jesus's identification as the Word and the Lamb, the "I am" sayings, and Jesus as the giver of the water of life, all of which appear in both the Gospel of John and Revelation. A further study on these parallels is needed.

Third, the examples provided by Charles can also be approached in a different model than proposed by Beale and myself. A helpful comparison would be utilized in a similar methodology of Richard B. Hays who, in his *Echoes of Scripture in the Letters of Paul*, provides seven criteria to determine the presence of biblical echoes between Paul and the Hebrew Scriptures.[6]

Conclusion

The end did not come immediately after the Shire had been scoured for the hobbits. It was nearly two years later that Sam and his beloved Master Frodo took their final journey together. The "Third Age was over and the Days of the Rings were passed, and an end was come of the story and song of those times."[7] Frodo and Sam, now accompanied by Merry and Pippin, rode to The

---

5 However, Chapter Three did briefly interpret the contents of Revelation from the canonical approach; yet, a more thorough examination of the book is needed. See, also, Brian J. Tabb, All Things New: Revelation as Canonical Capstone (IVP Academic, 2019). Tabb states that his work stresses the canonical context of Revelation and that it serves as the climatic conclusion to the biblical canon.

6 Richard B. Hays, *Echoes of Scripture in the Letters of Paul* (Yale University Press, 1989), 29–32. See also Hays works Reading Backwards: Figural Christology and the Fourfold Gospel Witness (Baylor University Press, 2014), and the expansion in Echoes of Scripture in the Gospels (Baylor University Press, 2016).

7 Tolkien, *Return of the King*, 309.

Grey Havens where they would say goodbye to Frodo and Gandalf. Frodo went aboard the ship and "then it seemed to him that as in his dream in the house of Bombadil, the grey rain-curtain turned all to silver glass and was rolled back, and he beheld white shores and beyond them a far green country under a swift sunrise."[8] The careful reader of *The Lord of the Rings* will remember this line, quoted almost exactly, from *The Fellowship of the Ring*, where Tolkien describes the Hobbits asleep in the house of Tom Bombadil.[9] The reader eagerly anticipates that Frodo will, at last, finally have his rest. So, it is with the ideal-reader of the Revelation who, after meditating on the Old and New Testament, looks forward with great anticipation for the end of all things to come to pass.

This volume has argued that the ideal-reader of Revelation is one who is familiar with both Testaments of the Christian canon. Considering that the author of Revelation employed Old Testament imagery and allusions without further explanation leads to the conclusion that he understood his readers as those who are familiar with the Old Testament. Likewise, this study argued that the author also used various New Testament texts and themes which he also believed that his readers understood. Although not every example proposed by Charles was validated, there is enough evidence to suggest that the author of Revelation was familiar with these texts. Therefore, we can conclude that the ideal-reader of Revelation is understood to be someone who faithfully reads his Bible and "meditates upon it day and night" (Ps 1:2).

---

8 Ibid., 310.

9 J. R. R. Tolkien, *The Fellowship of the Ring*, 2nd ed. (Houghton Mifflin, 1988), 146.

Bibliography

Aland, Kurt. *The Problem of the New Testament Canon*. A.R. Mowbray and Co., 1962.
Allen, Garrick V. "The Apocalypse in Codex Alexandrinus: Exegetical Reasoning and Singular Readings in New Testament Greek Manuscripts," *JBL* 135.4 (2016): 859–880.
Alexander, T. Desmond. *From Eden to the New Jerusalem: An Introduction to Biblical Theology*. Kregel, 2008.
Armstrong, Ryan Melvin. "Canonical Approaches to New Testament Theology: An Evangelical Evaluation of Childs and Trobisch." ThM thesis., Southeastern Baptist Theological Seminary, 2007.
Arnold, Clinton E. *Ephesians*. ZECNT. Zondervan, 2010.
Azure, Christopher P. "A New Humanity in the Risen Christ: Paul's Use of ΚΑΙΝΗ ΚΤΙΣΙΣ in 2 Corinthians 5:17 as a Metaphor from New Foundations." PhD diss., Midwestern Baptist Theological Seminary, 2017.
Aune, David E. "Apocalypse of John and the Problem of Genre." *Semeia* 36 (1986): 76–91.
Aune, David E. *Apocalypticism, Prophecy, and Magic in Early Christianity*. Mohr Siebeck, 2006.
Aune, David E. *Greco-Roman Culture and the New Testament: Studies Commemorating the Centennial of the Pontifical Biblical Institute*. Brill, 2012.
Aune, David E. "The Influence of Roman Imperial Court Ceremonial on the Apocalypse of John." *BR* 28 (1985): 5–26.
Aune, David E. *Jesus, Gospel Tradition and Paul in the Context of Jewish and Greco-Roman Antiquity*. Mohr Siebeck, 2013.
Aune, David E. *Revelation 1 – 5*. WBC. Thomas Nelson, 1997.
Aune, David E. *Revelation 6 – 16*. WBC. Thomas Nelson, 1998.
Aune, David E. *Revelation 17 – 22*. WBC. Thomas Nelson, 1998.
Balla, Peter. "2 Corinthians." Pages 753–783 in *Commentary on the New Testament Use of the Old*. Edited by G. K. Beale and D. A. Carson. Baker, 2007.
Bandy, Alan S. "The Prophetic Lawsuit in the Book of Revelation: An Analysis of the Lawsuit Motif in Revelation with Reference to the Use of the Old Testament." PhD diss., Southeastern Baptist Theological Seminary, 2006.
Bandy, Alan S. *Reading Revelation with the Church*. Forthcoming.
Barr, James. "Childs' Introduction to the Old Testament as Scripture." *JSOT* 16 (1980): 12–23.
Barr, James. *Holy Scripture: Canon, Authority, Criticism*. Clarendon, 1983.
Barrett, Matthew. *Canon, Covenant, and Christology: Rethinking Jesus and the Scriptures of Israel*. IVP Academic, 2020.
Barton, John. *Reading the Old Testament: Method in Biblical Studies*. Westminster 1984.
Bauckham, Richard. *The Climax of Prophecy: Studies on the Book of Revelation*. T&T Clark, 1993.
Bauckham, Richard. "Synoptic Parousia Parables and the Apocalypse." *NTS* 23 (1977): 162–176.

Bauckham, Richard. *The Theology of the Book of Revelation*. Cambridge University Press, 1993.

Bauckham, Richard. "The Worship of Jesus in Apocalyptic Christianity." *NTS* 27 (1980): 322–341.

Beale, G. K. *The Book of Revelation: A Commentary on the Greek Text*. NIGTC. Eerdmans, 1999.

Beale, G. K. *John's Use of the Old Testament in Revelation*. Sheffield Academic Press, 1998.

Beale, G. K. *A New Testament Biblical Theology: The Unfolding of the Old Testament in the New*. Baker, 2011.

Beale, G. K. *The Use of the Old Testament in Revelation*. JSNTSup 166. Sheffield Academic Press, 2015.

Beale, G. K. and Sean M. McDonough. "Revelation." Pages 1081–1158 in *Commentary on the New Testament Use of the Old Testament*. Edited by G. K. Beale and D. A. Carson. Baker, 2007.

Beyer, Hermann Wolfgang. "κανών," *Theological Dictionary of the New Testament*. Eerdmans, 3:596–602.

Bell, Albert A. "Date of John's Apocalypse: The Evidence of Some Roman Historians Reconsidered." *NTS* 25 (1978): 93–102.

Blaising, Craig A. "The Day of the Lord: Theme and Pattern in Biblical Theology." *BSac* 169 (2012): 3–19.

Blaising, Craig A. and Darrell L. Bock. *Progressive Dispensationalism*. Baker, 1993.

Blass, F. And A. Debrunner. *A Greek Grammar of the New Testament and Other Early Christian Literature*. The University of Chicago Press, 1961.

Blomberg, Craig L. "The Historical-Critical/Grammatical View." Pages 27–47 in *Biblical Hermeneutics: Five View*. Edited by Stanley E. Porter and Beth M. Stovell. IVP Academic, 2012.

Blomberg, Craig L. *Jesus and the Gospels: An Introduction and Survey*. B&H Academic, 2009.

Blomberg, Craig L. "Matthew." Pages 1–109 in *Commentary on the New Testament Use of the Old Testament*. Edited by G. K. Beale and D. A. Carson. Baker, 2007.

Blomberg, Craig L. *From Pentecost to Patmos: An Introduction Through Revelation*. B&H Academic, 2006.

Bock, Darrell L. *A Theology of Luke and Acts: God's Promised Program, Realized for All the Nations*. Zondervan, 2012.

Bock, Darrell L. *Luke 1:1–9:50*. BECNT. Baker, 2008.

Bock, Darrell L. *Luke 9:51–24:53*. BECNT. Baker, 2008.

Brett, Mark G. *Biblical Criticism in Crisis? The Impact of the Canonical Approach on Old Testament Studies*. Cambridge University Press, 1991.

Bruce, F. F. *1&2 Thessalonians*. WBC. Word, 1982.

Bruce, F. F. *The Epistle to the Colossians, to Philemon, and to the Ephesians*. New International Commentary on the New Testament. Eerdmans, 1984.

Campbell, Constantine R. *Verbal Aspect and Non-Indicative Verbs: Further Soundings in the Greek of the New Testament*. Peter Lang, 2008.

Carson, D. A. "Matthew," in *The Expositor's Bible Commentary*. Edited by Frank E. Gaebelein. Zondervan, 1984.

Carson, Don. and Douglas J. Moo. *An Introduction to the New Testament*. Zondervan, 2005.

Chafer, Lewis Sperry. *Systematic Theology*. Four Volumes. Kregel, 1993.

Charles, R. H. *A Critical and Exegetical Commentary on Revelation of St. John*. 2 vols. ICC. T&T Clark, 1985.

Childs, Brevard. *Biblical Theology in Crisis*. Westminster Press, 1976.

Childs, Brevard. *Biblical Theology of the Old and New Testaments: Theological Reflection on the Christian Bible*. Minneapolis: Fortress Press, 1992.

Childs, Brevard. *The Book of Exodus*. Westminster Press, 1974.

Childs, Brevard. "The Canon in Recent Biblical Studies: Reflections on an Era." Pages 33–57 in *Canon and Biblical Interpretation*. Edited by Craig G. Bartholomew, Scott Hahn, Robin Parry, Christopher Seitz, and Al Wolters. Zondervan, 2006.

Childs, Brevard. *The Church's Guide for Reading Paul: The Canonical Shaping of the Pauline Corpus*. Eerdmans, 2008.

Childs, Brevard. *Introduction to the Old Testament as Scripture*. Fortress Press, 1979.

_____. *The New Testament as Canon: An Introduction*. Fortress Press, 1985.

Childs, Brevard. *Old Testament Theology in a Canonical Context*. Fortress Press, 1985.

Collins, Adele Yarbro. *Crisis and Catharsis: The Power of the Apocalypse*. Westminster, 1984.

Collins, Adele Yarbro. *The Combat Myth in the Book of Revelation*. Scholar Press, 1976.

Collins, Adele Yarbro. "Reading the Book of Revelation in the Twentieth Century." *Int* 40.3 (1986): 229–242.

Cotro, Hugh A. "Could the Author of Revelation Step Forward, Please?" *DavarLogos* 14.1 (2015): 71–89.

Davids, Peter H. *The Epistle of James*. NIGTC. Eerdmans, 1982.

Dempster, Stephen G. "Canons on the Right and Canons on the Left: Finding a Resolution in the Canon Debate." *JETS* 52:1 (2009): 47–77.

Dempster, Stephen G. *Dominion and Dynasty: A Theology of the Hebrew Bible*. New Studies in Biblical Theology. Edited by D. A. Carson. InterVarsity, 2003.

Dempster, Stephen G. "The Prophets, the Canon, and a Canonical Approach: No Empty Word." Pages 293–332 in *Canon and Biblical Interpretation*. Edited by Craig G. Bartholomew, Scott Hahn, Robin Parry, Christopher Seitz, and Al Wolters. Zondervan, 2006.

DeSilva, David A. *An Introduction to the New Testament: Contexts, Methods and Ministry Formation*. InterVarsity Press, 2004.

DeSilva, David A. "A Sociorhetorical Interpretation of Revelation 14:6–13: A Call to Act Justly toward the Just and Judging God." *BBR* 9 (1999): 65–117.

Driver, Daniel R. *Brevard Childs: Biblical Theologian for the Church's One Bible*. Baker, 2010.

Dunn, James D.G. *The Epistles to the Colossians and to Philemon*. NIGTC. Eerdmans, 1996.

Eichrodt, Walther. *Old Testament Theology*. 2 vols. Westminster Press, 1961.

Emerson, Matthew Y. *Christ and the New Creation: A Canonical Approach to the Theology of the New Testament*. Eugene, Oregon: Wipf and Stock, 2013.

Emerson, Matthew Y. "Victory, Atonement, Restoration, and Response: The Shape of the New Testament Canon and the Holistic Gospel Message." *STR* 3.2 (2012): 177–194.

Enroth, A.M. "The Hearing Formula in the Book of Revelation." *NTS* 36:4 (1990): 596–608.

Eslinger, Lyle. "Inner-Biblical Exegesis and Inner-Biblical Allusion: The Question of Category." *VT* 42 (1992): 47–58.

Fanning, Buist. *Verbal Aspect in New Testament Greek*. Clarendon Press, 1990.

Farmer, William R. and Denis M. Farkasfalvy, *The Formation of the New Testament Canon: An Ecumenical Approach*. Paulist Press, 1983.

Fee, Gordon D. *The First Epistle to the Corinthians*. NICNT. Eerdmans, 1987.

Fekkes, Jan. *Isaiah and the Prophetic Traditions in the Book of Revelation: Visionary Antecedents and their Development*. Sheffield Academic Press, 1994.

Fiorenza, Elisabeth Schüssler. *The Book of Revelation: Justice and Judgment*. Fortress, 1985.

Fotopoulos, John. *The New Testament and Early Christian Literature in Greco-Roman Context: Studies in Honor of David E. Aune*. Brill, 2006.

France, R.T. *The Gospel of Matthew*. NICNT. Eerdmans, 2007.

Frei, Hans W. *The Eclipse of Biblical Narrative*. Yale University Press, 1974.

Furnish, Victor Paul. *II Corinthians*. Doubleday, 1984.

Gamble, Harry Y. "Canon." Pages 838–861 in *The Anchor Bible Dictionary*, volume 1. 6 vols. Edited by David Noel Freedman. Doubleday, 1992.

Gamble, Harry Y. "The New Testament Canon: Recent Research and the Status Quaestionis." Pages 268–294 in The Canon Debate. Edited by Lee Martin McDonald and James A. Sanders. Baker, 2019.

Garland, David E. *1 Corinthians*. BECNT. Baker, 2003.

Gathercole, Simon J. "Jesus' Eschatological Vision of the Fall of Satan: Luke 10.18 Reconsidered." *ZNW* 94 (2003): 143–163.

Gathercole, Simon J. *Luke*. ZECNT. Zondervan, 2011.

Gentry, Kenneth L. *Before Jerusalem Fell: Dating the Book of Revelation*. Rev. ed. American Vision, 1998.

Gentry, Kenneth L. Gentry, Kenneth L. "A Preterist View of Revelation." Pages 37–92 in *Four Views on the Book of Revelation*. Edited by Stanley N. Gundry and C. Marvin Pate. Zondervan, 1998.

Giblin, Charles H. "Revelation 11.1–13: Its Form, Function and Contextual Integration." *NTS* 30 (1984): 433–459.

Gignilliat, Mark S. *A Brief History of Old Testament Criticism: From Benedict Spinoza to Brevard Childs*. Zondervan, 2012.

Goodspeed, Edgar J. *The Formation of the New Testament*. The University Chicago Press, 1926.

Goppelt, Leonard. *Theology of the New Testament: Volume 1*. Translated by John E. Alsup. Eerdmans, 1981.

Goswell, Greg. "The Order of the Books in the Greek Old Testament." *JETS* 52 (2009): 449–66.

Goswell, Greg. "The Order of the Books in the Hebrew Bible." *JETS* 51 (2008): 673–88.

Goswell, Greg. "The Order of the Books of the New Testament." *JETS* 53 (2010): 225–241.

Goswell, Greg. "Two Testaments in Parallel: The Influence of the Old Testament on the Structuring of the New Testament Canon." *JETS* 56 (2013): 459–474.

Grudem, Wayne. *Systematic Theology*. Zondervan, 2000.

Gunkel, Hermann. *Creation and Chaos in the Primeval Era and the Eschaton: A Religion-Historical Study of Genesis 1 and Revelation 12*. Translated by K. William Whitney Jr. Eerdmans, 2006.

Guthrie, George H. *2 Corinthians*. BECNT. Baker, 2015.

Hagner, Donald H. *Matthew 1–13*. WBC. Thomas Nelson, 1993

Hagner, Donald H. *Matthew 14–28*. WBC. Thomas Nelson, 1995.

Hahneman, Geoffrey Mark. *The Muratorian Fragment and the Development of the Canon*. Clarendon Press, 1992.

Hall, Mark Seaborn. "The Hook Interlocking Structure of Revelation: The Most Important Verses in the Book and How They May Unify Its Structure." *NovT* 44 (2002): 278–296.

Hamilton, James M. *God's Glory in Salvation Through Judgment: A Biblical Theology*. Crossway, 2010.

Hansell, Peter Michael. "Why Was the Shepherd of Hermas Left Out of the New Testament Canon? A Contextual Study in Church History and Its Contemporary Relevance." *Bangalore Theol. Forum* 34.2 (2002): 38–57.

Harris, Murray J. *Colossians and Philemon*. EGGNT. Broadman and Holman, 2010.

Hays, Richard B. *1 Corinthians*. Westminster John Knox, 2011.

Hays, Richard B. *Echoes of Scripture in the Letters of Paul*. Yale University Press, 1989.

Hays, Richard B. *Reading Backwards: Figural Christology and the Fourfold Gospel Witness*. Baylor University Press, 2014.

Hays, Richard B. *Echoes of Scripture in the Gospels*. Baylor University Press, 2016.

Head, Peter M. "Graham Stanton and the Four-Gospel Codex: Reconsidering the Manuscript Evidence." Pages 93–101 in *Jesus, Matthews Gospel and Early Christianity*. Edited by Daniel Gurtner, Joel Willitts, and Richard A. Burride. T&T Clark, 2011.

Head, Peter M. "Is P4, P64 and P67 the Oldest Manuscript of the Four Gospels? A Response to T.C. Skeat," *NTS* 51 (2005): 450–457.

Hitchcock, Mark L. "A Defense of the Domitianic Date of the Book of Revelation." PhD diss., Dallas Theological Seminary, 2005.

Hoskins, Paul M. "Another Possible Interpretation of the Seven Heads of the Beast and the Eighth King (Revelation 17:9–11)." *BBR* 30 (2020): 86–102.

Hoskins, Paul M. *The Book of Revelation: A Theological and Exegetical Commentary*. ChristoDoulos Publications, 2017.

Hughes, Philip E. *The Second Epistle to the Corinthians*. NICNT. Eerdmans, 1962.

Hull, Robert F. Jr. *The Story of the New Testament Text: Movers, Materials, Motives, Methods, and Models*. Society of Biblical Literature, 2010.

Ibrahim, Philemon. "Pentateuch Authorship: A Critical Analysis of Existing Imaginations." *AJBT* 3 (2020): 177–195.

Keener, Craig S. *Revelation*. Zondervan, 1999.

Kempson, W.R. "Theology in the Revelation of John." PhD diss., Southern Baptist theological Seminary, 1982.

Klein, William W., Craig L. Blomberg, and Robert L. Hubbard Jr. *Introduction to Biblical Interpretation*. Thomas Nelson, 2004.

Knight, George W. *The Pastoral Epistles*. NIGTC. Eerdmans, 1992.

Koester, Craig R. *Revelation*. Yale University Press, 2014.

Koptak, Paul E. "Intertextuality." Pages 332–334 in *Dictionary for Theological Interpretation of the Bible*. Edited by Kevin J. Vanhoozer. Baker, 2005.

Köstenberger, Andreas J. *A Theology of John's Gospel and Letters: The Word, the Christ, and the Son of God*. Zondervan, 2009.

Köstenberger, Andreas J., L. Scott Kellum, and Charles L. Quarles. *The Cradle, the Cross, and the Crown: An Introduction to the New Testament*. 1st ed. B&H Academic, 2009.

Köstenberger, Andreas J., L. Scott Kellum, and Charles L. Quarles. *The Cradle, the Cross, and the Crown: An Introduction to the New Testament*. 2nd ed. B&H Academic, 2016.

Kristeva, J. "Word, Dialogue, and Novel." Pages 64–91 in *Desire in Language: A Semiotic Approach to Langauge and Art*. Edited by L.S. Roudiez. Translated by T. Gora, A. Jardine, and L.S. Roudiez. Columbia, 1980.

Kruger, Michael J. *Canon Revisited: Establishing the Origins and Authority of the New Testament Books*. Crossway, 2012.

Kruger, Michael J. "The Definition of the Term 'Canon': Exclusive or Multi-Dimensional? *TynBul* 63.1 (2012): 1–20.

Kruger, Michael J. *The Question of Canon: Challenging the Status Quo in the New Testament Debate*. IVP Academic, 2013.

Kyrtatas, Dimitris J. Pages 29–44 in "Historical Aspects of the Formation of the New Testament Canon," in *Canon and Canonicity: The Formation and Use of Scripture*. Edited by Einar Thomassen. Museum Tusculanum Press, 2010.

Ladd, George Eldon. *A Theology of the New Testament*. Eerdmans, 1993.

Lea, Thomas D. and Hayne P. Griffith Jr. *1, 2 Timothy, Titus*. NAC. Broadman Press, 1992.

Lockett, Darian R. *An Introduction to the Catholic Epistles*. T&T Clark, 2012.

Lockett, Darian R. "Are the Catholic Epistles a Canonically Significant Collection? A Status Quaestionis. *CBR* 14.1 (2015): 62–80.

Lockett, Darian R. *Letters from the Pillar Apostles: The Formation of the Catholic Epistles as a Canonical Collection*. Pickwick, 2017.

Lockett, Darian R. "Not Whether, but What Kind of Canonical Approach: A Review Essay." *JTI* 9.1 (2015): 127–136.

Longman, Tremper III. *Proverbs*. Baker, 2006.

Lunn, Nicholas P. "The Temple in the Wilderness: Allusions to the Hebrew Sanctuary in the Baptism and Temptations of Christ." *JETS* 59 (2016): 701–716.

Luther, Martin. *Luther's Works Volume 35: Word and Sacrament*. Fortress Press, 1960.

Lyons, William. *Canon and Exegesis: Canonical Praxis and the Sodom Narrative*. Sheffield Academic Press, 2002.

Marsh, Cory M. "Kingdom Hermeneutics and the Apocalypse: A Promotion of Consistent Literal Methodology." *JMAT* 20.2 (2016): 84–105.

Marshall, I. Howard. "Acts." Pages 513–606 in *Commentary on the New Testament Use of the Old Testament*. Edited by G. K. Beale and D. A. Carson. Baker, 2007.

Marshall, I. Howard. *New Testament Theology*. InterVarsity Press, 2004.

Martin, Ralph P. *2 Corinthians*. WBC. Word, 1986.

Mazzaferri, Frederick David. *The Genre of the Book of Revelation from a Source-Critical Perspective*. Walter de Gryuter, 1989.

McDonald, Lee Martin. *The Biblical Canon: Its Origin, Transmission, and Authority*. Baker, 2006.

McDonald, Lee Martin. "Canon." Pages 134–144 in *The Dictionary of the Later New Testament and Its Developments*. Edited by Ralph P. Martin and Peter H. Davids. IVP, 1997.

Meek, Russell L. "Intertextuality, Inner-Biblical Exegesis, and Inner-Biblical Allusion: The Ethics of a Methodology." *Bib* 95.1 (2014): 280–291.

Metzger, Bruce M. *A Textual Commentary on the Greek New Testament*. Deutsche Bibelgesellschaft, 1994.

Metzger, Bruce M. *The Canon of the New Testament: Its Origin, Development, and Significance*. Clarendon Press, 1997.

Metzger, Bruce M. *The Early Versions of the New Testament: Their Origin, Transmission and Limitations*. Oxford University Press, 2001.

Metzger, Bruce M. *The Text of the New Testament: Its Transmission, Corruption, and Restoration*. 4th ed. Oxford University Press, 2005.

Meyer, B.F. "Many (= All) Are Called, but Few (= Not All) Are Chosen." *NTS* 36 (1990): 89–97.

Milligan, William. *Revelation of St. John*. Macmillan, 1887.

Moberly, R.W.L. "Theology of the Old Testament." Pages 467–472 in *The Face Old Testament Studies*. Edited by David W. Baker and Bill T. Arnold. Baker, 1999.

Moo, Douglas J. *Galatians*. BECNT. Baker, 2013.

Moo, Douglas J. *The Letter to the Colossians and to Philemon*. PNTC. Eerdmans, 2008.

Moo, Douglas J. *The Letter of James*. PNTC. Eerdmans, 2000.

Morris, Leon. *Revelation*. IVP Academic, 2009.

Morton, Russell S. *Recent Research on Revelation*. Sheffield Phoenix Press, 2014.

Mounce, William D. *Pastoral Epistles*. WBC. Thomas Nelson, 2000.

Mounce, Robert. *The Book of Revelation*. Eerdmans, 1998.

Neman, Barclay. "The Fallacy of the Domitian Hypothesis." *NTS* 10 (1963): 133–139.

Niehaus, Jeffrey J. *Biblical Theology Volume 1: The Common Grace Covenants*. Weaver, 2014.

Nienhuis, David R. *A Concise Guide to Reading the New Testament: A Canonical Introduction*. Baker, 2018.

Nienhuis, David R. *Not by Paul Alone: The Formation of the Catholic Epistle Collection and Christian Canon*. Baylor University Press, 2007.

Nienhuis, David R. and Robert W. Wall. *Reading the Epistles of James, Peter, John & Jude as Scripture: The Shaping and Shape of a Canonical Collection*. Eerdmans, 2013.

Noble, Paul R. "Esau, Tamar, and Joseph: Criteria for Identifying Biblical Allusions." *VT* 52 (2002): 219–252.

Nolland, John. *Luke 9:21–18:34*. WBC. Thomas Nelson, 1993.

Nolland, John. *Luke 18:35–24:53*. WBC. Thomas Nelson, 1993.

O'Neal, G. Michael. *Interpreting Habakkuk As Scripture: An Application of the Canonical Approach of Brevard S. Childs*. Peter Lang, 2006.

Ortlund, Dane C. "'And Their Eyes Were Opened, and They Knew': An Inter-Canonical Note on Luke 24:31. *JETS* 53 (2010): 717–728.

Osborne, Grant R. *The Hermeneutical Spiral: A Comprehensive Introduction to Biblical Interpretation*. Baker, 2006.

Osborne, Grant R. *Matthew*. ZECNT. Zondervan, 2010.

Osborne, Grant R. "Recent Trends in the Study of the Apocalypse." Pages 473–504 in *The Face of New Testament Studies: A Survey of Recent Research*. Edited by Scot McKnight and Grant R. Osborne. Baker, 2004.

Osborne, Grant R. *Revelation*. BECNT. Baker, 2002.

Packer, J. I. *God Speaks to Man, Revelation and the Bible*. Westminster, 1965.

Pao, David W. and Eckhard J. Schnabel. "Luke." Pages 251–414 in *Commentary on the New Testament Use of the Old Testament*. Edited by G. K. Beale and D. A. Carson. Baker, 2007.

Parker, T. H. L. *Calvin's Commentaries on the New Testament*. 2nd ed. Westminster John Knox, 1993.

Parry, Robin. "Ideological Criticism." Pages 314–316 in *Dictionary for Theological Interpretation of the Bible*. Edited by Kevin J. Vanhoozer. Baker, 2005.

Pate, C. Marvin. "A Progressive Dispensational View of Revelation." Pages 133–176 in *Four Views on the Book of Revelation*. Edited by Stanley N. Gundry and C. Marvin Pate. Zondervan, 1998.

Pattermore, Stephen. *The People of God in the Apocalypse: Discourse, Structure, and Exegesis*. Cambridge University Press, 2004.

Patterson, Paige. *Revelation*. NAC 39. Broadman and Holman, 2012.

Patzia, Arthur G. *The Making of the New Testament: Origin, Collection, Text, and Canon*. InterVaristy Press, 1995.

Peckham, John C. *Canonical Theology: The Biblical Canon, Sola Scriptura, and Theological Method*. Eerdmans, 2016.

Pennington, Jonathan T. *Reading the Gospels Wisely: A Narrative and Theological Introduction*. Baker, 2012.

Pippin, Tina. *Apocalyptic Bodies: The Biblical End of the World in Text and Image*. Routledge, 1999.

Pippin, Tina. *Death and Desire: The Rhetoric of Gender in the Apocalypse*. Westminster John Knox, 1992.

Porter, Stanley E. and Andrew K. Gabriel. *Johannine Writings and Apocalyptic: An Annotated Bibliography*. Brill, 2014.

Porter, Stanley E. *Verbal Aspect in the Greek of the New Testament with Reference to Tense and Mood*. Peter Lang, 1993.

Poythress, Vern Sheridan. "Johannine Authorship and the Use of Intersentence Conjunction in Revelation." *WTJ* 47 (1985): 329–336.
Provan Ian. "Canons to the Left of Him: Brevard Childs, His Critics and the Future of Old Testament Theology." *SJT* 50 (1997): 1–38.
Quarles, Charles L. *Matthew*. EGGNT. B&H Academic, 2017.
Quarles, Charles L. *The Sermon on the Mount: Restoring Christ's Message to the Modern Church*. B&H Academic, 2011.
Rendtorff, Rolf. *The Canonical Hebrew Bible: A Theology of the Old Testament*. Deo Publishing, 2005.
Roberts, Colin Henderson and T.C. Skeat. *The Birth of the Codex*. Oxford University Press, 1983.
Robinson, J.M. "A Formal Analysis of Colossians 1:15–20." *JBL* 76 (1957): 270–287.
Robertson, A.T. *A Grammar of the Greek New Testament in Light of Historical Research*. Broadman Press, 1934.
Sailhamer, John H. "1 Chronicles 21:1—A Study in Inter-Biblical Interpretation." *TJ* 10 (1989): 33–48.
Sailhamer, John H. "The Canonical Approach to the OT: Its Effect on Understanding Prophecy." *JETS* 30 (1987): 307–315.
Sailhamer, John H. *First and Second Chronicles*. Moody Press, 1983.
Sailhamer, John H. *Introduction to Old Testament Theology: A Canonical Approach*. Zondervan, 1995.
Sailhamer, John H. "The Mosaic Law and the Theology of the Pentateuch." *WTJ* 53 (1991): 241–261.
Sailhamer, John H. *The Pentateuch as Narrative: A Biblical-Theological Commentary*. Zondervan, 1992
Sanders, James A. "Canon." Pages 837–851 in *The Anchor Bible Dictionary*, volume 1. Edited by David Noel Freedman. 6 vols. Doubleday, 1992.
Sawyer, John F.A. *From Moses to Patmos*. SPCK, 1977.
Schreiner, Thomas R. *Galatians*. ZECNT. Zondervan, 2010.
Schreiner, Thomas R. *The King in His Beauty: A Biblical Theology of the Old and New Testaments*. Baker, 2013.
Schreiner, Thomas R. *New Testament Theology: Magnifying God in Christ*. Baker, 2008.
Schnabel, Eckhard J. *Acts*. ZECNT. Zondervan, 2012.
Scofield, C.I. *The Scofield Study Bible*. Oxford University Press, 1999.
Seitz, Christopher R. *The Character of Christian Scripture: The Significance of a Two-Testament Bible*. Baker, 2011.
Seitz, Christopher R. *Colossians*. Brazos Press, 2014.
Seitz, Christopher R. *The Goodly Fellowship of the Prophets*. Baker, 2009.
Seitz, Christopher R. *Prophecy and Hermeneutics: Toward a New Introduction to the Prophets*. Baker, 2007.
Seitz, Christopher R. and Kent Harold Richards. *The Bible as Christian Scripture: The work of Brevard S. Childs*. Society of Biblical Literature, 2013.
Shepherd, Michael B. *Daniel in the Context of the Hebrew Bible*. Peter Lang, 2009.
Shepherd, Michael B. *The Textual World of the Bible*. Peter Lang, 2013.
Shepherd, Michael B. *Textuality and the Bible*. Wipf and Stock, 2016.

Sheppard, Gerald T. "Canonical Criticism." Pages 861–866 in *The Anchor Bible Dictionary*. Vol. 1. Edited by David Noel Freedman. 6 vols. Doubleday, 1992.

Soulen, Richard. *Handbook of Biblical Criticism*. 3rd ed. Westminster John Knox, 2001.

Smith, Brandon D. "Vision of the Triune God: Reading Revelation through the Father, Son, and Spirit." PhD diss., Ridley College Melbourne, 2020.

Spellman, Ched. "Colossians." *JETS* 58 (2015): 655–658.

Spellman, Ched. *Toward a Canon-Conscious Reading of the Bible: Exploring the History and Hermeneutics of the Canon*. Sheffield Academic Press, 2014.

Spina, Frank W. "Canonical Criticism: Childs Versus Sanders." Pages 165–194 in *Interpreting God's Word for Today*. Edited by Wayne McCown and James Earl Massey. Warner, 1982.

Stanton, Graham N. "The Fourfold Gospel." *NTS* 43 (1997): 317–346.

Stein, Robert H. *Mark*. BECNT. Baker, 2008.

Stevens, Gerald. *Revelation: The Past and Future of John's Apocalypse*. Pickwick, 2014.

Stenström, Hanna. "They Have Not Defiled Themselves With Women...": Christian Identity According to the Book of Revelation." Pages 33–54 in *A Feminist Companion to the Apocalypse of John*. Edited by Amy-Jill Levine. T&T Clark, 2009.

Stokes, Ryan E. "Satan, YHWH's Executioner." *JBL* 133.2 (2014): 251–270.

Stovell, Beth M. *Mapping Metaphorical Discourse in the Fourth Gospel: John's Eternal King*. Brill, 2012.

Summers, Ray. *Commentary on Luke*. Word, 1972l

Sundberg, Jr., A.C. "Canon Muratori: A Fourth Century List." *HTR* 66 (1973): 1–41.

———. "'The Old Testament:' A Christian Canon." *CBQ* 39 (1968): 143–155.

Swete, Henry Barclay. *The Apocalypse of St. John*. Macmillan and Co., 1907.

Tabb, Brian J. *All Things New: Revelation as Canonical Capstone*. IVP Academic, 2019.

Thielman, Frank. *Ephesians*. BECNT. Baker, 2010.

Thiselton, Anthony C. "Canon, Community and Theological Construction." Pages 1–30 in *Canon and Biblical Interpretation*. Edited by Craig G. Bartholomew, Scott Hahn, Robin Parry, Christopher Seitz, and Al Wolters. Zondervan, 2006.

Thiselton, Anthony C. *The First Epistle to the Corinthians*. NIGTC. Eerdmans, 2000.

Thiselton, Anthony C. *Hermeneutics: An Introduction*. Eerdmans, 2009.

Thomas, John Christopher and Frank D. Macchia. *Revelation*. Eerdmans, 2016.

Thomas, Robert L. *Revelation 1–7: An Exegetical Commentary*. Moody, 1992.

Tolkien, J. R. R. *The Fellowship of the Ring*. 2nd ed. Houghton Mifflin, 1988.

Tolkien, J. R. R. *The Return of the King*. 2nd ed. Houghton Mifflin, 1988.

Tõniste, Külli. *The Ending of the Canon: A Canonical and Intertextual Reading of Revelation 21–22*. Sheffield Academic Press, 2016.

Trobisch, David. *The First Edition of the New Testament*. Oxford University Press, 2000.

Trobisch, David. *Paul's Letter Collection*. Quiet Waters Publication, 2001.

Turner, David L. *Matthew*. BECNT. Baker, 2008.

Turner, Seth. "Revelation 11:1–13: History of Interpretation." PhD diss., University of Oxford, 2004.

Ulrich, Eugene. "The Notion and Definition of Canon." Pages 21–35 in *The Canon Debate*. Edited by Lee Martin McDonald and James A. Sanders. Baker, 2002.

Vanhoozer, Kevin J. *The Drama of Doctrine: A Canonical Linguistic Approach to Christian Theology*. Westminster John Knox, 2005.

Vanhoozer, Kevin J. *Is There Meaning in This Text? The Bible, the Reader, and the Morality of Literary Knowledge*. Zondervan, 1998.

Vawter, Bruce Francis. "The Colossians Hymn and the Principle of Redaction." *CBQ* 33.1 (1971): 62–81.

Vlachos, Chris A. *James*. EGGNT. B&H Academic, 2013.

Von Harnack, Alford. *The Origin of the New Testament and the Most Important Consequences of the New Creation*. Williams and Norgate, 1925.

Wall, Robert W. "Apocalypse of the New Testament in Canonical Context." Pages 274–298 in *The New Testament as Canon*. Edited by Robert W. Wall and Eugene E. Lemico. Sheffield Academic Press, 1992.

Wall, Robert W. "The Canonical Approach." Pages 111–130 in *Biblical Hermeneutics: Five Views*. Edited by Beth Stovell and Stanley E Porter. InterVarsity Press, 2012.

Wall, Robert W. "The Canonical Function of Second Peter." *Biblical Interpretation* 9.1 (2001): 64–81.

Wall, Robert W. "The Function of the Pastoral Letters Within the Pauline Canon of the New Testament: A Canonical Approach." Pages 27–44 in *The Pauline Canon*. Edited by Stanley E. Porter. Brill, 2004.

Wall, Robert W. "Reading Paul with Acts: The Canonical Shaping of a Holy Church." Pages 129–147 in *Holiness and Ecclesiology in the New Testament*. Edited by Kent E. Brower and Andy J. Johnson. Eerdmans, 2007.

Wall, Robert W. *Revelation*. Baker, 2001.

Wall, Robert W. "Reading the New Testament in Canonical Context." Pages 372–396 in *Hearing the New Testament: Strategies for Interpretation*. 2nd ed. Edited by Joel B. Green. Eerdmans, 2010.

Wall, Robert W. "The Significance of a Canonical Perspective of the Church's Scriptures." Pages 528–540 in *The Canon Debate*. Edited by Lee Martin McDonald and James A. Sanders. Baker, 2002.

Wallace, Daniel B. *Greek Grammar Beyond the Basics: An Exegetical Syntax of the New Testament*. Zondervan, 1996.

Weima, Jeffrey A.D. *1–2 Thessalonians*. BECNT. Baker, 2014.

Wendland, Ernst R. "The Hermeneutical Significance of Literary Structure in Revelation." *Neot* 48.2 (2014): 447–476.

Westscott, Brooke Foss. *A General Survey of the History of the Canon of the New Testament*. MacMillan and Co., 1889.

White, Joel. "Colossians." *Them* 40.1 (2015): 133–135.

Wilder, Terry. L., J. Daryl Charles, and Kendell Easley. *Faithful to the End: An Introduction to Hebrews Through Revelation*. B&H Academic, 2007.

Wright, N. T. *The Epistles of Paul to the Colossians and to Philemon*. Eerdmans, 1986.

Xun, Chen. *Theological Exegesis in the Canonical Context: Brevard Springs Childs's Methodology of Biblical Theology*. Peter Lang, 2010.

Index

Genesis
- 3:15 — 60
- 12:3 — 81
- 28:14 — 81

Numbers
- 22:22 — 104 n. 90
- 22:31 — 104 n. 90
- 23:22 — 104 n. 90
- 24:8 — 17

Deuteronomy
- 4:6 — 78
- 6:7-9 — 8
- 10:17 — 129, 130
- 11:9 — 8
- 32:43 — 71

Judges
- 17:6 — 28
- 21:25 — 28

Ruth
- 1:1 — 28
- 3:11 — 28 n. 128

1 Samuel
- 17 — 28
- 29:4 — 104 n. 90

1 Kings
- 16 — 86 n. 37
- 17:1 — 101
- 17:8-24 — 100

2 Kings
- 1:10 — 101
- 16 — 86 n. 37
- 19:21 — 106 n. 96

Psalms
- 1:2 — 144, 147
- 71:17 — 81 n. 21
- 88 — 118
- 118:17-18 — 120
- 118:22 — 134
- 145:6 — 108

Job
- 1:5 — 75–76 n. 295

Psalms
- 2:7 — 55
- 8:7 (LXX) — 49
- 40:6 — 75–76 n. 295
- 73:25–26 — 59
- 110:1 — 106, 124, 125, 130

Proverbs
- 2-7 — 8
- 3:18 — 135 n. 87
- 4:9 — 135 n. 87
- 5-7 — 28
- 31 — 28, 145
- 31:31 — 28

Isaiah
- 3-14 — 238
- 3:10 — 95, 96, 96 n. 68
- 6:3 — 67

6:5	66	Joel	
8:14	134	2:10	96
11:16	16	2:11	98, 99
28:16	134	2:31	96
31:10	96	3:15	96
34:4	96	3:16	27
34:12	97		
40:13	38 n. 23	Amos	
43:20	68 n. 87	1:2	27
46-47	138	2:9-11	8
52:11	130, 131	5:2	106 n. 96
61:1	100		
61:6	133	Micah	
		1:8-15	92
Jeremiah		2:6	92 n. 57
15:2	70 n. 97	6:1-8	92
18:13	106 n. 96	7:15	16
22:20	92 n. 57		
50-51	138	Nahum	
		1:6	98, 99
Lamentations			
2:13	106 n. 96	Zephaniah	
		1:14-16	68 n. 88
Ezekiel			
1:5	67	Zechariah	
1:10	67	4	101
1:18	67	4:3	101
1:22	67	4:11	101
1:27	67	4:14	101
9	127	12:10	81, 82, 102 n. 85
22:27	105	12:10-14	82 n. 22
24:16	92 n. 57	12:12	102 n. 85
24:23	92 n. 57	14:17	81 n. 21
31:1-3	69 n. 90		
32:7	96	Malachi	
48	72 n. 110	3:2	98, 99
Daniel		Matthew	
2:28-29	78 n. 10	1:1-17	144
2:47	129, 130	4:1-11	102, 113
4:34	107 n. 98, 108	4:1	113 n. 118
4:37	108	4:8	102-103, 112-113
7:13	65, 81, 82 n. 22, 102 n. 85	4:20	107
		5:2-12	111
7:13-14	2, 103, 120	5:12	111, 112 n. 114
7:9-10	72	7:15	105-106
7:9-12	81	7:26	19 n. 86
7:18	126 n. 48	8:1	107
7:21	109	10:16	106
7:22-27	72	10:17-22	93
7:25	100	10:32	77, 89-91, 113
7:27	126 n. 48	10:34	92-93
8:17	66	10:34-37	93
12:7	100	11	85
		11:15	85 n. 33, 86 n. 35
Hosea		11:15	84-85
2:16-17	16	13:5	122, 123 n. 37
10:8	98	13:9	84

13:43	84	14:16-17	112
17:1-9	101, 119 n. 20	14:35	84-85
17:2	83-84	18:2	94
19:28	68 n. 87	18:7	109 n. 107
22:1-14	109, 112 n. 115	18:7-8	94-95
22:14	108-110, 129 n. 62	18:9-14	99
24	81	18:11	99-100
24:6	77-78	18:12	100
24:29	95-96	21:8-12	76 n. 6
24:30	77, 80-82, 96	21:9	77-78
24:42-43	87-89	21:25	95-96
24:43	77	21:34-38	98
25:32-33	106	21:36	98-99
26:6-7	76 n. 6	22:29-30	126 n. 52
26:9	76 n. 6	23:25	109 n. 107
26:18	80, 113	23:27	97
26:29	76 n. 6	23:30	97-98
26:31	106, 136	23:38	92
28:19-20	29	24:44-48	10 n. 39

Mark

2:14	106		
2:15	107		
4	85		
4:5	123 n. 37		
4:9	84-85 n. 33		
4:23	85 n. 33, 86 n. 35		
5:4	122		
7:16	85 n. 33		
9:2-8	101		
10:21	106		
13:7	78 n. 10		
13:20	109 n. 107		
13:22	109 n. 107		
13:24-25	95-96		
13:27	109 n. 107		
14:27	136		

John

1:1	61		
1:6-7	61, 146		
1:14	61		
6:35	61		
7:24	83		
10:2	136		
10:11-12	136		
10:14	136		
10:16	136		
10:27	107		
11:44	83		
14:21	119		
17:24	83 n. 30		
19:35	65, 66 n. 76		
21:24	65		

Luke

4:25	77, 100-101
7:13	91-92
8:21	79
8	85
8:7	94
8:8	84-85
8:52	91-92
8:54-55	91
9:28-36	101
9:57	106-107
10:7	19
10:18	105
11:27	79
11:28	78-79, 113
11:37-54	110
11:50	110-111
12:8	77, 89-91, 102 n. 85, 113
14:16	112 n. 116

Acts

1:8	29
2:23	137
4:24	107-108, 128 n. 57
7:60	94
14:15	107-108
14:19	120
15:28-29	85-87, 122 n. 34

Romans

1:2	132
1:3	3
1:7	116
1:25	132
2:4	125
2:13	19 n. 86
2:29	68 n. 87
5:3-5	19 n. 86
6:9	117
6:23	19 n. 86
8:29	117

8:33	109 n. 107	3:8	121
8:37	119	3:18	122
8:39	122	3:20-21	118
9:23	125	4:13	127
11:33	122	4:17-32	127
16:13	109 n. 107	4:17-19	127
16:20	133	4:20-24	127
16:25-27	118	4:25-31	127
		4:30	126-127

1 Corinthians

		5:2	119 n. 18
1:3	3, 116	5:7	131
2:7	122	5:11	130-131
2:8	122, 123	5:25	119 n. 18
2:10	122-123	6:24	132
2:10-13	122		
4:9	120	Philippians	
6:9	113 n. 121	1:2	3
7:30	92	3:8	121
11:17	33	4:23	133
11:23-26	120		
15:30	120	Colossians	
16:9	77, 89-92	1:2	3, 116-117
16:23	133	1:13	132
		1:15-20	117
2 Corinthians		1:15	123-124,
1:2	3	1:18	117-118, 123-124
1:8-9	120	1:24-29	125
1:20	77, 80-82, 113 n. 121	1:27	124-125
1:22	127	2:2	125
5:14-6:2	120	2:12-13	126
5:16-21	131	3:1	125-126
5:17	131-132	3:12	109 n. 107
6:3-10	120	4:18	132
6:9	119-120		
6:10	115, 121-122	1 Thessalonians	
6:14-16	130	1:1	3, 116
6:17	130-131	4:16	128
8:2	122, 125	5:2	77, 87-89
10-13	44	5:28	133
10:13-16	49		
11:12	106 n. 96	2 Thessalonians	
13:14	133	1:2	3, 116
		2:13	70
Galatians		3:16	119
1:3	3, 39, 116		
2:9	22	1 Timothy	
2:15-21	119	5:18	19
2:20	118-119	5:21	109 n. 107
3:27-29	68 n. 87	6:15	129-130
6:16	49, 68 n. 87	6:21	133
6:18	133		
		2 Timothy	
Ephesians		2:10	109 n. 107
1:2	3, 39, 116	4:8	135 n. 86
1:3	127	4:22	133
1:7	121, 125		
2:6	125-126	Titus	
2:7-8	121	1:1	109 n. 107

1:4	3, 116		116-117, 133
3:15	133	1:5	117-119, 124
		1:6	117, 126, 133-134
Hebrews		1:7	80-82
1:6	118 n. 11	1:8	61
9:14	57	1:9-20	65
13:20	136	1:9	65 n. 75
13:25	133	1:10	64, 65 n. 76, 71
		1:11	66 n. 80
James		1:12	65 n. 76
1:2-4	19 n. 86	1:14	118
1:2-11	135	1:16	83-84, 119 n. 20
1:12	135	1:17	120
1:18	70	1:18	119-120
1:22-25	78	2-3	52, 66 n. 80
1:22	19 n. 86	2:1	66 n. 80
2:5	115, 121-122	2:2-3	66
5:17	77, 100-101	2:7	66 n. 80, 84-85
		2:8-11	121, 135 n. 84
1 Peter		2:8	66 n. 80
1:1-2	134, 138	2:9	121-122
1:1	109 n. 107	2:10	135
1:2	3, 116	2:11	66 n. 80
1:18-20	137	2:12	66 n. 80
1:19-20	137	2:14-15	66
2:1-10	134	2:17	66
2:1-3	134	2:18-29	122 n. 34
2:4	109 n. 107	2:18	66 n. 80
2:6	109 n. 107	2:20	66, 85-86
2:9	109 n. 107, 133-134	2:24-25	85-86
2:25	136	2:24	87, 122-123
5:13	138	2:26	66
		2:29	66 n. 80
2 Peter		3:1	66 n. 80, 116
1:2	3	3:2	87
1:12	116	3:3	87-88
3:10	88 n. 45	3:5	66, 89-91
		3:6	66 n. 80
1 John		3:7	66 n. 80
1:1	61	3:8	90
1:1-2	61	3:12	66
1:1-3	65 n. 75	3:13	66 n. 80
		3:14-22	124 n. 44
2 John		3:14	66 n. 80, 123-124, 126
1	109 n. 107	3:17	124-125
2	109 n. 107	3:21	66, 125-126
13	109 n. 107	3:22	66 n. 80
		4	37, 39 n. 32
Jude		4:1-2	65 n. 76
2	3, 116	4:1	66, 78 n. 10
24-25	118	4-5	38
		4:2	64, 71
Revelation		4:5	116
1:1-8	65, 67 n. 81	4:11	67
1:1-2	61, 146	5:1-2	65 n. 76
1:1	61, 77-78, 84	5:4	65 n. 76
1:3	78-80, 84 (145)	5:5	91-92
1:4	3, 65 n. 75, 66 n. 80,	5:6	65 n. 76, 70, 93, 136

5:9	93	12:5	104
5:10	126	12:6	104
5:11	65 n. 76	12:7-8	105
5:12	93	12:7	104
5:13	65 n. 76	12:9	103-105
6:1-17	61	12:10-12	70
6:1-8	67	12:10	66 n. 76
6:1-3	66 n. 76	12:17	69
6:4	92-93	13:1-18	70, 97, 105
6:5-8	66 n. 76	13:1	66 n. 76
6:9-11	67, 94	13:8	93, 137-
6:9	93, 94	13:9-10	70
6:10	70 n. 97, 71, 94-95	13:9	84
6:11	94	13:11	66 n. 76, 105-106
6:12-17	95, 127	13:12	105
6:12-13	95-96	13:13	105
6:12	66 n. 76	13:14	105
6:15-17	96	13:15	105
6:15-16	97-98	13:16-17	37 n. 18
6:16	68	13:17	127
6:17	67, 98-99, 106	14:1-20	69, 70
7:1-17	61	14:1-5	37 n. 18
7:1-8	72, 106	14:1-2	66 n. 76
7:1-2	66 n. 76	14:1	98, 106, 127
7:3	126-127	14:3	106
7:4	66 n. 76	14:4	70, 4, 106-107, 109
7:9	66 n. 76, 136	14:6-7	107 n. 98
7:14	66 n. 76	14:6	66 n. 76
7:17	136	14:7	107-108
8:1-4	61	14:11	70, 127
8:2	66 n. 76	14:12	128
8:3-5	94	14:13-14	66 n. 76
8:8-9	70	14:13	66 n. 76, 128-129
8:13	66 n. 76	15:1-8	70
9:1	66 n. 76	15:1-2	66 n. 76
9:13	66 n. 76, 94, 99	15:1	70
915	99	15:5	66 n. 76
9:16-17	66 n. 76	16:1-21	70, 138
9:18	99	16:1	66 n. 76
9:20	99-100	16:2	127, 138
10:1-11:19	69	16:5	66 n. 76
10:1-11	69	16:7	66 n. 76
10:1	66 n. 76	16:15	66 n. 76, 87-88
10:4-5	66 n. 76	16:18	95
10:8-11	66 n. 76	16:19	138
11:1-14	69, 100	17:1-2	71
11:1	66 n. 76	17:1	112 n. 117
11:3	66 n. 76, 100-101	17:2	109
11:6	100-101	17:3-6	71
11:7	69	17:3	64, 65 n. 76, 112 n. 117
11:11	100	17:5	108
11:12	100	17:6	66 n. 76
11:15-19	69	17:7	108
11:15	102-103	17:8	137 n. 92
12:1-15:1	69	17:14	108-110, 112, 129-130
12:1-17	69	18:1-24	71, 130
12:2	104	18:1	66 n. 76, 110
12:4	104	18:3	109

18:4	66 n. 76, 130-131
18:9	109
18:24	93, 110-111
19:1-5	111
19:1-4	71
19:1	66 n. 76
19:6-10	106 n. 96, 111
19:6	66 n. 76
19:7	111, 112
19:9	112
19:10-11	66 n. 76
19:13	61
19:16	129
19:17	66 n. 76
19:19	66 n. 76
19:21	72
19:20	127
20:1	66 n. 76
20:4-6	72
20:4	66 n. 76, 126
20:6	66 n. 76
20:11-15	72, 127, 131
20:11-12	66 n. 76
21-22	60
21:1-3	66 n. 76
21:1	131
21:2	131
21:3	131
21:4-5	131-122
21:9-10	112 n. 117
21:9	113 n. 118
21:10	64, 71, 112-113
21:13	83
21:22	66 n. 76
22:5	126
22:6	78 n. 10
22:7-8	66 n. 76
22:7	66 n. 76
22:8	66 n. 75, 73
22:10	144
22:12-16	73
22:14	66 n. 76
22:17-18	84
22:21	132-133

www.ingramcontent.com/pod-product-compliance
Lightning Source LLC
Chambersburg PA
CBHW072013110526
44592CB00012B/1284